SECTARIAN CHILDREARING

THE DUNKERS

1708-1900

Alvin E. Conner, M.D.

The Brethren Heritage Press

©Brethren Heritage Press
24 Chambersburg Street
Gettysburg, Pennsylvania 17325

ISBN 0-943429-00-5

Library of Congress CIP Number 87-71483

Typesetting and graphics by REF Typesetting, Manassas, Virginia. The text typeface is 11 point Melior.

Preface

The isolated German Baptist Brethren subculture as it existed prior to 1900 offers a valuable forum in which to study childrearing. The author, from his unique perspective as a pediatrician and as one who was reared in this subculture, has devoted years of study to this subject. He has explored the status of the child in the German Baptist Brethren sect, and has delineated the principles of childrearing used by that culture. His data reject the contention of early Brethren historians that members of that era were ignorant and backward. Rather, his data suggest that the children were reared according to psychologically sound principles of parent-child interaction which were appropriate for that environment. Of interest is that these principles are being rediscovered today as appropriate for use in our society.

Childrearing of the past is poorly documented. Much of this documentation consists of subjective interpretations of the meaning of ancient records and artifacts. The present study goes deeper. With meticulous methodology, it attempts to discern the thoughts and feelings of children, the relationship between parent and child, and to a degree, the resultant effect of these upon the child in his adult life.

A good research study should raise more questions than it answers. This study is not an exception. The quality of the research is excellent and the author's conclusions provide a point of departure for further investigation. The text is readable despite its scientific nature, and the author's interpretation of the data quite logical. This is an important addition to the literature of the Brethren and contributes significantly to the understanding of the child in Brethren history.

Marcus Miller, M.D.
Old German Baptist Brethren

Appreciation

Many people contributed suggestions and material as the work evolved from a casual reading of the history of the Brethren to a study of the child's place among the Old Brethren and, finally, to organizing the gathered material. Among these were William Rankin, Oneida Lawrence, Humbert Kahle, Edward K. Ziegler, and Arlene May. R.B. Young, M.D., Professor of Pediatrics, Medical College of Virginia, commented from his perspective as a pediatrician and as a non-Brethren. Emmert Bittinger, Ph.D. of Bridgewater College, offered suggestions in the early stages, and John A. Hostetler, Ph.D., then of Temple University, provided insights relative to the theological differences between the Anabaptists and Pietists. Sadly, Mr. B.O. Wakeman did not live to see the completion of this study. He, through his love and appreciation of our Brethren heritage, awakened in me a similar appreciation.

Introduction

Children are the conduits through which the old is passed to the new. This was especially true in the subculture of the German Baptist Brethren, a Protestant sect of Pietist and Anabaptist roots, founded in Shwarzenau, Germany in 1708. That this ordered group of religious people endured for almost one hundred and fifty years in an essentially unchanged sociological mode attests to the soundness of their childrearing practices.

This study uses the record established by diaries and autobiographies as well as other documents and church records to present the sectarian child in his environment. These personal recollections of childhood should picture the child more accurately than observations of others. Except for three, the references used are from Brethren born prior to 1900 from a family where at least one parent was a member of the sect. Since the way these subjects were raised reflects the parenting practices of the two previous generations, we can infer that these practices are representative of the period from 1750 to 1900.

Sectarians are thought to continue their way of life through "brain washing" their children in a family atmosphere of strict behavioral rules and oppressive religious dogma. This aspect of the childrearing practices of the German Baptist Brethren (known as the Dunkers because of their baptism by trine immersion) is examined to see to what extent this perception existed and to determine to what degree the religious beliefs of the sect affected the way the children were reared.

Finally, the interaction of the parents and children is analyzed for principles of parenting and for how these molded the lives of the young on their path to maturity. As with similar studies, this investigation is hampered by the paucity of records. However, valuable insights are gained and may provide a stimulus for further study. And perhaps the principles of childrearing used by the Brethren can be measured by the reader against those recommended for parents of the present era.

Table of Contents

About the Author

Alvin E. Conner was born in Manassas, Virginia and is at least fourth generation Brethren on both sides of his family line. He received his early religious training in the Manassas Church of the Brethren, a conservative congregation served by free ministers in his youth. Most of its members were related, with links to the Shenandoah Valley and Pennsylvania Brethren. Dr. Conner was baptized at fourteen and has continued as a member of his home church. Educated in the public schools, he earned a B.A. from Bridgewater College, an M.D. from the Medical College of Virginia, and is a Fellow of an American Academy of Pediatrics Among his community and professional activities, he served on the Manassas City School Board and as a trustee of George Mason University. Currently, he is a trustee of Bridgewater College. His practice of pediatrics involved anticipatory guidance and family counseling which, in part, led to his interest in the child of the Old Brethren.

PLATE 1. Three generations of a typical Dunker family—1914

1

The Child and the Sect

The German Baptist Brethren sect was formed in Germany in 1708 out of the chaos resulting from the religious and economic upheavels of the previous two hundred years.[1] Its early members were almost entirely Germanic, were poor and alienated, and, to some extent, suffered from the religious persecution of that era. Many of them represented the dominant culture of that section of Europe; a few were educated; and many of them were skilled tradesmen who needed only economic chance and stability to be self-sufficient. From these capable people, a subculture formed around religious principles derived from the Protestant Revolution, particularly the Anabaptist and Pietist movements. These religious principles were applied to their daily lives, further shaping the form of the subculture and dictating the values by which these hardy people lived. Transplanted to America in 1719, the subculture thrived in the atmosphere of freedom and plenty and adapted to this environment as the population built up from a scattered frontier nation to an emerging industrial giant. These changes placed stresses on the sectarians who wanted, above all, to maintain the purity of their religion through its expression in their daily lives. And when urbanization infringed on their rural way of life, additional stresses threatened their existence as a group "set-apart" from the general culture. The lives of the children were shaped by the parenting practices these people derived in the early period from secular culture of their native land. In the nineteenth century, these parenting practices were influenced by a mixture of secular influences of their heritage, secular influences of their adopted land and religious values as defined by their order.

A comparative study of the Dunker sect and its children with similar contemporary groups would be most interesting. However, it is beyond the scope of this study. Furthermore, except for the Puritan children of New England, there are few solidly researched accounts of the child in early America. So the life of the Dunker child will be studied within his environment with minimal reference to the outside world. However, a brief review of the following areas will provide background for a better understanding of the material as it portrays the somewhat puzzling position of a free child in a restrictive society. These areas are: the evaluation of the concepts of childhood; the nature of sectarianism; and beliefs of the Pietists and Anabaptists. Finally, the influence of the sect's polity and policies (collectively known as the "order") on the children will be discussed.

Three Stages in the Historical Evolution
of the Concept of Childhood

The position of children in history may be divided into three periods. Roughly, the first period ended about the time of Christ. During this period, the child was a non-entity, a pawn in the adult world. The second period began when, under the influence of Christianity, the child was proclaimed to have a soul. This provided the theological basis for child conservation. The third period, the child as an individual, began somewhere around 1400 A.D. and by 1700 A.D. had reached a maturity in which children had achieved a status where the sentimental nuclear family was possible. In certain strata of society, he could be compared favorably with a child of the latter part of the nineteenth century.

Prior to the third period, there were two divisions among the populace: children, until the age of five years; and after that, adults. Adolescence was unknown. Five- and six-year old boys were officers in the armed forces of the day. Schools were ungraded; beginners were in the same class with adults and studied the same curricula. The schools run by the church educated future priests; the humanist schools focused more on the total life of the person. The concept of the child as a developing organism with age-related capabilities had not yet caught on. Promotions and an end-point to education were yet to be conceived. Some societies, though, had made a beginning in the development of the concept of childhood.[2]

The semi-barbaric German tribes, said to be influenced by the early Christian missionaries, passed child protective laws around the fourth century A.D. These laws provided for fines which related to the age of the child, with the heavier fines levied against those who killed young people over the age of twelve years. Above this age, the children were considered adults. The fine for killing a pre-pubertal girl was the same as killing an older woman incapable of childbearing. A girl of childbearing age commanded the heavier fine. This system of punishment indicates that the life of the young was threatened and that age-related values were assigned to them. Their utilitarian worth was more important than their intrinsic worth. Even though the reason for these laws was not humanitarian, the people in this area of Europe seemed to have an advanced perception of the nature of the child.[3]

In France, by the beginning of the sixteenth century, the age-related capabilities of the child were recognized, and classes in school were formed that progressed from the younger to the older with increasingly difficult subjects. School discipline had begun. Training the child to be a useful and Christian citizen became the purpose of these schools. Martin Luther was a strong advocate of child instruction, but he believed that outside agencies, as well as the parents, should be involved in the children's education.[4] By the eighteenth century, the industrial revolution had begun in England which caused children to be worked in an inhuman way, pricking the conscience of both the people and the government to provide safeguards for their care. In America at this time, children were generally well-treated within the imported customs from the various countries of the immigrants.

When the Dunkers emigrated to America in 1719, the child had become a valued member of society, albeit mostly on an ecomomic basis. He occupied a position of sentimentality, as opposed to distant objectivity, in the nuclear family. But he still was subject to the will of the father. Interjection by the state of child protective measures was several centuries away. In the Dunker subculture, the economics of the frontier farm contributed to the child's value and standing along with the religious values of their theological progenitors, Pietists and Anabaptists. To better understand these heretical groups and the form under which the

Dunker children were raised, the nature of sectarianism will be reviewed.

The Nature of Sectarianism

There are differences between a church and a sect.[5] A sect is a group of people whose religious concerns are turned inward; a church is a group of people whose religious concerns are directed towards the world in which they live. The sect is governed by a narrow view of religious principles directed mostly at the individual; it attempts to capture the apostolic way of worship and life; the members accept the scriptures as inerrant; they are more against than for; the ministers are not trained; and rigid ethical principles govern the life of the members. The church is more of a social institution for its members; the ministers are apt to be professionally trained; the scriptures are not interpreted literally; and the program is directed towards the concerns of the society around them as expressed in the issues of the day. Sects tend to put much emphasis on an inward experience; churches value liturgy and sacraments.

Each society has people whose emotional needs are not met by the existing churches. These people are usually poor and their lives are full of unfulfilled desires and ummet expectations. Unhappy, they search for something to fill the emotional void of their lives and lighten the loads that they carry. These people may coalesce from general circumstances into a group, or they may be drawn into a movement by a charismatic leader. In either event, the luxuries which they cannot afford are placed in the evil category; wealth is a roadblock to salvation, hard work is a virtue, and frugality, which is a necessity for them, also becomes a virtue. This process is based on a foundation in scripture. A sect is born.

Clarke says that all churches, even the Roman Catholic church, began as sects. Why did these sects become churches? Economics is said to be the cause. The work ethic and frugality of the founders of the sect produced material wealth, which improved their standard of living and enabled them to raise their children in more affluence. The children, then, did not develop the needs born of poverty, disaffectation, and deprivation; consequently they were less receptive to the work ethic. In addition, either through improved economic circumstances or through more opportunities, the children received a better education. This provided them with the cognitive ability to evaluate more critically the scriptures and made literal acceptance less likely. Unattainable luxuries, formerly assigned a sinful value, became attainable and were classified as permissible to the members under specific circumstances. Later, the specific circumstances were eliminated. Because life in the present was better, the psychological need for the promise of a better life in the hereafter was lessened. Therefore, the sectarian looked to the outer world to express his religious feelings through an ethical system developed to keep him in harmony with his introspective system of religious beliefs. Finally, when the group developed programs of relief and missionary activities with the management structure to implement these programs, the sect became a church. The rate at which this process took place depended on the rate at which economic improvement occurred. Economic improvement of the sects was inexorable, and the sectarian mode gave way to the church mode unless self-preserving rules of society were developed to prevent this. These rules were far-reaching, governing the life of the members and, in the aggregate, were commonly called the "order."[6]

While sects have usually grown exogenously, they may and do grow from within. For this to happen, the children of the sectarians must be trained to accept the beliefs and customs of their parents, and to resist the powerful call of the outside world, i.e., other churches or a non-religious life. There are three crucial times in the young person's life that especially relate to this training. The first crucial period is the pre-school years. Basic patterns of thought are established from the values presented to the child. This is the time when the child can be indoctrinated with the sectarian reactive and affective patterns. The second period, adolescence, is crucial also, because the rebellion of young people emerges and the indoctrination of the earlier years may be shed. These periods were important; the Dunkers recognized this. The proper application of love, discipline, and tolerance kept many of the young men and women close to the family values. The third period, that of deciding whether or not to make the commitment to join the group through baptism, was critical to the survival of the sect because it was at that time that the discipline of the group had to be accepted. One Dunker youth progressed satisfactorily until he reached the third stage; then he refused to be baptized because he said the sect wanted only to make a preacher out of him.[7] But many of the Dunker youth accepted baptism with its commitment to beliefs as expressed by the order of the German Baptist Brethren and helped to continue their sectarian way of life.

Sectarians protected the integrity of their group and its growth by training their children in the values and customs of the past; by emphasis on the community of believers; by controlling education of the children; by using excommunication as a disciplinary tool and as a means of weeding out non-conformers; by adhering to a specific limit of permissibility of actions, and, in some, by a principle unique to that group. These were used, in part, to indoctrinate the children so that survival of the sect by endogenous growth would occur as well as to preserve the cultural integrity of the sect.

The German Baptist Brethren were sectarians from 1708-1900. In Germany, members were generally poor. They were also alienated from the community life of the area. Their beliefs were developed through study and introspection, and were individually oriented. Further, the sectarians looked back on the primitive church and tried to emulate its practices. They developed a discipline with many things indicated as worldly, and therefore not acceptable to a true follower of Christ. In addition, they had a strong work ethic, had one social rank, and had a method of purging the nonconformers from their group. Their societal conscience was limited primarily to fellow members and, to a lesser extent, their neighbors. They had no concern for the world at large. They allowed outsiders to join their sect as long as they accepted the order. Because of their isolated agricultural base and aided by the order, they continued in the sectarian mode many generations past the time it usually took a sect to mature into a church.

Scholars set different dates to mark the beginning of the Dunkers as a church. The earliest time suggested was in 1853, when they reluctantly accepted a denominational magazine. Others thought church status was achieved when Sunday schools were permitted around 1870; the first missionary, in the 1880's; the elimination of the dress code in the early 1900's; and the acceptance of the various youth programs of the 1920's, respec-

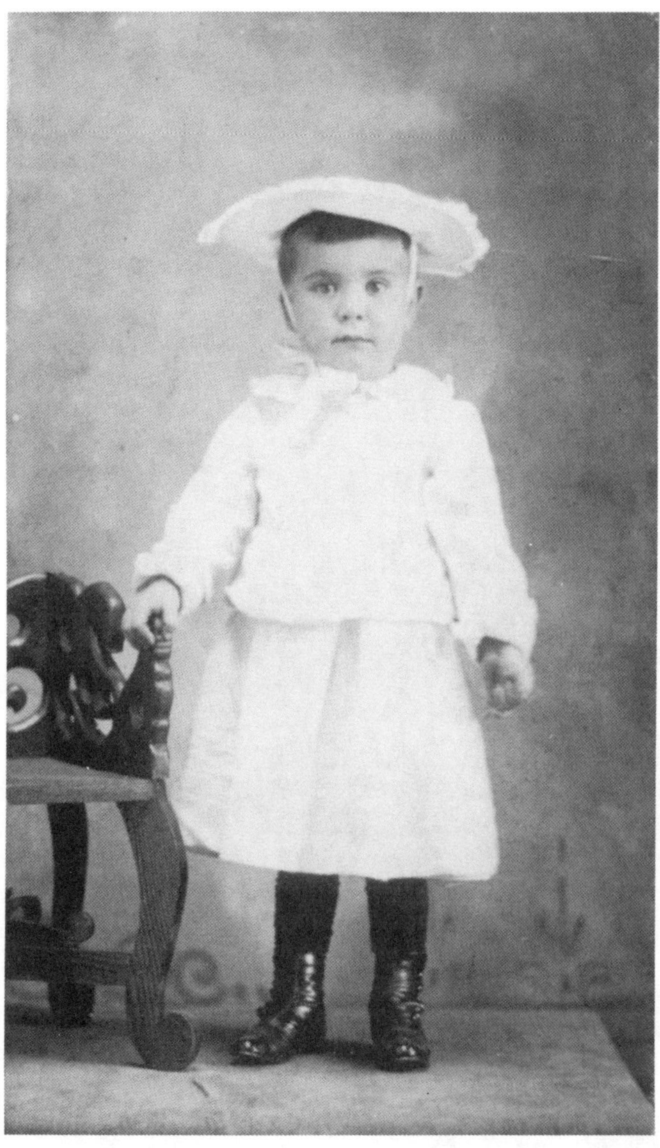

PLATE 2. A little Brethren boy aged 3 years—1906

PLATE 3. Dress-up play—1925

tively. One thought that church status was reached in 1941, when the Church of the Brethren became a member of the National Council of Churches. Since a church is not precisely defined, a precise time of beginning cannot be given. By most criteria, the changing of the name to the Church of the Brethren in 1908 was appropriate—church status had been reached.

As befitted sectarians, a religious atmosphere was pervasive in the home and life of the Dunker children. Their upbringing reflected the influence of basic religious principles. The child-rearing practices used were shaped by interpretations of the Old and the New Testaments, which were formulated into rules making up the order of the German Baptist Brethren. This order governed the lives of the parents, and, therefore, the early lives of the children.

The principles of the scriptures used in constructing the order were the most significant influences derived from this religious environment and were reflected in the parents' lives. In the tacit and non-verbal Dunkers', their lives as examples stood as the primary method of value transference allowing these principles of the scriptures to be effectively passed to the next generation. A major principle, obedience to God, was considered a model for the relationship of the father and the children and its authority derived from that primary relationship. The "good" and "bad" labels inherent in early theology were useful to the parents, as they molded the sensitive consciences of their children. Specific instruction, e.g., spare the rod, feed the hungry, swear not, was followed with exactness in many of the families, with compassion in others, and with selectivity in a few. On the more positive side, the New Testament stress on the value of each person can be seen clearly in the Dunkers' childrearing methods. However, there was a distance between parent and child, strange to the present generation and somewhat strange to the love theme of the scriptures. This, perhaps, could have been a continuation of the parent-child relationship derived from secular factors of past generations.

As the Dunker sect grew in the wilderness of the new world, it followed most of the parameters of sectarianism. However, there is no evidence that only the poor and lonely joined; and, to the contrary, there is no evidence that the affluent became members. Rather, the loneliness of the frontier and the attraction of the

German background to other Germans of mixed stations in life seemed to be the main cause of growth from without. Growth from within was significant, but has always been disappointing to the German Baptist Brethren, later called the Church of the Brethren.

Pietiest and Anabaptist Contributions
to the Concept of Childhood

Many societal forces contributed to the evolving concept of childhood. Among these the Anabaptist beliefs were instrumental in the societal change; how much has not been determined. Belief in adult baptism carried with it the implicit recognition that a child was not born with adult faculties, did not acquire them soon, and because of this, did not have the same relationship with God and His Word as did the adult. They believed that an age of innocence, because of the inability to reason, lasted from four to seven years of age. During this time, the child was not capable of wilful disobedience, and, therefore, was not held accountable for his actions. This period was a time of forbearance on the part of the parents, and corrective punishment was used to train. Religious instruction could begin at five or six years of age when the child had matured to the reading stage. It was at this time that the child was expected to begin to conform to the values of the parents. This was in keeping with both the Anabaptists and the Pietistic beliefs, faith through reasoning.

Whereas Luther believed that education of the child was for both religious and social purposes, the Anabaptist separated the two. Education provided the rudimentary intellectual skills; the greater duty of the school was to train the child in the ways of the community in which he belonged and in which he was to become an adult member. Both the school and the home were to "filter down" the culture of that particular group. The principles of community and limited education continue in the two foremost derivatives of the Anabaptist movement, the Hutterites and the Old Order Amish. These children are taught that their societal group has both a theological and a support function. Education beyond the eighth grade disqualifies them from membership.[8]

The Pietists placed less religious value on the community than the Anabaptists. Rather, they felt that salvation was an individual effort, so much so that the individual was to read and interpret the scriptures without pressures from the outside to change or alter his interpretation. This stress on the individual role in the search for salvation in an era when the state churches and the noblemen wielded so much power was a stimulus to the developing concept of the individual as an important factor in society. This is not to say that only the Pietists projected individualism. The Anabaptists, within their concept of community, assigned worth to each member and collectively, according to Holloway, were the spearhead of the democratic religious movement.[9]

This lesser emphasis by the Dunkers on the importance of the community of believers aligned them with Pietistic beliefs. Their application of the order to the lives of the sect's members was more pragmatic and less doctrinaire. This had tremendous implications for childrearing as the Dunker young skirmished with the order on their way to maturity.

Church Polity

The polity of the German Baptist Brethren reflects that their roots drew from the somewhat antagonistic concepts of Pietistic individualism and Anabaptist community. At times very democratic, at times authoritarian, the rules of the church produced policies that were designed to uphold the integrity of the community of believers while, at the same time, giving full range to the conscience of the members.

A central belief of the newly organized sect was that there should be "no force in religion." This derived from the throttling of individual conscience by the organized religious groups prior to the sixteenth century. In the Dunker's view, the individual should be guided by his conscience, not by secular or ecclesiastic fiat. He should, however, abide by civil rule unless he thought it contrary to the scriptures. In that case, the scriptures must be obeyed. But the sect did recognize a group role for the community of believers. This role had many facets, one of which was to establish policies for individual behavior so that this behavior would reflect the principles of the apostolic church. This function of the group, the community of believers, was well founded in the scriptures. This role also required the group to offer guidance to its members in the interpretation of these policies and to discipline those who violated the mores of the body of believers.

The organizational structure of the sect affected the lives of the children. It provided a framework for their lives that was well-defined, democratically administered, and had the capability for change as the conditions required. The purpose of this organization and the rules which it formalized was to enhance the spiritual purity of the individual member, a distinctly Pietistic concept. The sanctity of the group as a theological instrument was secondary. Therefore, the children saw the rules enforced as a reaction to personal behavior more so than to a violation of group rules. This was not absolute. These group rules were known as the order, in time, the Order of the Ancient Brethren, and they were referred to from time to time in the abstract.

The order of the Brethren was established through a case law approach. Congregational in form, the denomination's authority was vested in its members in the local churches. This authority was exercised in a democratic fashion through council meetings presided over by an elected elder. These congregational council meetings established policies through majority vote. These policies could be in the area of dress, slaves, liquor, divorce, church attendance, that is, in all areas of the member's life. Each year, the sect had an Annual Meeting (AM) to which elected representatives from the local congregations were sent as delegates. Thorny problems were referred to this AM for debate and answer. These questions were referred to as "queries," a term borrowed from Quaker polity. The answers to these queries were considered advisory, but they were the main ingredients in the order. Local decisions containing the current perceptions of scriptural revelations fleshed out the order.

This process of establishing and updating the order was democratic with each member's vote counting as much as another. And there was no higher authority than the members of the congregation in council—not the presiding elder, the district meeting, nor the Annual Meeting. This has significance for childrearing. The rules by which the child was expected to live were formulated by his family, extended family, and friends of his family. They were not handed down from above. Therefore, when the child violated a rule, he tampered not only with God's law but also the beliefs of his aunts, uncles, cousins and neighbors. Under these circumstances, the pressure to conform was enormous. And since the child was not a member of the church, this pressure to conform was designed to shape the value system of the child so that, at maturity, he would and could accept the order of the Dunkers.

Resolution of Violations of the Order

The Dunkers were not committed to endogenous growth as the primary way of expanding the membership rolls. This was shown by their easy acceptance of the converts from other denominations and, in later years, by the acceptance of revival services. The order tolerated, within limits, congregational options for conforming to the decisions of the AM, a situation not likely to obtain if the emphasis had been on group purity. The Dunkers did not have a principle or rule beyond which the person was automatically dismissed from membership. They had no complex marriage, as did the Oneida Community, no celibacy and ritualistic living pattern that characterized the Ephrata Cloister group, and no absolute ban on higher education, as did the Old Order Amish. Rather, they settled problems in the context of the times: they reacted to conditions. Since absolutes and inflexibility, with its connotation on childrearing, seem always associated with sectarianism, it is worthwhile to review this system of resolving problems.

There are two fields in which the Dunkers have held constant: war and slavery. In these areas, one would think that their rules would be inflexible, but they were not. If a member joined the army he lost his membership, but it was restored as soon as he left the service and petitioned for reinstatement: a reaction to a condition. Slavery was equally prohibited; yet, if a person had just acquired a slave and then joined the church, he could keep the slave until the slave worked off the purchase price. If that man owned children of slaves, he kept them as servants until they were of age. During this time he had to teach them to read and write and to provide them with clothes when he freed them. If a slave could not exist on his own when freed, the brother kept him as a hired hand.[10] Those who were squeamish did not have to give the kiss of charity to a "colored" member. A reaction to an absolute value may have required the immediate freeing of all slaves, but this was not feasible in every instance. The conditions of each case were considered and solutions arrived at which preserved the integrity of the slave as an individual and worked towards the absolute—sanctity of the individual which called for freedom for the slave.

The use of liquor required some compromises with the ideal. Starting in 1781, the AM took a stand against the making and selling of ardent spirits and against the intemperate personal use of the stronger alcoholic beverages. They considered it wrong even to sell grain to a distillery particularly if the food supply that year was low. However, if the farmer could not dispose of his grain in any other way and if he had to convert it into cash, sale to a distillery was permitted.[11] Working in a store was considered dangerous exposure to the world. A brother or sister should not do this type of work; but if no other work could be found, store clerking was permissible.[12] The use of tobacco defiled God's temple, but all the admonitions of the successive AM's failed to curb the habit. After sixty years of trying, the AM rather lamely concluded that a brother or sister should not use tobacco during worship service or in situations where its use offended others.[13]

The Dunkers did not ride ideological white horses; rather they reacted to the conditions of the day, showing a sensitivity to the needs of the individual at that point in time. Rather than displaying a lack of conviction, this approach to problems demonstrated a maturity of reasoning and a realization that a partial victory may be the first step to the ultimate solution. It was in keeping with their understanding of the scriptures: God did not require perfection; he required them to strive towards perfection.

The ultimate, and most effective, means of protecting the purity of a group is to cast out the ideological deviants. This practice was in the armamentarium of the Dunkers, first used in the Hoecker case around 1716, and reaffirmed in 1892 by the AM as being consistent with their beliefs. Unlike some of the other sects, this practice was not used extensively, and when used, was directed towards restoration of the member, rather than rejection. It did not seem to be a ruthless weapon, and the members apparently did not fear it to any great degree.[14]

To provide the background necessary to understand the position of the Dunker child in his life in America, these areas have been reviewed: the child as an individual; sectarianism; very briefly, the Anabaptists and the Pietists; and the polity of the sect.

The material to follow will substantiate, to the limited extent possible in historical research, that, 1. despite sectarian governance, the Dunker child was viewed as an individual with the freedom to develop his life according to his desires and motivation; 2. this attitude towards the child resulted primarily from Pietistic dogma and was made possible by the sect's rural life; 3. the Dunkers followed, although probably not unique to them, well-defined principles of childrearing that were suited to their era; 4. these principles recognized the characteristics of the essential child; 5. the Dunker subculture, and thus their attitude towards children, remained essentially unchanged from 1723 to 1900; 6. the Dunkers' attitude towards their children was an enlightened position, not only for their time in history but particularly for sectarians.

Finally, a child can only be understood within his world. In the interest of space, a detailed description of the total environment is not given. This is remedied, however, by the references throughout the study, which give a reasonable portrait of the Dunker child's world.

Summary

The child has been the lowest rung on the economic ladder and, therefore, has been shamefully treated in times of famine or low food production. Maternal influence, where present, has offered protection to the child. The confluence of the needs of the state and church resulted in an improved environment for the child. Education was provided and laws were passed which offered minimal protection. From that of an adult at age six years, the perception of the child changed to where age and size capabilities were recognized. The sentimental nuclear family concept developed. The child held a position of importance within this family setting by the early 1700's.

The Dunker sect was formed in Germany in 1708 with a theology derived from the Pietists and Anabaptists. This affirmed the worth of the individual. They emigrated to America in 1719 and lived on the fringes of the settled country for the next 180 years. A system of governance of the Dunkers evolved called the order, the chief function of which was to guide the everyday life of the member. The religious beliefs, the position of the women in the sect, and the economic value of the children provided an excellent environment for sectarian childrearing of that day.

2

Values

What sort of people were the Dunkers? What did they live by and what did they believe? An outsider described them in 1787:

> Such Christians as they are I have never seen. So adverse are they to all sin, and to many things that other Christians esteem lawful, that they do not only refuse to swear or go to war, but they are so afraid of doing anything contrary to the commands of Christ that no temptation would prevail upon them, even to sue a person at law, for either name, character, estate, or debt, be it ever so just. They are industrious, sober, kind, temperate, charitable people, envying not the great, nor despising the mean; they read much, they sing and pray much, and are constant attendants upon the public worship of God. Their dwelling houses are all houses of prayer. They walk in the commandments and ordinances of the Lord blameless, both in public and in private. They bring up their children in the nurture and admonition of the Lord. No noise or rudeness, shameless mirth, loud, vain laughter we heard within their doors. The law of kindness is in their mouths; no sourness or moroseness disgrace their religion; and whatever they believe their Savior has commanded, they practice without inquiring or regarding what others do. I remember the Rev. Morgan Edwards, former minister of the Baptist Church in Philadelphia, once said to me, 'God always will have a visible people on earth, and these are His people at present, above any others in the world.' In a word, they are meek and pious Christians, and have justly acquired the title of the Harmless Tunkers.[1]

These statements, accurate or inaccurate as they may be, described the way the values of the Dunkers were displayed in their daily lives, at least as perceived by a non-Dunker. The Meek and Harmless Tunkers. Children brought up under this value system should have required strenuous training to keep them within the system. Many of the values had to be accepted by rote, rather than by understanding, and many youthful exuberances had to be subdued, at least this picture given by an outsider would have us believe.

A little less than two hundred years later, Kermit Eby, brought up under this system, reflects on the impact of the values on him:

It has been almost thirty years since I left home for good, but my thoughts constantly return to Dad's farm at Baugo; it is here where my real roots are. The reasons are not merely sentimental or because the experiences of one's youthful days become more poignant in later years. It is deeper than that—at Baugo we were taught, in season and out of season that we are born for a purpose, and this purpose was declared by men and women who believed that their lives too had meaning. To these neighbors and ancestors of mine the sins of omission were as deadly as the sins of commission, and life was a serious business indeed. Today, in my weaker moments, I often wish I could escape this sense of purpose. I know that life would be easier if I could. But this cannot be so easy, for this sense of conviction grew out of a total experience: our family life, farm life, and the religious life centered at Baugo. Each of us was judged as much by his actions and the conduct of his family as by his prayers and his preaching. There was no compartmentalization of life at Baugo, no separation of theory and practice, no place where one could escape the all-seeing eyes of God and the gossip of the sisters.[2]

Perhaps the most succinct statement relating to the value system of the Dunkers was a follow-up observation made by Kermit Eby to the paragraph given above:

Someone once said that both whiskey and a sense of purpose are a curse, but one can get over whiskey. If he was right, the Brethren are inescapably cursed. We cannot escape the haunting sense that we were born to leave this world of farm and church better than we found it.

The moral "ought to" is very deep in Brethren hearts. We are inclined to see the world in blacks and whites. Perhaps that is why Martin G. Brumbaugh, a birthright Brethren who served as governor of Pennsylvania, was said to have broken in health under the pressure of politics.[3]

Those born into the Dunker sect will recognize truths in both the outside observation and Eby's account of the impact of the value system on him. They will agree that the Dunker children were reared by closely held ideals within a seemingly rigid system, one which related to the purposeful life according to the dictates of the Bible and to the requirements of rural life. But the rigidity of the system did not always extend to the lives within that system. Considerable flexibility was allowed, in some instances taken, as the members sought an accommodation between what the system required and what they believed. That a certain measure of hypocrisy seemed to present itself from time to time was inevitable as this accommodation took place. The story, perhaps apocryphal, is told of the time when a congregation voted on the issue of whether the members should be allowed to own automobiles. The majority agreed that they should. The meeting adjourned and the church lot emptied of the horse-drawn vehicles. Within an hour the lot was filled with cars of assorted types.

This would appear to indicate a lack of moral fiber in the Dunkers but this was not so. Rather, it is an illustration of the looseness of the order, a lack of definite boundaries, and the space within the order for individual expression. The pressure to conform to the current rules is clearly evident by the buggies in the church yard; the cars in the garages at home indicate the looseness of the order. This pressure on the child to conform to the established order was real; generally he had to choose between the "automobile" and the "buggy" many times before his adult value system formed.

Although the Dunkers felt the pressure to conform to the order, their response to this pressure varied according to the degree with which they believed in the rules currently in force. They were not a homogenous group of people walking in lockstep down moral mainstreet. There was general agreement on the major issues, but within this consensus, the degree to which these views were held spanned the spectrum from minimal to maximum. Some believe in pacifism; some in temperance; some worked hard; others slipped off to cock fights; and many felt that the letter of the law was the core of true belief, while others thought the spirit of the law was of more importance. To some, the love of the group far outweighed its drag on their lives. To others, this drag was not compensated for by the advantages of the support of the group. Yet, from the outside, the Dunkers appeared to be a separate society with an identity of its own, sometimes called the "peculiar people," a society which lived as much by a common law as did the military. This identity was brought about undoubtedly by the garb and some of the other standardized practices. What was not readily visible to the outsider was the latitude for life allowed within the group.

To relate this style of value enforcement to childrearing, the difference among the three terms, forbidden, permitted, and allowed, must be considered. Forbidden is absolute; escape from this has to be through rebellion. Permitted gives approval and the practice may or may not be incorporated into the child's life. Allowed can exist with disapproval or approval. When a parent allows his child to do something which is not approved of, the child has the opportunity to explore with the parent pressure still intact. Of equal importance is that there is no need for rebellion; therefore, the relationship between the child and the parent remains whole. This allowed behavior was most evident in the teenage years of the Dunker young and, even within the looseness of the order, seems somewhat of an aberration to the general rules of their subculture. But when the relationship of these values to the individual is examined, this allowed behavior fits within their approach to childrearing.

Theology of the Dunkers

The "moral ought to" of Eby's reference derived from the place of the Bible in the Dunker family's life. It was used for recreational reading, for inspiration, and for surcease from hopelessness and depression. It also provided the basis for their ethical and religious life. The value system of the Dunkers derived from this and companion scriptures:

> Luke 6:45   A good man out of the good treasure of his heart bringeth forth that which is good; and an evil man out of the evil treasure of his heart bringeth forth that which is evil: for of the abundance of his heart his mouth speakest.

Man was made in the image of God and was "little less than the angels." His relationship with God was a personal one which needed no intermediary. Because of this Pietistic statement, the church organization, in the present-day form, was resisted for almost one hundred years. Man should study the Word of God, converse with him through prayer, seek out His will and His way in all things. He should recognize the weakness of the flesh, the existence of the Devil, and the Devil's preying on the flesh-centered weakness of man. The Dunker theology included a vengeful God, a corrupting Devil, and either a pleasant reward in Heaven or a distasteful punishment in Hell. This statement, representing the theology of the time, was made in a private letter by W.K. Conner (b. 1873, PA), a Dunker preacher who also taught Bible at Bridgewater College:

> But from what they told me at home, I fear you are getting farther away from God and heaven. I tell you, there is a heaven and there is a hell. And you are going to spend eternity in one place or the other. You are more than a horse or a dog or any other animal. You will live forever in happiness or in misery just as you choose now. Now is the time you must decide where you are going to spend eternity and I am writing this to help you decide to spend it in heaven.
>
> You are going to die some day. That you know. And you know too that you are not ready to die. And death may come suddenly. Your work is dangerous. One of these days you may come down from a building and never go up another, and where will you be then? I want you to think about this life until you do prepare yourself and live a Christian life, then you need not fear death, and can think of our death time with joy. As it is you don't like to think of it because you know you are not ready.
>
> When you come to die it will be too late, even if you do not fall to your death. So do now what you'll then wish you had done. You know I'm right, that the Bible is back of me, and your own conscience tells you that you should do something. May God help you.[4]

This letter was written in 1917 to his brother whom he thought disregarded the order too often. Among these lapses, he put up lightning rods on barns. This was frowned upon because the reliance of the rods showed a lack of trust in God's protection and mercy. As the letter shows, their theology included the existence of Heaven and Hell. Despite this general belief, one member was not sure of the rules that governed the two entities. He asked the elder whether one could go to Heaven chewing tobacco. The elder pondered a while and then observed that if one chewed tobacco in Heaven, he would surely have to go to Hell to spit.

If God was in the heart, the life would reflect this; if the life concerned itself with matters and pleasures not of God, then God was not in the heart. From this concept came many of the legalisms of the Dunkers that so affected the lives of its members and influenced the way in which its children were raised. From clothes to buggies, from occupations to avocations, from church buildings to home buildings, from speech to singing, and from all other aspects of the Dunker life, Luke 6:45 held supreme, and a violation of this scripture was a serious matter.

The cardinal violation of Luke was pride. The external revealed the internal; therefore, external factors—such as dress, houses, methods of transportation that call attention to the self— could be manifestations of pride, and their use by the members was carefully scrutinized. This was the basis for the avoidance of showy dress, ornaments of various kinds, personal photographs, household furnishings, and other items whose looks spoke of pride and whose expense was out of proportion to their useful- ness. Anything above utilitarianism had to appeal to the sense of pleasure and, therefore, was an instrument of pride. For some reason, this rule did not apply to horses. One could not put bells on the horses at Christmas, paint the buggy a bright color, have ornate harness, or decorate sleds gaily; but a team of horses as fine as money could buy was not a manifestation of pride. This was not accepted by some of the other sects. Dunkers who exhibited this pride and gave into temptation for the trappings of the world were sometimes referred to as "gay dunkers;" this had no connotation of sexual preference. Luke was applied to many areas of the Dunker's life.

A young man who aspired to preach could not ask the congregation to elect him to the ministry. This labelled him as prideful and immediately called for purging this pride before he could be considered. His call had to originate within the congregation, unsolicited. "He was a self-made man and he loved his creator" instantly condemned a person as prideful and therefore ungodly. Even to write about oneself was considered putting the person above God. H.C. Early (b. 1855, VA) defended his motives for writing his ministerial memoirs:

PLATE 4. Sunday School picnic at White Rock, Masentown, Pa.—1919

PLATE 5. A group of young people on a hiking party—1921

Whatever may be said that may appear as self-adulation is not written in this spirit, I assure you.[5]

Pride as a cardinal sin produced a self-effacing people. Brother Daniel Saylor protested that he was empty, had nothing for the people, and was unqualified.* Saylor said this when he was asked to stand for election to the ministry. He was elected, nevertheless, and went on to become one of the influential leaders of the denomination and a confidant to Abraham Lincoln.

The Set-Apart Feeling

It has been held that the members of the Dunker sect, coming from generations of people who had this self-effacing stance, suffered from feeling of inferiority. This is possibly true. However, it related to their position in society and was caused by the comparison with those outside of the sect who did not have the laid-back attitude that the Dunkers had. In addition, the Dunkers may have felt inferior because their theology called for repeated comparison with their God and with repeated statements in their prayers that they were sinful and unworthy. Actually, when comparing their personal worth as defined by their state of grace, they felt superior to others. Their set-apart feeling was conditioned by their rural life and by their distinctive lifestyle. It became a significant factor in the life of the young people as the changing economic environment required them to compete with the young from other cultures. Despite this well-known state of the Dunkers, the literature speaks little of it. Only Dan West and Kermit Eby expressed the feeling when they said that they did not like the culture from which they came. Others spoke more eloquently by leaving the culture. A recent speaker at the AM chided the Dunkers for having a denominational sense of inferiority, citing their peace witness, their heifer project which

---

* One brother said that there were three things he did not like in a preacher. One was for him to begin his sermon with the statement that he was ignorant and empty. If he was, said this brother, he didn't have to tell the congregation—they would find out after five minutes. The second was a preacher who talked twenty minutes after he said what he had to say. And the third was a preacher who prayed for divine guidance as he began his service and then spoke from notes.

grew to a nationwide movement, and their relief work, as examples of denominational maturity and effectiveness. He called for them to "toot" their own horn. Were the Dunkers to do this, they would set aside one of their long-held and cherished values, the sin of pride.

Reconciliation of Economics and Religion

The balancing of economic needs against the teachings of the scriptures presented many thorny problems to the church in council and at their annual meetings. The resolution of these problems, detailed by the answers to queries in the eighteenth and nineteenth centuries, provides some evidence that the church had to engage in painful soul-searching to be equitable to the members and, at the same time, true to the scriptures. These queries, aimed at tobacco, alcoholic beverages, slaves, and the charging of interest, had a very direct and substantial impact on the economic well-being of the members. There were no relief or unemployment benefits. A person who made his living from raising tobacco had an adjustment to make when ordered not to continue to grow that crop. Distilling the grain into alcohol meant the difference between selling his crop, storing it, or perhaps selling it at a lower price. But the harm of tobacco to the body, the disharmony produced by excessive use of alcohol, the inhumanity of slave-holding, and the lack of love in charging interest under certain circumstances had to be dealt with by the scriptural Dunkers. They dealt with it in the context of its effects on the individual and this was based on the evolving business life of the country.

Tobacco was viewed as a lesser evil that was offensive to those around the user and defiled the body—"God's Temple." It was against the order of the church, but it was dealt with by persuasion, not by expulsion. Tobacco was used by men and women alike:

She always wore a little white cap and for a time, she smoked a small clay pipe.[6]

Oh, the stuff that people put into their mouths, I remember when I was a child, some of the elderly women kissed me and I did not enjoy it because they smoked pipes. I did not like smoky kisses.[7]

An elder in Pennsylvania owned a cigar factory; many grew the tobacco as a cash crop. Of the males born in 1880, 71% had smoked; 1900, 54%; and in 1920, 51%.[8] Apparently the AM became frustrated in dealing with the problem, for in 1864 this question was answered in this manner:

Y.M. 1864 Art. 9 Inasmuch as all that our annual meetings had hitherto done to suppress the excessive or intemperate use of Tobacco in smoking and chewing, has virtually proved a failure, could not this meeting adopt some method by which the excessive use of this growing evil could be suppressed in our brotherhood?

Ans. As the use of Tobacco is offensive to some brethren and sisters, and the excess of it an evil, we advise and counsel brethren not to use it in time of worship so as to be either filthy, or offensive to others; and we think our ministering brethren should admonish their members not to indulge in the excessive use of it in any way, because it is wrong to do so.[9]

The use of alcohol was viewed more seriously than the use of tobacco. In addition, the private use was viewed very differently from distilling for sale. And distilling liquor was viewed with more gravity than brewing beer. Many brethren owned distilleries to process their grain into alcohol. The expense of transporting this to the market was less than raw grain. With the query of 1781, the Dunkers incorporated into the church order a prohibition against the ownership of distilleries. Later, selling grain to a distillery was discouraged. The private use of alcohol was advised against; but temperance was required, not abstinence. Because alcohol produced so much human misery, it was considered advisable that the Dunkers not operate taverns. The church eventually took the stand that temperance would not work; abstinence was the solution to the problem. However, this did not become part of the order until 1862. In the generation of 1880, 53% thought the use of alcohol wrong; in 1900, 88%; and in 1920, 100%.[10] The outside cultural stand of abstinence influenced the subculture of the Dunkers.

Nonviolence and Slavery

The Dunker position on taking a human life has stood firm throughout the history of the church, and, therefore, its opposition to war as a means of settling disputes. There were a few voices heard during the War Between the States who declared that, since governments were ordained of God, perhaps governments could engage in war where groups of individuals could not. This meant that a person could take a life if he acted on the order of the government. But other voices countered with the argument that a person owed his allegiance to God first and to the government second. Although the government was ordained of God to provide peace and harmony for the general well-being of God's children, infallibility was not conveyed upon it since the government's judgment is that of men who are subjected to the errors of the human mind. Therefore, they were to obey the laws of the land, but only when these laws were not in conflict with the law of God. This view has held constant.

The principle of nonviolence in settling disputes, compared with pacifism, did not hold with equal force. These instances were found. The first occurred in Indiana around 1860. The elder was a big, burly man:

> On one occasion a ruffian started to 'clean up' a crowd. Elder Berkey went to him, took him by the arm, and set him down, telling him to sit still and he did.[11]

In the second instance, George Wolfe followed the first step of conflict resolution according to Matthew: he went to the person. When that failed he reverted to the wild:

> His problem resulted from his marriage to a young lady who was coveted by a lawyer. Wolfe attempted to reason with him. When this failed, he invited the "spindling lawyer" to settle the matter with his fists.[12]

Elder Wolfe, Jr. was not a minister at the time of this story. He later was elected to the ministry and served effectively for many years. Even the youngsters were slow to anger, but eventually they did with some "Dutch" temper. D.L. Miller (b. 1841, MD) went to his tormentor, but in a combative way:

> A lot of boys used to throw stones at me, as I rode out of town. One day I got off "Old Fan" the bay mare—and settled the score with them.[13]

However, in the plurality of their beliefs some adhered to nonviolence in conflict resolution. J.H. Moore tells about the time a man threw a handspike at his father's head. His father dodged and received the blow on the shoulder. "Father never attempted to strike back."[14] Another story of the nonviolent approach is told. This occurred in Maryland in the late 1800's:

> John Herr demonstrated in his daily life that a minister lives the message he preaches to others. One night, while still living on the farm, he was awakened by the noise of some one robbing the smokehouse. Brother Herr had a very stealthy way of carrying his large body, and unbeknown to his family he got out of bed and appeared very unexpectedly at the door of the smokehouse. The thief on the outside in his fright ran to safety as soon as he spied the owner of the home, without alerting the thief on the inside of the smokehouse. Brother Herr quietly took his place, and without saying a word continued to receive the hams. Finally the thief asked how many hams they should take, to which Elder Herr replied that they might as well take all of them. It was only then that the thief discovered that his buddy had left him, and that Brother Herr was receiving the hams. Then he wanted to run away, but Brother Herr insisted that he take a ham for his family. When he refused by saying that he did not need a ham, Brother Herr reminded him that surely a man who goes to his neighbor at midnight for ham must need ham very desperately, and he compelled the man, who was his neighbor, to take a ham along home. He further reminded him that any time in the future, when he needed a ham he was not to bother to come during the night, for he could have as much as he needed any time he would ask. Needless to say the man never needed ham so much after that.[15]

The principle of nonviolence ran deep in the Dunker tradition and, for the most part, left no place for guns in the family except for hunting purposes. The age to receive a knife or a gun was a milestone of maturity. Kermit Eby's grandfather felt that, at the age of six years, a boy could carry a knife. (Of course, this was not for protection; it was useful on the farm.) At fourteen, in some families, he was capable of handling a gun. This gun was used to hunt game for the table.

While there were a number of instances where Dunkers were gunsmiths, this was not a wholly approved occupation of the members. Other families would not allow a gun in the house. But, in some cases, they did rely on guns as a defense against the Indians:

The congregation for years carried their guns regularly to church, stacked them by the door, and placed a sentinel to them to give the alarm, so that the men could rush to their arms.[16]

This refers to the Antietam congregation in the days of the Indian forays and massacres. In Maryland, farmers took their guns to the fields with them in case they were attacked by the Indians. But the official position of the church never permitted this. Though this position of pacifism has held for over two hundred years, at no time has there been one hundred percent agreement among the members. A high percentage of the members support the concept on a theoretical basis and, as such, impart the value to their children as they grow to adulthood. Some accounts suggest that, over the years, less than half of the Dunkers supported the peace position to the extent where they would not serve in the armed forces. In practice, this percent has been very low, perhaps as low as ten percent. However, this may not show the true extent of the pacifistic stand of the Dunker youth; some remained on the farm and did not have to declare their belief.

Character, Ethics and Economics

The worth of the individual as a child of God was central to the German Baptist's theology, and the individual was asked to merit this regard. His personal integrity must be without blemish, his word should be his bond. Kermit Eby describes his Grandfather Schwalm and the community in which he lived:

> In this day of short cuts, the Brethren are very right in yet another matter. They know there is no substitute for integrity, and no contract is as binding as the world of the man who signed it. My Grandfather Schwalm never signed a note at the bank where he did business. To be asked to do so was a reflection on his integrity. Sometimes, he went a step further and gave his approval for loans to young men of the community, always judging them by their character. Signing notes and swearing oaths were for lesser men.

> Furthermore, when members of our church community violated their and the community's integrity, it was a violation of the respect held for the whole. For example, there was the case of one of our neighbors who added a little water to his milk and therefore some extra weight which enhanced his milk check by a few pennies. He was caught and made to repent before the whole congregation. It was something terrible for a Brethren, whose word was as good as

his bond, to commit such an act. There there was the case of the neighbor who sold my father a kicking horse as a gentle worker. The first time I went to harness her, she nearly kicked my head off and we were able to work her only at the risk of our lives. Dad told the story to Grandfather, and once more the community went to work and the seller was asked to take his horse back and publicly repent his sins. These lapses were looked upon as a reflection on the whole community, for the Brethren were extremely conscious that an individual's performance was the concern of the whole group. Thus, the shame of the transgression was each man's shame. Because of this kind of attitude, those who took short cuts were frowned upon and the weight of the whole community kept them from going astray.[17]

Note the line of authority and position of influence. The father was in his mid-thirties at the time, yet he reported to his father who called for community action.

While the extent to which these values were held according to Eby's account may have been overstated, the form was there and the substance was considerable. This community pressure, augmented by the fact that many in that community were related, influenced the Dunker young people with an intensity approaching that of the nuclear family. In addition, it provided a uniformity of values beyond the immediate family. Eby mentioned this pressure by remarking on the difficulty of escaping the eyes of God and the all-seeing eyes of the sisters. That the actions of the individual were a reflection on the group is specific to close-knit groups with identities such as the Dunkers; the operative phrases to work with this concept are "group influence" and "group pressure." While the Dunkers did not recognize formally these psychological mechanisms, they used them quite effectively as they clustered in neighborhoods and localities, molding the lives of their young.

The Dunkers held dearly two concepts: that the individual was second only to God in intrinsic worth; and that labor, mostly manual, was the best expression of a purposeful life under God's direction. From these, it was easy to conclude that the manner in which a person worked and the quality of the product he produced expressed the worth of the individual. His work showed what sort of man he was and what was in his heart. Hard, clean work which produced good that benefitted mankind showed that God was in his heart. Working in a tavern that aided drunkenness and "disharmony" indicated that God was not in his heart. This interpretation of the scriptures was evident before 1900; it is still evident in the vocations that many of the young people of the church choose. As the opportunity to enter non-farm occupations became available to the youths, their indoctrination towards the purposeful life caused them to enter service vocations; the service occupations became the farm work of their grandfathers.

Regardless of the occupation of the old Dunker, his work carried his identity as an individual and as a churchman. In Pennsylvania, E.K. Ziegler (b. 1903, PA) observed of his father:

> I know father took quiet pride in having the best butter, meat, and vegetables (the father sold to the city dwellers).[18]

A man should give an hour of work for an hour of pay. Not only should his product be without flaw, the amount contracted for should be there. D.L. Miller (b. 1841, MD) said this of his father:

> He always sold guaranteed goods and in every particular lived up to the pledge. His measures were the "heaped up and running over" kind.[19]

Keeping one's word was not an attribute just of the Dunkers. Legal talent was scarce on the frontier where transactions crucial to survival were made frequently. Consequently, it was important that a handshake seal a business deal. The Dunkers had little use for legal contracts and lost land claims because of this. But their reputation for honesty brought them customers for their produce and became the collateral for borrowing.

Other Applications of Personal Integrity

If obedience was the cardinal value of childhood, personal integrity was the cardinal value of adult life. This was reflected in two practices which had wide currency in the life of the Dunkers, not ideals which were given lip service and ignored. First, to sign a promissory note was a reflection on the integrity of the signer, and, until bank and commerce practices demanded it, the Dunker would not do this. "A Dunker's word was his bond" and was respected by the outside community. Second, although civil law required that oaths be taken in certain instances, the Dunkers refused to do this; rather, they used the term "affirm" which was accepted by the civil authorities. This response was in accordance with the scriptures:

> James 5:12   But above all things, my brethren, swear not, neither by heaven, neither by the earth, neither by any other; but let your yea be your yea; and your nay, nay; lest you fall into condemnation.

This insistence on personal integrity served the Dunkers well in their business life; in their relations with the other members of the sect; and in conflict resolution within the sect. In addition to its use in verbal agreements on various aspects of the business and religious community, the strength of character needed to make "your word your bond" also was needed when a member was called before the church council for commissions of sin or violations of the church order. Weak, threatened individuals could not handle this; strong individuals who had a sense of personal worth could. This, perhaps, was a selective factor in retaining members who continued the sect, despite the absence of coercive measures, for the several hundred years that it lasted.

The perception by the outside community of the character of the adults of the sect was also a stimulus to the young to conform to this model.

Cultural Values: Gender, Birth, and Death

The values passed from father to son, through example, role model, or through instruction, came not just from the scriptures. Ethnic and general cultural traditions and practices were also part of the life of the German Baptist Brethren and were reflected in their childrearing. Gender designation and expectation, death, and birth showed the effects of these influences. H. Stover Culp (b. 1984, MD) wrote:

> In a day when all babies wore dresses, I remember the great day when I passed from neuter dresses to masculine pants.[20]

This was not a "Dutch" custom, but was one observed by many groups of that time. The transition to gender specific clothes occurred around four years of age, and, with this transition, the male stereotype was imposed on the child. This story from the midwest is remembered:

Grandmother Hildebrand took great delight in telling a story about her oldest son, Joe, whom I imagine was a very handsome little fellow. Whenever he cried, Grandmother tried to console him by saying in Pennsylvania Dutch, "Pretty boys don't cry." Apparently little Joe didn't understand the language because she said he would follow her everywhere wailing at the top of his voice in Pennsylvania Dutch, "Pretty boys don't cry." Although more than sixty years have passed since Grandmother last told that story, I can hear her laughingly tell it as though it were only yesterday.[21]

Gender expectation followed generally that of the surrounding culture. So did the attitude towards birth, reflecting the ancient superstitions and projections that concerned sex. This was somewhat surprising in a Biblical-oriented group who thought that birth control was an interference with the natural order, and who lived in the environment of the farm where sexual practices of the animals were there for the children to observe. But the children were shielded from this event and, as Ruel Pritchett (b. 1884, TN) said, were uninformed about the whole process:

It was no unusual thing for us children to get up of a morning and mother wouldn't be at home; nobody to fix breakfast. Daddy couldn't cook; he couldn't boil water without scorching it. And we'd inquire about mother. He was a little delicate about telling us, but he'd finally say, "She has gone up to Uncle Daniel Bowman's. Aunt Sue is sick." We were uninformed about the whole process, but Mother was a midwife.[22]

The use of the term "sick" to describe the most natural of processes represents the triumph of cultural values over scriptural ones. But the Tennessee children were not the only ones who were uninformed; so were those in Pennsylvania. Despite a house which was big enough to keep the children separated from the birthing area, the Zieglers, in 1913, sent their children away:

That evening my brother Jesse was born. We older children had gone to Grandma's house . . .[23]

The Blough children fared even worse:

On April 21, I think, another baby came to our house. This was in 1871. Mime and I were sent out into the fields and woods with Silas who was three years old. The weather was raw and damp, and we all got cold and he began to cry for us, and finally when we ventured home, we were told that a baby boy had come. We named him Elijah.[24]

Jerome Blough was ten years old at this time. Note that he included himself in selecting a name for his little brother. This has the flavor of not only a close family but also that even the ten-year-old thought of himself as an important part of the family who was included in the decision making.

Though the Dunkers followed the world in reacting to childbirth, they were much more scriptural in their attitude towards death and at the event of death. It is probable, though, that most people of that time had a similar attitude.

Only recently has death been regarded as a postponable event. During the period under study, there was a fatalism about the ultimate outcome of life that called for the acceptance of the death of the loved ones as it happened. This was particularly true of the young in whom infectious diseases were deadly and which required the adults to develop a defense mechanism against the inevitable loss of a child. The Dunkers' religious beliefs provided this, because the innocence of childhood in their minds was only a short step away from the purity of angels. They were confident that the children would be accepted, not rejected. Harry Ziegler's son, Mark, was terminally ill, and when he died the father went into the room of E.K. Ziegler, who was eight years old, and said, "Mark has now gone to be with Jesus."

With this acceptance of death from a faith basis, the children were not shielded from the event of death. They attended funerals, viewed corpses, participated in wakes as they grew older, and were part of the family mourning system. This mourning system, within the religious beliefs of the sect, provided the environment for the children to learn to accept death in increments of their emotional development. That the dead go to be with Jesus can be understood by the youngest, while the concept that life is a journey necessary to live with God can be understood by the teenager. Death was truly a victory, not a defeat, to the Dunkers.

Primary Scriptural Values and Derived Values

The life of members of the German Baptist Brethren was a religious experience, drawn from values derived principally from the New Testament. These values were manifested in the church order, a structure which governed the lives of the Dunkers. Both the core values of recognizable Biblical origin and the derived values more closely identified with the secular were assimilated into the lives of the children and made up their value system. Some of these will be listed.

The principal belief of the Dunkers was to love and obey God. From this, the children were to love and obey their father and mother, and to observe the rules of the family and of the church. Obedience to the established order became a derived value from the primary one of obedience to God.

God must be in the heart. By the interpretation of the elders, clothes other than those of the order were a manifestation of pride, the antithesis of God in heart. From this and other interpretations, a concept of stewardship developed where resources should be used for the greatest good, rather than for satisfaction of one's personal desires. This derived value produced conflict with the young, because they wanted those things that other young people had.

The main purpose of life was to develop a relationship with God. To do this, one had to believe in and follow the dictates of the scriptures. Farm life was the ideal place to implement these beliefs, because manual labor not only expressed Christian attributes but also it shielded the member from the temptations of the world. Farm life developed a sense of responsibility, appreciation of nature, patience, compassion, and sharing that became part of the growing child. The seasons and the harvests were symbols of the renewal of life. The products of the farm were tangible evidences of the partnership between nature and man, between God and man.

The individual is made in the likeness of God. From this core belief came the derived value of democracy which gave each member an equal voice in church organization and called for the use of Matthew's way of conflict resolution. This core value perhaps caused the Dunkers to view their children as individuals in their own right.

Life is to be lived according to the Gospel. The semi-literate Dunkers accepted, at face value, the Biblical commands. From these developed the mindset, augmented by the isolated rural life, that rules were white or black, right or wrong, correct or incorrect.

Read the Bible, stay with the order, and heaven was the reward. This provided a security and a sense of safety for many of the young people, because they did not have to think. For others, it was quite perplexing and stifling.

The order of the Dunkers, with its leaning towards the rural life, provided many secondary values which guided the lives of the Dunker youths, and which they recorded into their basic value system. Observing the order was a visible sign to the parents that their children were in conformity with the teachings of the Bible and of the church. As the order slowly dissolved in the period before 1900, the parents lost their sign, and they began a frantic search to find solutions to their "youth problem," one which seemed to be more in the minds of the parents than in the beliefs and behavior of the children. As Paul Bowman said in 1928, "Mistrust of youth is usually born in the conferences of those whose contacts with young people have been broken. The best panacea for this attitude of mind is in the comradeship of young people. They are better and finer than rumor would have us believe."[25] As the order dissolved, the youth discarded the garb; they did not discard the essential values of their ancestors.

Recreation Within the Culture and the Order

The use of leisure time speaks to the values of a group. In the world of the Dunker, recreation was spelled with a small "r"; for the most part, it was hyphenated with purpose. The serious Dunkers, believing that they lived for a purpose, tolerated poorly the waste of time. They disapproved even more the use of time which "tickled the senses," did not produce a recognizable economic gain, or did not produce spiritual growth. Many of the recreational exercises of the day, fairs, carnivals, dances, not only failed to meet the criteria of the purposeful life but also produced "disharmonies" which were contrary to the scriptural admonition for love between persons. Therefore, the group had a narrow list of acceptable activities which could be used as relief from the everyday routine.

Those activities within the list generally met the criteria of permissible recreation: labor, purpose, and spirituality. For most of the period under study, an additional factor was weighed in determining if an activity was permissible: whether the group was all Dunkers or whether it also had "outsiders." If all Dunkers, the activity became an extension of the church and, therefore, was approved. But when held in conjunction with those of the neighborhood, it was seen as a "social" gathering, highly suspect. The ideal recreational exercise, then, was one which combined labor, purpose, and spirituality within the Dunker group.

But there was an additional restriction: never on Sunday. This was the designated day of rest and worship, commanded by the familiar scripture of Exodus 20:8, 9, 10, 11:

> Remember the Sabbath day, to keep it holy. Six days shalt thou labor, and do all thy work. But the seventh day is the Sabbath of the Lord thy God: in it, thou shall not do any work, thou, nor thy son, nor thy daughter, thy manservant, nor thy maidservant, nor thy cattle, nor thy stranger that is within thy gates.

Although a number of the Dunkers joined the Ephrata Cloister and the Snow Hill Nunnery, Sabbitarian communes in Pennsylvania which worshipped on the seventh day, Saturday, these were not part of the Dunker sect. It never approved of seventh day worship. The Dunkers' interpretation of this scripture was in harmony with the reasoning of the Pennsylvania Supreme Court in 1848, in Specht versus the Commonwealth. The court ruled that the state had the authority under the Pennsylvania Constitution, without violating the religious liberty clause, to establish Sunday as a civil holiday during which all unnecessary work was banned as long as the state did not forbid anyone from worshipping on any given day. The ruling turned on the interpretation that the imperative in the above scripture was to observe one day of rest, not to work six days or to worship on one particular day. They further observed that, since the majority of the citizens observed the first day as their Sabbath, it was logical that the state designate that day as the state-mandated day of rest.[26] A reference indicates that one Dunker father found two imperatives in the scriptures: work six days and worship on the seventh. His son concluded sadly that this would make him a dull boy.

The Dunkers observed the Sabbath to the extreme with their insistence on only worshipful or restful activities. Their reluctance to approve Sunday Schools was based partly on the fear that these schools would be social instead of worshipful.

But the Dunkers, as have all groups, found ways to relieve the tedium of their daily lives with a minimum of conflict within the order. Dancing produced the most problems, deemed by the Dunkers to have a potential to harm the spirituality of the members by appealing to the flesh and "tickling the senses." It was strictly forbidden by the order, not only for the above reasons but because dances were held in taverns and other public places where drunkenness and fights often occurred. This disharmony could not be tolerated. As the school system developed and as dancing became part of the social program of the schools, the youths of the church wanted to participate. The order was very slow in changing in reaction to this pressure, even though one of the main reasons why they objected to it was no longer a factor— the place in which the dances were held.

Many of the members of the sect ignored the order and attended dances as the minutes of local church councils and the several AM's show. It was not until the youths put continuing pressure on the parents that the opposition to dancing gradually disappeared. This did not happen until the fourth or fifth decade of the twentieth century.

Essential work, such as milking the cows, was permitted on Sunday, but not haymaking. The day was used by some for relaxing, but non-purposeful activities certain of which, such as fishing and sports, received reluctant approval. As extra-curricular activities became a more important part of the school life, further accommodations were made in the order. The attitude towards singing was a major one.

Singing has always been a big part of the life of the Dunkers, both in their meeting houses and in their homes and schools. They not only wanted to be better at it, but some were good enough to teach voice. Queries to the AM for clarification of this matter were frequent. The time frame and progression of the reasoning illustrates the sect's adaptability to current circumstances, including the current mood of its members. Again, this is relevant to childrearing because it shows that the order was not rigid and unchanging, but was responsive, however slowly and reactively, to the beliefs of its members. These references will be given consecutively for ease of comparison, and to follow the progression of thought:

Y.M. 1825 Art. 4   Whether a brother may teach singing schools was considered, that the musical schools, as they are generally conducted, have nothing to do with the services of God, and that a brother should teach none.

Y.M. 1838 Art. 2   Whether it is considered proper to hold singing schools in our meeting houses? Chiefly considered, that meeting houses are no proper places for holding singing schools therein.

Y.M. 1849 Art. 22   Can a brother be allowed to teach singing schools on Sundays, and take money for the same? Considered, that much as we are in favor of correct singing, we still think it best for a brother not to teach singing schools.

Y.M. 1857 Art. 22   Is it agreeable to the gospel for brothers brethren to teach singing schools? Answer: We consider it best for brethren not to teach singing schools on Sabbath or at night.

Y.M. 1862 Art. 7   Is it allowed by the brethren in annual council for the members of the church to attend singing schools on Sundays, or at night, or in the week? While we could caution our members, especially the young, against the abuses of singing schools, we would not absolutely forbid them if conducted orderly, and if they do not conflict with the time of preaching.[27]

In the period of thirty-seven years, the Dunkers went from prohibiting a member from teaching in singing school to permitting him to do so; in addition, singing schools on Sunday were permitted. The important point of this progression of thought is that it was reactive. The delegate body, after being pressured repeatedly in the form of queries, finally gave in over a short period of five years.

Unfortunately, there are no references to establish precisely what this reactive rule did to the young of the sect, but it can be surmised that two things occurred: there was bitterness created in their minds and/or the rules were broken. This may have contributed to the developments of the 1920's because, as the Dunkers perceived that they had a "youth problem," their rule-making became less reactive and the administration became more active in guiding the youth through programs.

The specific description of the types of recreation do not tell as much about attitudes toward childrearing as do the reasons why these activities were approved and permitted. In analyzing these reasons, it is useful to consider them from the standpoint of the number in the activity, whether the activity was productive, and whether it was church-related. This applies primarily to those activities of the teenage years. The physical limitations of the preteens not only removed them from the criteria of usefulness, but also kept them close to home and in activities which could not be considered worldly. However, the story is told of a very little Dunker boy, Samuel A. Kahle of West Virginia, who managed to combine recreation with purpose and, in the process, disturb a worship service. It seems that young Sam was not allowed to go to the Sunday morning worship at the Smith's Chapel because he had misbehaved. He was seven or eight years old. However, after his parents had left, he decided to go down to a little creek, which had to be crossed on the way to church, and fish. Eluding whoever was watching him, he started on his way. He was successful in his fishing, because ten or fifteen minutes later the little fellow walked proudly up the aisle of the church while services were in full session and loudly proclaimed, "Hey, Pa, I caught a fish!" displaying the fish for all to see. He said that he was not spanked for either his disobedience in leaving the house or for disrupting the church service.

Fishing and reading were the activities most frequently mentioned involving only one person. Both of these, although they were purposeful, were generally prohibited on Sunday unless the reading concerned religious material. While not mentioned as frequently, the boys hunted a great deal when the season was in; some trapped. This was a combination of recreation and work because the game was used either for the table or for skins. The majority of the social activities of the Dunker youth was group, purposeful, and church-related. Lester Flory described in a reference to be given how work can be play. Mary Early Davis[28] described group activities which included sleigh riding and walks in the fields. Jerome Blough[29] described the many activities of the very young and, in addition, the spelling bees and Christmas festivities in the schools. Austin Cooper describes two activities which were group, purposeful, and religiously-oriented:

> Large crowds of Brethren would meet at a central meeting place and walk many miles; as many as twenty-miles to the "Big Singing," the Love Feast, or the "Big Meeting." The strong married men and the middle aged men would always walk in the vanguard. There was not one of them armed, save with a staff. Next in order would

come their wives, mixed with the young girls and "young sisters" who were eligible and prospective wives. Next in order came the older couples with the boys and young women who needed an eye on them to keep them in the order. However, there are many stories, and we certainly may see that they had a tinge of truth in them, that the adults occasionally looked the other way if the son or daughter or kinsman had a "crush" on one or the other of the group. Secret songs, hymns, noises, were given at certain times to attract the attention of either the boy or the girl by the opposite sex in the walk (though Brethren were not to hold secrets from the group). In the back of the group were other young or middleaged men who kept an eye on the rear of the procession for danger.[30]

This arrangement was primarily for protection, but it also served as a social outing to be enjoyed by the young and the old; furthermore, the walk kept the young people under the eyes of the older couples so that they could be kept "in the order" without imposing formal courting rules on these young couples. The conditions of the day required the form; group pressures provided the discipline.

The second activity is unique in that it is an example of some of the occasions in which the Dunker youth socialized with the young of other denominations:

Another favorite group gathering was the "Scripture Bee" when large crowds would assemble when the teams would form, or challenges would be given to other denominations to see who could answer the most questions about the Scriptures. There are many stories that such gatherings almost got out of hand. About Civil War time there were many debates and Scripture Bees planned between the Brethren and "Albrighters" or Evangelicals. This was usually a very active and boisterious session.[31]

Despite this intermingling with members from other denominations, not all Dunker communities agreed. The minutes of the Midland, Virginia church around 1890 suggest that it was wrong for Brethren to invite non-members' youngsters to their social gatherings.

Spelling bees, fishing parties, weddings and corn shuckings provided recreational opportunities, group and productive, but were not related to church activities. Weddings provided, as a social gathering, visiting time for members who saw each other infrequently. A festival spirit at the wedding was permissible and

PLATE 6. Swimming in the Cheet River near Morgantown, West Virginia

PLATE 7. Ice skating near Great Falls, Virginia—1929

proper, but infares were not. These occurred on the evening of the wedding while the couple was still at the bride's home preparing for their wedding trip. A group of the couple's friends would steal up and surround the house. On signal, the young people made noises by every conceivable means, sometimes even with dynamite. This noise continued until the bride and groom appeared at the window and acknowledged the presence of the crowd, which was then invited into the house for refreshments. According to church order, this should not happen:

> Y.M. 1827 Art. 11   Whether we may be allowed to hold infares? Considered that it belongs to pride, extravagance and vanity, and should not be among members.[32]

The attitude towards this type of entertainment changed. Several decades later Otho Winger, who was to become one of the leaders of the church, took a bride. The household of the bride's parents had settled down for the night:

> But all was not quiet for the night. For at an unexpected moment, there burst in wild discord. Dynamite and circular saws lent their discordant noise to increase the music. The youthful party was then invited in, and after they extended congratulations, they were treated to pie and cake.[33]

The infare was a group activity and perhaps the group was made up of the youth of the church. But infares, like dancing, were identified with worldly and disruptive behavior and, as such, the form was not acceptable to the Dunkers. As the substance of the activity changed and as the behavior of the group conformed to the order, the method of honoring the newlyweds became acceptable.

There were communities in Pennsylvania made up almost entirely of members of the German Baptist Brethren, so their activities became the community's recreational activities. These members came together at the various church functions and fun was mixed with church work:

> The men and boys of the community held their horse races, their carriage races, and in earlier days foot races, as a means of group participation and amusement. Many members still living can relate stories when during Council Meetings, Love Feasts and

Church Services, such races were held from Berling to Brotherton and back or the Pike Church to Roxbury or to Shankville and back. This was a time when axle nuts and all wheels were well examined to see if anyone had tampered with them. The lust for speed existed in 1770 or 1800, just as it does among the young people of today. Certain of the elders took great pride in having horses which were capable of a good gait too and occasionally talked about how much time it took between appointments.[34]

The Dunkers departed from their doctrine when they permitted races among their members, because winning a race, be it between men or between horses, has only one reward—the pride of winning. Again, it is noted that this doctrine did not extend to the horse; they could own and display and brag about the best horse they could afford.

As the modern age approached and team sports were formed, the Dunker youth was allowed to participate. L.W. Schultz (b. 1890, IND) said of his father:

> He allowed me to play ball—on Sunday afternoons. A happy memory I have of him (father) is our playing croquet together in our farm yard.[35]

Ruel Pritchett (b. 1883, TN) and his brother were permitted to play baseball.[36] Ernest Wampler, who was born in Virginia at about the same time, was also allowed to play ball, not only in his neighborhood but also in college. Playing ball was not sinful; that it was played on Sunday afternoon constituted the objection of the church to that activity. All three of these men came from traditional Dunker families and would become outstanding in the church.

Summary

The Dunker children were reared under a system of values derived from the scriptures, from the environment, and from the demands of the economics of the day. Obedience was a prime virtue of children; integrity was demanded of the adult. Their concept of the simple life included industriousness, frugality, and the wise use of assets. Respect was required from the members for the established order of the church and the values of that order. These included temperance, lack of pride, non-violence, and adherence to the Biblical method of conflict resolution. Other values were present in a pervasive way to mold the characters and personalities of the young as they grew into womanhood and manhood within the sectarian form.

3

Organization and the Child

The German Baptist Brethren Church was made up of congregations loosely tied together through the media of travelling elders, Annual Meetings and District Meetings. These were nestled in the order, a pervasive system of customs and beliefs which provided guidance to the members. These beliefs and customs were codified by the query and answer process and recorded in the proceedings of the local, district, and national meetings. Examination of some of the queries with their answers provides insights into the minds of the members of the sect.

Since the children were not members, the codification of beliefs (the order) had little direct effect on the children until around 1870. After this, institutional influences increased slowly until 1900, rapidly after that. But until 1900, the references indicate that the church related to the children in four ways: advisory, baptism, programs for the youth, and helping the unfortunate. The change in the age of baptism and the programs for the youths were developments after 1900.

The foremost influence of the early organized church was advisory. Through answers to queries submitted to the AM the parents were directed on the several aspects of the care of their children. The answer to a query of 1789 gives surprisingly modern advice on how best to teach. While directed toward religious instruction, the methodology applies to other areas and speaks to an advanced concept of the child and his capabilities. In addition, the answer gives a sense of appreciation for the worth of the child. It also affirms the responsibility of the parents to provide religious instruction for their children. The Dunkers' position in 1789 was more remarkable when one considers that, at that time, the child was still shamefully treated in the world at large. Child labor sweat shops, punitive discipline, swaddling, and infanticide were present in England. In the United States protective laws of significance would not be passed for another hundred years, these spurred by the inhuman use of children in industry.

Parents of that time had no one to look to when concerns about their children arose. Government was not interested in the minutia of childrearing; it was hardly interested in the child, certainly not as a child. There were no community support groups. Even were these facilities available, the Dunker parent would not have used them, because they answered only to the order of their sect. So, when their parenting practices seemed inadequate they looked to their organization for help. This was particularly appropriate since it was assumed that the parenting inadequacies resulted from the failure of the parents to carry out the mandate of the scriptures. To them this was significant. While all parents are apprehensive that their children will not follow family traditions, to the Dunkers, failure of their children to stay in the order represented a personal failure as well as a loss of "a sheep from the flock." No matter that the youth followed the essentials of religion. If he did not conform to the peripherals as prescribed by the order, the parents had failed to meet their responsibility to "bring him up in the fear and admonition of the Lord," that is, in the Dunker way. It is from this perspective that the query was sent to the AM in 1789. Because it is one of the most important references, the complete query and its answer are given:

> AM 1789 Art. 2 . Inasmuch as many of our children and young people fall into a coarse life, and a great occasion of it seems to be a want that there is not sufficient diligence used in instructing the children according to the word of the Lord given by Moses in Deut. 6:7 where we read: "and thou shalt teach them (these words I command thee this day) diligently unto thy children, and shalt talk of them when thou sittest in thy house, and when thou walkest by the way, and when thy liest down, and when thou risest up"; and also the apostle Paul says (Eph. 6:4), that parents should "bring them (their children) up in the nurture and admonition of the Lord."

> It is our opinion (and advice) that there should be used more diligence to instruct our dear youth and children in the word of truth to their salvation, and that it is the special duty of the dear

parents, as well as of the pastors and teachers, to be engaged herein, inasmuch as the apostle teaches, "Feed the flock of God which is among you, taking the oversight thereof." (1 Pet. 5:2). And inasmuch as the children of the faithful belong to the flock of Christ, just as naturally as the lambs belong to the flock of sheep; and inasmuch as the word can be brought nearer to the hearts of children in a simple conversation or catachisation or however it may be called, than otherwise in a long sermon, to that they apprehend the word of divine truth, believe in Jesus Christ, and accept his doctrine and commandments, and walk therein to their eternal salvation— hence we admonish in heartfelt and humble love all our in God much loved fellow laborers, in the dear and worthy name of our Lord Jesus Christ, who has given himself into death for us, that we should die to ourselves, and live to him forever, that they would use all possible diligence that our dear youth might be provoked to love God, and to appreciate his Word from their childhood. Do not spare any labor and toil to convince them by our teaching and by our lives, not after the manner which is almost too common nowadays, then to rehearse it in a light, thoughtless manner, and then are permitted to go in a life as thoughtless as before—but that they may give themselves up to God in an earnest life. The great Rewarder of all good will undoubtedly remunerate you; for those that have done right shall live forever, and the Lord is their reward, and Most High provides for them; and they will receive a glorius Kingdom and a beautiful crown from the hand of the Lord. (Sap. 17:17)[1]

The position of children expressed in the answer is a high one: teach by example, simple conversation without memorization, begin instruction early, constancy, give weight and meaning to instruction. Note the failure to mention discipline, punishment, and the child characterization of the ages—bad, sin, wilful, self-centered and others. This statement suggests that the Dunkers indeed viewed their child as an individual within a sentimental relationship. But this should be considered: does the statement represent the prevailing group perception of the child or is the statement the view of one man or of a small group of men? A review of the process of handling a query sheds some light on this.

The Significance of an Answer to a Query

At this time in the sect's development, queries originated from the local churches and were presented to the Standing Committee of the Annual Meeting. The Standing Committee was made up of senior elders, selected from the elders residing in the area in which the meeting was held. This Committee considered the queries on their merits within the beliefs of the Dunkers, drew up an answer, and reported this to the delegate body. After full debate, the answer was accepted or rejected. Or it may have been modified and accepted. Either way, the acceptance had to be almost unanimous. After this, it became part of the rules of the church, the order. Near unanimity was required to ensure that each decision had a broad base of support among the members so that conflict, disharmony, and splintering would not result.

In this process, the elders of the Standing Committee had a significant influence on the content of the answers; however, the delegate body had the final approval. These elders represented generally the more conservative views of the brotherhood, had the most intimate contact with the previous generation because of their age, and tried to keep the present order of the brotherhood in harmony with the practices of the founders, the Order of the Ancient Brethren.

The Standing Committee of the Yearly Meeting of 1789 was of this composition and represented essentially the next generation from the founders of the sect. The first generation died around the middle of the century: Mack, Sr., 1735; Naas, 1741; Becker, 1758, and Michael Frantz, 1748. Of the fifteen men on the Standing Committee of 1789, three were born shortly after the formal beginning of the sect and thus had close exposure in their youth to Mack, Sr., Becker, and the others. Daniel Letterman was born in 1706; Martin Urner, 1725; and Jacob Stoll in 1731. Other names mentioned as members of the Committee were those of first generation Dunkers: Brumback, Eby, and Schrieber. These undoubtedly were the sons of the founding members or of early converts. The Standing Committee of 1790 is more revealing of the lineage and therefore of the direct link with the founders: Sander Mack, son of the founder; Peter Keyser, whose family dated back to the Mennonites in Switzerland in the 1500's; and Michael Frantz. Christopher Sower, Jr., one of the most influential Dunkers of the 1700's, died in 1884, just five years before the meeting under discussion.

It is likely that the answer to the query of 1789 expressed a sect-wide perception of the child. The query had to be examined and an answer formulated by a representative group of the senior elders with links to the founders. These elders did not acquire their perception of the child in academic isolation nor perch it on esoteric theories of their own formulation. Therefore, it can be assumed that their contribution to the answer represented the first generation perception of the child. Because the query had to be approved by a large majority of the delegates present, it can be further assumed that the perception of the child inherent in the answer to the query was indeed the prevailing view of the members of the Dunker sect.

Again, we come to an oft-repeated warning: care must be taken to distinguish what was said from what was done. Even though the Dunkers stated a high position intellectually, their actual practices certainly had not erased in two generations all of the parenting practices inherited from the people of northern Germany. But if they perceived the child as it seems in the answer to the query, this is evidence that the sentimental child with a place of his own in society existed in that area in the late 1600's.

Even if that perception of the child was original to that group of elders, it received support from the next generations. References a hundred years later indicate that example was the major method of value transference. J.M. Henry and others speak of their father's talking to them in simple conversation about beliefs that the parents held. Accounts which did not meet the criteria of this study tell of the fathers who carried the Bible to the fields where the father and sons used work breaks and lunch to study its meaning.

The 1789 Art. 1 query signals, most likely, a beginning shift in parenting from the secular patterns of Germany to that of a parenting practice molded from Anabaptist and Pietist belief. The generational change from secular parenting practices influenced by a religious structure to that of parenting practices derived from internalized religious convictions produced a more disciplined environment for the children. To a certain extent, this narrowed their intellectual and physical horizons, but did not necessarily destroy their freedom of thought, individual expression in its many aspects, and motivation.

The Age of Baptism
In a second way, the church related to the children in its

requirements for baptism. During the period from 1723 to 1900, it was considered advisable for them to be baptized at the age of understanding—the late teens in the earlier times, and after marriage in the middle times. This was in recognition of the limited cognitive ability of the young and with the freedom of choice inherent in baptism of the older person, it met the requirements of the Pietist theology. This practice also allowed the adolescent the time to experience the self-centered and explorative teen years before accepting the commitment to the order with the discipline required.

The Dunkers had shown a remarkable awareness of the nature, capabilities, and limitations of the child. Towards the end of the nineteenth century, however, they fell prey to the temptations of the ages. They used the child not for his welfare, but for institutional gain. They lowered the age of baptism to increase the membership of the church. In doing this, they violated three of their previously-held beliefs: first, emotionality should not be the basis for acceptance of Christ—early teens are notorious for the emotionality of their decision-making; second, informed, reasoned acceptance of the church and its rules, obviously impossible in the early teens; and third, freedom of choice. Even in the matured child of the frontier farm, freedom of choice was an empty phrase when their susceptibility to parental pressure is considered. Von Hochenau had warned that the institutional church would fetter the religious life; he probably did not foresee the rationalization which would allow these earnest Christians to think that they were acting in the interest of the children when they were actually acting in the interest of the institution.

This movement to earlier baptism began before 1900; it escalated sharply after that, essentially on the same curve as the professional ministry and church programs for the youth developed. In addition to the abrogation of the three beliefs, early baptism represented a shift in perception of the child. Throughout most of the period from 1723 to 1900, the concept of adolescence, with the special immaturity associated with that age, was being accepted.

But who had the truer perception of the child? The 1850 Dunkers who worked their teenagers as adults but did not think that they had the maturity and knowledge to make the decision to accept Christ through faith and reasoning? Or the 1920 Brethren

PLATE 8. A Brethren baptism—1924

PLATE 9. Cannon Branch Public School in Manassas, Virginia—1890

who viewed adolescence as a time to prepare for adult life through developing their minds and bodies, but thought that they had the cognitive ability to accept Christ through faith and reasoning? This question will have to be explored when the childrearing practices of the Brethren after 1900 are studied.

Programs for the Children and Youths

The third area of church involvement in the life and training of the children was in religious instruction. This began with the Sunday School movement and was an admission on the part of the Dunkers that the organized church had a legitimate role in the religious training of the child. This rcognition developed slowly in church councils. In 1838, the AM advised that the Dunkers should "take no part in Sunday Schools." Twenty years later, in 1857, Art. 2, the blessing was given to attending Sunday Schools "if they were conducted in gospel order."[2] The permission of the AM for children to attend Sunday Schools is an example of the reactive nature of their decisions: it was given because the members were going to Sunday Schools of other denominations or to "union" Sunday Schools sponsored by several denominations.

The need for the church as an institution to take over part of the responsibility for the training of the children was said to be due to the weakening of the family structure caused by the dispersal of the members from the farm to the cities. This was only partially true, because Ziegler, in future references, indicates that the Dunkers remained predominantly rural up into the twentieth century and farm families traditionally have been strong. James Quinter, the leading Dunker in 1858 when the movement was gaining force, stated in an article in the Gospel Visitor: 1) Sunday Schools were not a positive force. 2) They should not supplant home or ministry. 3) They might reach those who were not taught at home. 4) They would provide a good social setting. 5) He implied that some people are better teachers than others; these could be used for the benefit of all.[3] His words reflect the concern the Dunkers had for the proper spiritual preparation of their children. They were not yet ready to discard the mandate that families should provide primary religious instruction.

This will be discussed later, but it appears that city flight had little to do with the acceptance of outside religious instruction.

Rather, the major reason appeared to be the basic dynamics of the Dunker family. In the absence of effective controls like excommunication and limited education, the Dunker had the freedom to utilize community resources as they became available. The ties within the Dunker family were loose enough to permit this.

Care of the Unfortunate

The fourth area in which the church related to the children was in the care and nurture of the unfortunate. From its beginnings, the church, as an oganization, accepted the responsibility for the care of the widows, orphans, and those who needed help for one reason or another. This was not a right of the recipients; the giving of help was in response to Biblical injunction. A poorhouse was established in Germantown in the 1770's for the adults. At the AM of 1812, Art. 3, the church acknowledged that it was responsible for the widow and to put her children out in good places (homes). Child rescue work was started, and orphanages were established in the last twenty years of the nineteenth century. These areas of church involvement in the life of the Dunker child represent an institutional or group perception of the needs of the sect's children. But before 1900, the parents were the prime influence, not the church, on the Dunker child.

Summary

From 1723 to 1800, the sect as an organization played a real but peripheral role in the life of the member's child. This role was for the most part advisory. After 1800, the order strengthened and had a more pervasive influence on the lives of the adult members of the sect. Through the adults, the children were influenced. Around 1850, the Order of the Ancient Brethren was tested more and more by those who believed that the family structure was not enough to train the children—outside help was required. Reluc tantly and through schism, the sect adjusted. Yielding part of the responsibility for childrearing to outside agencies was permitted and made possible by the dynamics of the Dunker family, an essential ingredient of which was Pietistic individualism. Programs for the children were developed by the organized church in the decades prior to 1900. This movement was accentuated after 1900.

4

Children

Certain doctrines and events have been credited with determining the course of the evolution by which parenting patterns have been developed. This is not entirely true. The culture-dependent patterns can be likened to a highway which traverses a mountainous state. As one rides along this highway, a peak here, a valley there, a stream, later a pass through the mountain range, each seems to have a decisive influence on the course of that road. One gets the impression that the engineer, in his planning, has been captive to these features. However, a view from an airplane in which one can see long stretches of highway gives a more accurate picture of the road in relation to the topography of the area. From this perspective, it is apparent that the road generally follows a course determined by many factors; the individual features of the topography play a minor role.

The progress of the child in society is the highway; it is influenced by the broad cultural forces. The Catholic Church, the Protestant Reformation, Louis XIV, Gerson, Locke, and Rousseau have influenced the child's place in society, but none have had a decisive effect. Rather, they have had a molding effect permitted by the economics and political balances of the times in the continuum of generations. To say that Pietistic attitudes decisively established the parenting patterns of the Dunkers would be simplistic; to say that the Anabaptists had no influence would be wrong. The parenting patterns of the Dunkers, and therefore the status of the children, should be seen as a continuation of the cultural pattern of the groups from which the early members sprang. They were shaped into a pattern reasonably distinctive for the Dunkers, but not unlike those of other groups with similar religious views and economic circumstances. This progress was gradual; the highway of progress in society has few sharp turns.

History generally accords a specific event or a person's work as the start of a movement. But note this: a Dominican monk in 1405 stated that children were like soft wax that takes whatever imprint is put on it.[1] Locke proposed his tabula rasa (empty slate) as part of the intrinsic nature of children in the 1600's, but Rousseau's writings were needed in the next century to set the tone for children's education. The Anabaptists of the sixteenth century thought children from the beginning were "ignorant, simple, childish, and disposed to evil." A group of elders of the Dunker church thought, in the eighteenth century, that children should learn the scriptures, not just memorize them in an empty fashion, an advanced concept for the time. Yet, a hundred years later, P.H. Beery (b. 1888), a prominent member of the church, voiced what was essentially the sixteenth century Anabaptist position:

> After making due allowance for inbred and heredity principles in human nature, in the child is to be seen a striking illustration of our bias for lawlessness. Among the first manifestations of their part is that of self-control which if licensed and unrestrained, results in a highly developed character of stubborness, self-will, petulance, and incorrigibleness, which is very undesirable and injurious, and as the wise man says, "A child left to himself bringeth his mother to shame." Prov. 19:15[2]

So the progress of the child has not been one of straight line progression. Events in isolation mean little. Rather, the composite of events and the trend which it establishes are meaningful. In evaluating the trend, qualifiers must be used. Schwartz, in his discussion of the Anabaptist's perception of the nature of the children, adds this towards the end of his article:

> It is difficult to tell how sixteenth century attitudes about the nature of children and the prescriptions for child rearing were translated into practice.—Until court records and similar sources concerning the treatment of minors are explored or until an earnest researcher turns up a library of early Anabaptist diaries, one can hope only to describe sixteenth century perceptions of child nature and ideas about childrearing.[3]

It is hoped that the first person method of this study will give an accurate, though limited, insight into the status of the child in the Dunker society before 1900, and that this status of the child can be related to the progress of the child in history as he moved from essentially a non-entity to a child with a soul to a child as an individual.

The Dunkers began their sectarian life in 1708 in a German society formed in part by these shifting perceptions of the nature of the child. Eleven years later, the first group of sectarians left this society and sailed to a neutral new land to develop their own lifestyle with guidelines made by them, not by governments and all-powerful churches. They could not leave their ingrown heritage; it came with them. According to Durnbaugh, it seems that the Old World attitude towards childen may have preceded them to their new home:

> Our people are all getting along well, one better than the next, but no one has scarcity. I was amazed at what I heard concerning those indentured emigrants, about the young and strong people and artisans, how rapidly they are gone as masons, carpenters, and all other trades, and even old people with grown children who can do only farm work. There the child takes over the indenture for both his and his father's or mother's passage for four years, and is able in that time to earn all the necessary clothing and finally a handsome outfit from head to foot, a horse or a cow with a calf; small children take on one and a half's year indenture. When they are twenty-one years old they have to be taught reading and writing, and leave well-dressed and with a horse and cow.

> One find few houses in the city or country where the people are rather prosperous where there are not one or two children. The matter is always discussed at the city hall with great seriousness. Often parents and children are ten, eleven, . . . twenty hours from each other. Often those indenturing themselves are better off than those who paid their passage, as they get their expenses paid by others and learn the peculiarities of the country.[4]

This is taken from a letter from John Naas, one of the early leaders of the sect, to his son in Germany, Jacob William Naas. It speaks to the status of children in Philadelphia in 1733. Note the conditions which were to be met when the young person became twenty-one. These same conditions are mentioned in Dunker cases spanning the period under study. There is no evidence that the Dunkers indentured their children, although later in the period, orphans were placed with families under essentially the same terms but without the legal ties. If the Dunker children were not indentured to pay their passage, it probably speaks to their practice of mutual aid rather than their attitude toward working children.

Four factors influenced the parenting practices of the first and second generation sectarians. The first was the freedom in America which allowed them to adapt the precepts and practices of their heritage to the life in their new environment. The second was the relatively new concept of religion which stressed the application of the New Testament teachings to their daily living. Their order had begun to form, which gave some guidance along Biblical lines to their life. These two, cultural background and religious beliefs, were the main ingredients which affected their pattern of childrearing as it developed in comparative freedom in the sparsely settled areas of western Pennsylvania and northern Maryland.

The third influence, which had a lesser impact on the parenting patterns of these first and second generation immigrants, was the lack of sociological tension in their environment. There was a constant influx of immigrants, the government was weak, and the population sparse. In addition, the Germans settled close to other Germans. Therefore, there were no significant outside forces to change the lives of these early Dunkers. They continued their European way in the new world. But, as America grew, and the population became more dense, conditions presented by the surrounding environment put the parents and children in tension: the parents wanted things to remain the same; the children wanted to adopt a way of life similar to that of others in the neighborhood. So while the European pattern of living did continue, forces of cultural evolution were at work.

The fourth factor involved in molding the life of the Dunker, and thus their children as they passed through successive generations, was the harsh frontier environment. Those who stayed in the "old states" remained on the farm under an environment which was not as hostile, but still difficult, and which called for the same attributes of character and the same values. The isolated life of both kept the family intact, which, with the structure of the farm, dictated the childrearing methods used by the Dunkers. This setting provided the means by which the Dunker child could both be moderately controlled and yet be given considerable freedom of thought and activity. Again, the status of the Dunker child must be seen in the light of what was possible in the economic setting of that day, not by present standards. Accordingly, control and authority were necessary for survival, not necessarily reflecting an attitude. The Biblical injunction of obedience to the parents was used to provide control so that the work demands of the day would be met.

Unfortunately, the literature of the Dunkers does not give a comprehensive account of the child in their culture. Therefore, what is available will be grouped under independent headings not necessarily flowing one to the other. From each of these, though, a different aspect of the child will be seen.

Influence of Biblical Principles on Childrearing

The Pietistic principle of religious individualism and the application of the scriptures to daily living established a basis in thought for the rearing of children. The writings of the Old Testament, and, to a certain extent, the New Testament, provided a basis in fact, in that they outlined the childrearing practices of a two thousand year old culture. The literalistic Dunkers, at times, heeded these admonitions to the letter. At other times, they did not. The concept of obedience to the father, in the nature of a blind, unquestioning attitude, was of the intensity of the Old Testament. The punishment allowed for minor or major transgressions was more in keeping with the New Testament. A Biblical basis can be found in many of the relations of the parents with the children:

> Even a child is known by his ways: whether his work be pure and whether it be right. Proverbs 20:11

> Chasten thy son while there is hope, and let not thy soul spare for his crying. Proverbs 19:18

> Train up a child in the way he should go; and when he is old, he will not depart from it. Proverbs 22:6

This last scripture was observed in principle in handling the adolescent, but it applied also to the young. Abram Conner (b. 1850, PA) would not allow his children to speak at the table unless they wanted food passed. They ate quietly while he and his wife talked in the Dutch. A constructive by-product of this method was that the children learned some of the dialect. The obedience and respect theme, dear to the Dunkers as well as other cultures and subcultures, is mentioned in both the Old and New Testaments:

> And he that smiteth his father or his mother, shall be surely put to death. Exodus 21:15

> Whoso curseth father and mother, let him die the death. Mark 7:10

More Evidence of Equality of Sexes

Despite the explicit statements in the Old Testament about the value of the male over the female, the Dunkers regarded the sexes equally. There is no evidence to suggest that the boys were given preferential treatment, that they were viewed as evidence of the father's manhood, or, despite their greater usefulness on the farm, that the boys were preferred over the girls. The female assumed the Biblical position after she married. It may be that the parents protected their daughters more than they did the sons. This incident occurred in New Jersey around 1737:

> The (Brethren) at Amwell are also split now. They, too, began to insist on discipline and agreed to curtail the socializing and pairing off of the young people. Now Naas' (daughter) was found guilty of sitting with a man who tried to force her to immorality and of not removing herself from his person. Rather she remained in his lap for about an hour as if she were asleep. Therefore, all of the Brethren found it necessary to exclude her from the breaking of bread and the kiss of love. However, her father thought, since she had not actually committed fornication, this would not do. He sided with her and accused all the Brethren of judging wrongly. Thus he separated himself, later attracted many to his side, and is now holding a separate meeting. I wrote to him urgently concerning this and faithfully admonished him; however, it was to no avail.[5]

There was considerable unrest among the Dunkers at that time over discipline. This may have been a dispute between Naas and his fellow church members over larger issues; it appears though that Naas acted to protect his daughter from punishment which she did not deserve.

In Jerome Blough's account of his early life, he tells how his sister and her baby were deserted by her husband and, until he returned from California to rejoin his family, she stayed at her father's home.[6] On the other hand, a family in the western area had a sixteen-year-old daughter who married by elopement without the permission of her father. He would not speak to her, in fact disowned her, until reconciled five years later through the efforts of the mother.

Social Freedom of the Adolescent

The control of the adolescent is spoken to in three areas. First, in the discord in the early church in the 1730's:

> But the sectarian spirit of the Brethren thwarted them, and they could not join the Brethren congregation because they not only believed that too much emphasis was put on outward things like baptism, breaking of bread, etc., but they also realized that discipline was lacking and that in marriage, the raising of children, etc., too much disorder prevailed. The matter was brought up and the Brethren began to insist more on discipline. But this disconcerted most of the older members, who cannot reconcile themselves to this, for they are in favor of the matter, are supported by the Lord and are succeeding, although they must overcome many a difficulty.[7]

It was in this conflict that the actions of Naas' daughter caused her father to start his own congregation. In a letter dated 1738, a further comment is made:

> As regards the Old Brethren, whom I mentioned earlier, they are, for their part, separated into two factions. One insists on introducing a stricter discipline, and especially forbids young people to court and make love freely in the manner of the world; the other, however, thinks the matter should not be dealt with so strictly, for then too many would have to be rejected, (in fact) the matter would have to be begun with the children of the elders (Vorsteher). They so completely disagreed on this point, that some of the latter were put in the ban by the former because they would not give in . . .[8]

From this it can be inferred that the Dunker youth were acting in the way of the surrounding culture and perhaps their European background, not according to the mores of a set-apart community. The younger adults wanted to clamp down on the activities of the younger people as well as undesirable activities of the members.

The older adults were more cautious. They wanted to follow a mode of decision-making seen in a number of AM decisions—they wanted to react to the conditions at hand. In this instance, a less drastic correction was called for because too many of the young people were involved. It is probable that the behavior of the young was more in keeping with the cultural heritage of the older adults, and was not as offensive to them. The younger adults had begun to assimilate the religious views of the Anabaptists and the Pietists into their daily lives and could not reconcile these with the behavior of the young people.

Control of the young people was spoken to in a second source—the record of the AM's. This is scant. There are only four references to children in the index of Kurtz's Encyclopedia. One has been given; the other three refer to education and to dress. Towards the end of the nineteenth century, there were numerous queries concerning the proper role of the various outside agencies in the lives of the young people. Many of these, when the question of who would direct the young people arose, put the burden on the father "while the child was under the lawful age."

The third comment on the control of the young people is in these references:

> Years ago one of our ministers held a meeting in one of our strong churches in whose membership there was a large number of young sisters, and in speaking of the meeting he said: "When I looked at these young and devoted sisters and then at their wild and profligate brothers I was made to weep. The thought came to me, Where will these young sisters get husbands? Must they indeed marry such ruffians as these young men are, and they Brethren's children?" He said, to him it was a dark picture. They had wealth and brains, but lacked common sense and culture, such as a good education gives. And he decided then and there that the church must have schools where our young people can be educated and cultured under influences that will lead them to the Truth and the church. It was a dark picture, indeed, that he gave of these young men. And as such pictures were being reproduced, in places, all over the Brotherhood, we too were deeply impressed with the thought of what would become of our young men, and how the church was to be perpetuated.[9]

This appeared in 1895 in The Gospel Messenger in an article arguing that Dunker Sunday Schools would provide some polish for the young men. It may be that the church elders of that time thought that early teen baptism would corral the boys before they became profligate.

The concern for the actions of the adolescents was well-founded. Other instances show that the Dunker young men "sowed wild oats." Joseph Hostetler (b. 1797, KY) was one:

> It was supposed that one brought up under such circumstances would readily walk in the way of the righteous. But he was naturally of a very mischievous disposition; at times highly passionate; and "prone to evil as the sparks to fly upward." When, therefore, he grew older and became less in the presence of his parents, he often set at naught all their counsel to walk in the counsel of the ungodly.[10]

Jacob Bower, born into a Dunker family ten years earlier, caroused around until he finally accepted the religious view of his family. A half a century later, D.L. Miller (b. 1845, MD) caused his mother heartbreak and anguish:

> On coming home from an evening with his associates, he often found his mother praying and weeping for him. Certainly, that sight would do much to keep him in the straight path.[11]

The three young men eventually became ministers.

As previously mentioned, the children, through most of history, became adults at five years of age. However, under the Humanist and Anabaptist influence, instead of adults at five years, they became youths, capable of some understanding. The general Germanic culture thought adulthood began at twelve or thirteen years of age. The concept of adolescence had not developed. It may be that the Dunkers carried this perception of the nature of the child into the eighteenth and nineteenth centuries, in that he was given, except in the economic world, the freedom of an adult after the onset of puberty. Since the child of those days was able to earn his keep after twelve years, his status became more independent. Owing his work to his father until set free, then, was a contract, rather than an exercise of parental authority.

The Dunkers believed in an understanding and informed candidate for entrance into the church. Those adolescent years provided the young people with the opportunity to partake of the outside world. However, since they were not bound by explicit rules in the social matters, the activities of Bower, Hostetler, and Miller cannot be viewed as rebellion, and therefore are not indicative of overly-controlled children. Rather, these activities were of an adult nature and provided an outlet for youthful exuberance. Bestowing this freedom of social activities on the teenagers made it easier for the outside culture to infiltrate the Dunker sect as the country built up and the children were exposed to worldly practices through the schools and through other organizations. One must remember, though, that this "freedom" was subjected to a conscience which had been effectively developed in their younger years.

Male and Female Stereotypes

Though there is no evidence that one sex was favored over the other, the boy followed the male stereotype and the girl the female stereotype. The children were brought up that way as part of their culture. Minor Miller (b. 1888, VA) observed:

> She (his mother) was living under the influence of the nineteenth century pattern for bringing up boys; this pattern reflected the general idea that boys do not like or need all of the niceties which girls ought to have.[12]

The girls were concerned with things of beauty and with the expression of the maternal instinct. The boys wanted to became a man. E.K. Ziegler (b. 1903, PA) was one:

> About this time (five years of age) I thought I was too big to play with my dolls; the well worn stuffed clown and Foxy Grandpa. One morning Mother built a hot fire under the caldron to boil apple butter. I threw my aged and grimy toys into the fire. I was ready for manly toys.[13]

Jerome Blough (b. 1861, PA) had similar feelings:

> One cold windy day we were going to church. Mother had made me a little overcoat out of the material of one of father's discarded ones which I was to wear that trip. I was always ashamed to bundle up when it was cold, so I would not put on my coat when we started. But when we got out pretty well towards Johnathan's and the wind was pretty sharp, I yielded reluctantly and donned my little home-made overcoat.[14]

As did Minor Miller (b. 1888, VA):

> She thought the cape a wonderfully protective garment, but I thought it an abomination for a boy to wear.[15]

This account of children's play by Ruel Pritchett shows how the children conformed to the usual male-female roles in their world of make-believe:

> Father had a big pictorial Bible. We children weren't supposed to handle it, but when Mother and Father would be away, I'd carry out that old Bible, rest it on the bottom of a chair, and open it up. We'd have church. The other three children were younger, and I always did the preaching. I'd stand by, pound on the Bible, and preach out. My sisters would have their dolls in the meeting. John would bring the cat and hold him. When we prayed, we got on our knees. The dolls readily went down on their knees, but John always had a hard time getting the cat to pray.
>
> We had our funerals too. If a chick or kitten died or a rat was dead or we found a dead bird, we had a service. We'd dig a grave in our children's graveyard and wrap the little corpse in a rag or paper of some kind, lay him down in the middle and fold it around him gently. We'd preach and pray. I would describe this poor little bird who would never fly away any more; it had to die and leave its mother. And we'd have Father and Mother's old hymnal without any notes. I knew a few of the hymns. I'd heard them sung so much; and even when I couldn't read, I could rehearse them any how. We would deposit the dead, put some little sticks in to hold the dirt up off of its body, line that with a piece of paper, cover over the dirt, and set up a headrock. The girls would strew wild flowers from nearby. We'd sing and have a dismissal service.[16]

In addition to the gender-related roles the children assumed in their play, note that they used the Bible against their father's command, suggesting that either his discipline was not firm or that there were some areas in which the prohibitions were tentative.

Roles in the Economy of the Farm

Though the Dunkers did not favor one sex over the other, the responsibilities of gender in the economic structure of the farm were well-defined. The mother and daughters were responsible for the house and its functions, the garden (the younger boys worked the garden, also), and for gathering the produce, preparing the vegetables and meat for winter, and, quite often, for the poultry. In some families the mother and daughters helped with the milking. The father shopped at the store for staples, while the mother periodically went to the store for extraordinary items like cloth and household furnishings. The father and the older boys were responsible for the field work, for gathering wood, repairing buildings, and for much of the harvesting. An analysis of these tasks will show that the work assignments did not discriminate; the heavy work was given to the male and the light work was given to the female.

This is not to say that the Dunkers felt that the sexes were equal in their capabilities. Because of her patience, her tenderness, and her ability to relate to children, they thought that the female made the better teacher. Because of her sensitivity and gentle nature, she was better suited to give religious instruction to the children. The male, because of his physical strength, was an obvious choice for heavy work; this perception of strength was transferred to the decision-making field where the steadiness and lack of emotion associated with this strength were thought to make the male superior. Perhaps the misconception of this position created the "sharp tongue deaconess" and the "neck that controls the head,"* as the women attempted to assert themselves despite the scripture and the traditions of their group.

Factors Relating to the Status
of the Dunker Child

The children of the German Baptist Brethren were well cared for, considering the environment in which they lived, and their care was infinitely superior when compared to the childrearing practices in many other areas of the world. This resulted from the confluence of five factors: 1) the men esteemed their wives; 2) the church was interested in growth; 3) the theology of the Dunkers contained the concept of religious individualism: 4) the soil of the new nation was fertile and there was an abundance of game in the forests; and 5) the government needed a growing population for work and for protection. Points one, two, and three have been,

---

* There is an old saying that the man is the head and the woman the neck; everyone knows that the neck controls the head.

or will be discussed in other sections. Points four and five are related, and will be discussed now.

The Role of the Government

The various levels of government affected the children of America through promoting measures which improved the economic setting, such as the homesteading acts, setting up school systems, land grant colleges, and others. There were no negatives, even though child protection laws came late in the period under discussion. The Dunker children benefitted from these, particularly the homesteading acts, as their parents continually pushed towards the frontier. When public schools were started, Dunker children attended, but their use of the colleges was delayed by suspicions of higher education. During the Revolutionary War and the War Between the States, the young men faced conscription laws which some of them were unwilling to abide by; the laws were adjusted to allow them their freedom of conscience.

Of the five factors, the land and other natural resources worked in favor of the children the most, because food could be produced in abundance. This removed the children from a negative position in the fight for survival and made them a positive force, an economic asset, a factor which worked for the good of all the children in America, not just the Dunkers.

The Abundance of Natural Resources

It took many rough hands to handle the plough and the lines. These hands developed from the soft hands of the children; the age of machines had not arrived. Wheat was cradled; wood was chopped and sawed; gardens were hoed; cows were milked by hand; and there were no automatic feeders for the livestock. The care of animals went on seven days a week. Harvest time had to be observed for each crop. On the average farm, there was too much work for the mother and father to handle and hired hands were expensive and in short supply. A large family was not only desirable; it was almost a necessity. Although the children were consumers the first five years of their life, for the next sixteen years they became, except for their room and board, unpaid hired hands. This balance between available labor and the requirements of the farm was addressed by Eby's Grandfather Schwalm who said that the proper size farm was one that could be worked by the family and that provided enough food for them. Anything more was derived from pride and the desire for worldly goods. How widespread this was among the brotherhood is not known; his was the only reference found. In any event, the problem generally was not that of excess production; it was that of producing enough to survive. To do this, the children had to work. As the life of the child is seen on the Dunker farm, this must be restated: the position of the child was dictated by this necessity for survival; the parents had no alternative except to work their children. And this they did.

The children, boys and girls alike, were required to do their share of the work on the farm, and they started at an early age. Daniel Long (b. 1847, ILL) commented on the value of a youngster in a letter:

> I think you could do much better here then you can in Maryland and liv with more satisfaction in every way the land is as good as can be and everything that we sow or plant produces in a bundanc and the land is so easy to farm that a boy that know any thing about horses can plough my little John can plough as good as a man he helped to do all the ploughing last spring and farming is done with so little spens.[17]

The same, according to Kermit Eby, was true fifty years later in Indiana:

> Woe to the boy who couldn't milk a cow at eight, handle a team of ten, and do a man's job at fifteen.[18]

The Duty and Obligation of the Oldest Child

Hard work, climate, disease, and childbirth took its toll on the parents and many went to their "long home" prematurely. To the eldest boy fell the responsibility, with the mother's guidance, of running the farm when the father died. This was true in the case of James Quinter (b. 1816, MD), and sixty years later in the life of Otho Winger (b. 1877, IND):

> Five years of toil and the father, through exposure, was stricken down and died in 1829. James, though but thirteen, manfully took up the burden of assisting in supporting the family.[19]

Several years before that I wanted to go to Mt. Morris to take up my academy work. All plans were made for that when my father met with a serious accident and spent part of that year in the hospital. This not only used up the funds that were planned for me to use to go to college, but it also broke my father's health. Since I was the oldest son, it was my duty to remain at home on the farm.[20]

The girls assumed the household duties when the mother was sick. Mary Early (Davis) (b. 1885, VA) remembers:

My mother was sick: As I was the oldest girl at home, it fell to my lot to be housekeeper and nurse.[21]

Work Away from the Home Farm

Not all soil was rich; not all Dunkers were good providers; in this instance, the father deserted the family, so arrangements had to be made for the care of the child. Philip Moore (b. 1826, VA) was the victim:

When eight years old, Philip was put out from home to a farmer, on the common terms of receiving a horse, saddle, and a bridle when of age.[22]

It is possible that if Philip had been older, he and his mother could have kept the farm going, but even though an eight-year-old was expected to work, he could not do the work of a grown man. Note the similarity between this and the terms of indenture of the 1730's.

If there was not enough work to do on the farm, or if additional cash was needed, the father hired his son out to another. All wages were paid to the father. D.L. Miller (b. 1841, MD) began his outside work at a young age:

Being the eldest of a large family of children, a good deal was expected of D.L. He learned to work early in life, and soon was able to help his father about the mill and on the farm. At twelve, D.L. was hired out to Philip Hammond for $2.50 per month. He worked for him for seven months. He was very homesick and spent many nights crying for home, but in spite of that he stuck to his task and proved such a good worker that the next year he was able to get $4.50 per month with Jacob Sword, "on the rockiest farm in our parts."[23]

It is said that the first child generally is more successful because more is expected of him or her, and expectations by the parents are a powerful force in the life of a child. D.L. Miller met these expectations in his later life as an author, businessman, educator, and churchman.

Choice of Work by the Children
Indication of Individuality

This account gives the picture of the usual work life of the children. Note that the girls were given a choice in the work that they were required to do. Albert Cassel Wieand (b. 1871, OH) recalled his life on the farm:

> The early home life of Albert Wieand, as described by him in his later years, probably with a nostalgic interest, was wholesome and interesting. Children were early given responsibility. His earliest duty was to keep the woodbox by his mother's cookstove full. Later, it was to crawl into the haymow and throw down hay for the horses, to get straw to bed the cattle, and to lead the horses to water.

> In busy seasons the daughters, too, helped with the farm work, especially in harvest and haymaking. One of the most interesting seasons was that of making maple sugar. The girls preferred to help gather the buckets of sap from the trees and haul them to a central point where in huge iron or copper kettles, the sap was boiled to syrup; this was much more fun than dishwashing. Then there were the special occasions such as sewing bees, reaping, or threshing, when neighbors exchanged help. What thrilling days for farm boys and girls.[24]

The Dunker Child and Education

The Dunker children were required to work, but they were allowed to go to the elementary schools of the day. Their exposure to education proceeded along this line up to the last decade of the nineteenth century. Elementary school started at the age of five or six years in a one-room schoolhouse where all the classes studied together. The "scholars," a term used to denote pupils as far back as the thirteenth century, started their term in the fall, usually after the harvest, and went five or six months in the winter. Because of the weather and sickness, the scholars missed many days. Private schools, called subscription schools, and not necessarily taught by the Dunkers, were attended before public schools were established. It was difficult for the little "Dutch" children to keep

PLATE 10. Four children at play

PLATE 11. Two children going to school—1924

up if the teacher was "all" English (some spoke both English and German), but soon, through exposure, they learned English and were on a par with the other students. The elementary course ended when the children were between twelve and fourteen years, after which the young person worked for his father until the age of "setting free." If he wanted to go to the normal school which corresponds to the present high school and accepted those of around sixteen years, he had to get the permission of his father. After finishing the course of study in the normal school, he was eligible to take an examination which qualified him to teach in the public school or to start his own school. This also prepared him for entrance into a four-year college. Many of the Dunker youth taught for several years to earn the money to go to college.

The Dunker boy had a problem to overcome if he wanted to continue his education after elementary school. Many of the members of the German Baptist Brethren did not believe in advanced education. Even if they could afford to they would not help their children, so the children had to earn their own money. But the father took their wages until they were set free. Either they relied on their mother to intercede with their father or they asked him for their freedom so that they could keep their wages and save towards their college expenses. This attitude toward school was not held by all fathers; some did help their children. Vernard B. Browning (b. 1879, IND) had a sympathetic father:

> The young man had an ambition for a college education, and, by the consent of his father (he was seventeen years old) launched out to earn sufficient money . . .[25]

Kermit Eby does not state whether his father enforced the custom of the day and whether he had to ask permission to leave the farm after high school. However, a deal is suggested by the fact that Eby would get a farm if he worked for his father until the age of twenty-one:

> After I finished high school, Dad wanted me to stay on the farm. Education beyond high school was impractical, he insisted. I never will forget how, years before this, he had showed me the farm which would be mine if I stayed at home and worked until I was twenty-one, giving up my ideas about college. I didn't give them up,

but one Sunday afternoon left home to get a job at the Studebaker plant in South Bend and to live with a married cousin who had left the farm and moved to that city.[26]

From the accounts of his father's thrift and business acumen, there was enough money in the family to finance Eby's education, but when the "feet were out from under the family table" the young people made their own decisions; they financed them, too.

The age of "setting free" was set at the discretion of the individual father as opposed to a time set by either tradition or by the order of the church. In this account, the son is allowed a choice of working for his father or getting an education of his own. It is not told whether Roland F. Flory would have to pay room and board out of that one hundred dollars salary per year:

> My father, with meager means, was not able to provide funds for a college education for the children. It was quite common in those times that the children, especially the boys, owed their parents their services until 18 years of age, while others required their services until their 21st birthday. Father had the policy of a choice when the boys became 16 years of age. One choice was to remain working on the farm and receiving 100 dollars per year or if we desired to get a better education, we were free to do so, providing we were able to finance our educational program. My older brother Samuel chose the farm, while I decided to proceed with my education. In the year 1910, I began my secondary education, first at Jewell High School and later at Defiance College Academy, graduating in 1913 with the equivalent of a High School diploma. (He later attended Manchester College.)[27]

Eby's father thought that education was impractical; Abraham Harley Cassel's (b. 1820, PA) father thought it a sin:

> Born on his father's farm in Montgomery County, Pa. he was the eldest son of Yelles and Polly Harley Cassel. His mother was a granddaughter of Christopher Sower and Peter Becker, the latter being the first bishop of the Church of the Brethren in America. His father thought it a sin to acquire any learning, and sought to stamp out such a desire in his children. He succeeded in all but Abraham.[28]

Cassel taught school and was a leader in the church; his fame resulted from the library he collected which preserved the accounts of the early years of the church. This collection, numbering thousands of documents, is housed in part in the library at Juniata College in Huntington, Pennsylvania.

Stover Kulp's parents were of Mennonite background who had joined the German Baptist Brethren. His father did not believe in education beyond public schools, but he allowed Stover to work his way through normal school and Juniata College. At one critical time in Stover's finances, his father loaned him enough money to stay in school. Stover, along with Jacob Bower (b. 1786, PA), remembered that they were able to read the newspaper and New Testament respectively before they were six years old.

As the twentieth century approached, the bias against higher education began to disappear, but even with the removal of the arch conservatives by the schism of 1881-1883, there still remained an element which distrusted education beyond grade school, and, in one instance, a distrust of the grade school. Minor Miller (b. 1888, VA) was sent to a country school because his parents did not want him to go to the city school. It is surmised that the country school had a larger number of Dunker children in it than did the city school. This same type of reasoning was applied to the colleges. The young people of the church went to state universities, since there were no Dunker schools. Men of the church interested in education started schools (of a liberal arts type within a Christian lifestyle) in a number of areas. The old Dunkers reasoned that if their children were going to college anyway, it would be best for them to go to a Dunker-affiliated and supported college.

They were still unsure of the value of higher education. Particularly, they did not want the colleges to teach religion; this should be left to the local churches and to the families. To further safeguard their children in their own colleges, whose faculties were made up of members of the church, they appointed a three-man oversight committee of elders for each college. This was to ensure that the curriculum was not offensive to the church and that campus life was suitable for children reared in a Christian home. Religion was introduced into the curriculum after a decade or so, and the elder committees were disbanded.*

---

* The acceptance of the oversight of the committee of elders by these independent, but church-related colleges, is a striking example of

However, the colleges have kept their liberal arts orientation to this day. Perhaps, the opposition of the members of the church to a curriculum which contained religious studies prevented their turning into parochial schools.

Considerable freedom was given the adolescent not only in the social sphere but also in his selection of schools. However, it was not unusual for the parents to insist that their child at least try the church college in the area. L.W. Schultz (b. 1890, IND) was so coerced:

> But father said I should go to Manchester College for one term of ten weeks and then, if I did not like it, I could go elsewhere in later years.[29]

One would think that children who were reared in a home environment where discipline and obedience were values of the first order would be model students in school. E.K. Ziegler's father suggested that when he misbehaved more work would straighten him out. A.C. Wieand (b. 1871), OH) had a similar problem:

> As a lad Albert attended the country school one-half mile from his home. It was a one-room school in which one teacher taught all grades and which at one time had as many as sixty-six students. Albert sat in one of the smallest seats with "another naughty boy" for a seat-mate. No busy work was provided for students; so he whiled away the time after getting his lessons he occupied himself at rolling slate pencils down over the seat, shooting paper wads, or making faces at other students to make them laugh. "All very dumb," he commented later, "but I didn't know what else to do."[30]

Wieand, with E.B. Hoff, established Bethany Biblical Seminary in which many ministers of the Church of the Brethren have been trained. Aside from indicating that school children do not change. Wieand's behavior was not that of an overly controlled child, although it could indicate that his parents did not build up his sense of self-worth.

---

wisdom displayed in a difficult societal adjustment. It provided a means of pacifying the opponents of higher education either until they accepted the value of college training or until they passed from positions of influence. Were the same wisdom present in the earlier conflicts, the schism of 1881-1883 may have been avoided.

Vocational Freedom of Choice of the Young

The references do not spell out clearly how easy it was for the youth to escape the farm life that had been the way of the Dunkers since their arrival from Europe. Church order prohibited occupations that, at a particular time, were considered worldly, but sanctions were invoked only in those instances where the occupations were perceived to be frivolous, immoral, or contributed to disharmony. Just as in any other organization, a member's position and relationship with the group were altered if he moved too far from the center of approved activities, but there was no absolute boundary between membership and non-membership. Of equal importance, a member was never permanently disqualified; he was with the proper application and apology, accepted back into membership and fellowship. Even when the ban was invoked, the members observed it half-heartedly. Therefore, because of the freedom given the adolescent in his social life, due to the parent's perception that he was essentially an adult; from the lack of specific parameters that disqualified them from membership; from the sharp endpoint of their responsibility to their parents, the setting-free age; and from reference quoted, it appears that the Dunker youth had the opportunity to go into a vocation of his choice. This, of course, required money, which he had to raise to finance the venture, and he had to accept a new environment and perhaps a new life style.

This right of free choice of vocation was consistent with the principles inherent in faith through understanding and through informed and free-will baptism. It was also consistent with the belief that the scriptures should provide life guidelines; that the most important goal was to have love and righteousness in the heart; and that the life of the individual should show this. The farm provided the safest setting to live this relationship with God and man; however, there was nothing in the scriptures to indicate that only on the farm could one live the simple and righteous life. It was up to the individual to find his setting and live the life according to his own conscience. Through the order, which was formulated by a group of representative elders, the individual used the collective conscience to guide him in his interpretation of the scriptures.

This order, an organizational discipline, held while the outside world seemed so threatening. As the land filled up and the society became more civilized, as the education of the Dunkers improved, and as their economic standing became firmer, the threat of the outside world lessened. The order was enforced with less diligence. The youth of the sect found it easier to go off the farm into other vocations and professions. Even so, there were two factors of selection which screened out those who were not highly motivated to make a change from the parent's way of life. The first was the hypersensitive conscience that had been formed in the children and that tended to prevent them from acting contrary to the expressed or implied wishes of the parent. The second was the very narrow horizons that resulted from the sectarian life. Neither of these can be called organizational; they were psychological and cultural. This is why the children of successive generations found it easier to leave their family backgrounds and enter into other occupations and professions.

They did not, however, leave their religious heritage. From the farm, which provided the setting for the simple life, they entered service occupations that satisfied their need to show and to feel that they were right "within their hearts." It is in this light that Bridgewater College, an affiliated school, was said to produce teachers, preachers, and country doctors.

The Dunker youths were not discontent with their life on the farm. Neither were they frustrated by the order of the church and by the customs of their people. These Germanic people loved the land and gained satisfaction from their rural life. In the earlier years, few of those who went to college returned to the farm, because they were highly motivated to escape the perceived drudgery of working with their hands. In later years, education became accepted in a liberal arts sense as a means of expanding the mind for an informed, challenging life. The youths who went to college with this motivation returned to the farm as more effective citizens, church people, and as professionals in farming and in other related occupations.

Instances of Degrees of Control of the Children

This reference which follows relates to group behavior; the two previous ones concerned individual behavior. The three do not suggest that the controlled child of the sectarian household was less exuberant in school. Only one reference is given, but the author has heard more shocking tales from his father's generation.

It was customary in those days for the teacher to treat the pupils at Christmas. To secure this treat, the pupils often locked the teacher out of school until he was willing to promise the cakes and candy.[31]

These schools were attended primarily by children from German-speaking families. This behavior does not suggest overly-controlled children. However, the practice of teacher harassment was not confined to Dunker schools. It occurred generally in all schools of the time.

The home as a place of entertainment held special joy for the young who were able to play away the Sunday afternoon with the neighbors' and relatives' children. Home from church with many invited guests, the thoughtful mother would allow them to play until the adults had eaten. Occasionally, the children were allowed to eat in the kitchen while the adults ate in the dining room. But the children ate last, both time-wise and anatomically:

At love feast time visiting elders and others driving from a distance found rest and comfort in the three guest rooms in the house, and the children perchance sleeping on the floor. On these special occasions the dining table was so long that there were "two of everything" on the table. On any ordinary Sunday, it was customary to invite members of the congregation home for dinner, much to the delight of the children, even though they sometimes had to wait their turn to get a place at the "second table." In those days, there were more fellowship meals in the home than in the church.[32]

L.W. Schultz remembered:

Our turn as children usually came at the second or third sitting. In this way , I learned to eat and like chicken backs and wings.[33]

Christopher Sower, Jr. (b. 1721, Germany) was famous in both Dunker and Pennsylvania history for his German printing press which competed with the English press of Benjamin Franklin. Sower was one of the early members of the sect and this account shows that he was bound by custom to his father:

In 1743, in harmony with the custom of the day, he removed himself from his father's house and began to plan for himself. He was of age.[34]

Christopher Sower joined the Dunkers when he was sixteen years old. When he was ten, his mother left the family and joined the Sabbitarians and later the Ephrata Cloister as a single sister, leaving Christopher to be raised by his father. She stayed there about fourteen years and rejoined her husband a year later. Educated in the school of the Mennonite, Christopher Dock, he married at the age of thirty and was an effective churchman and successful businessman. He may have been the first, and certainly was the most famous, of the Dunker children from a single parent home. The dominion of the father over the son until the age of setting free as exemplified by the Sowers was observed among Dunker families for over two hundred years. It was not a unique German custom. In a dinner conversation one night, a young man said his father took all of his money until he was eighteen. This was in an Italian Catholic family in Chicago around 1950.

Control of the Girls

Among the Pennsylvania Germans of the eighteenth and nineteenth centuries, the daughters of the family owed their services to the father until they were eighteen years old. Despite a specific search, no statement could be found to suggest that this was the practice among the German Baptist Brethren. However, Lavina Kinsel (b. 1849, PA) was eighteen when she broke Dunker custom and went to work as a seamstress in a neighboring town. This may indicate that that was her age of "setting free" since she finished school at twelve to fourteen years of age. The following reference, though it doesn't speak to the custom of release from the economic obligation, does show the authority which a mother had over her daughter. Sister E.J. Onkst (b. 1830) was trained for domestic duty at the insistence of her mother.

> The writer of this article about forty-five years ago was united in marriage to an intelligent farmer, a widower with a number of small children. At the time of her engagement she was twenty years old; for three summers prior to that time she had taught district school. Her prudent mother, with commendable foresight on learning of her daughter's engagement, deferred the wedding day one year that she might remain in the home nest to improve on her

domestic education so it would be equal to the occasion. At the expiration of one year's special training she entered upon her life work, adapting herself readily to her farmhouse sphere.[35]

Despite having taught school for three years, the authority of the mother still prevailed. This is believable; Ziegler found that approximately one-half of the boys of the generations of 1880, 1900, and 1920 thought that obedience was always due parents.[36]

Summary

What then was the position of the child of the Dunker? Eagerly awaited, they were enjoyed as infants, controlled as toddlers, worked from the age of five or six until they finished their obligation to the parents. They were used as economic assets. The parents assumed the responsibility for their religious training as a mandate from the Bible and by delegation from the order of the church. The labor which they provided the family farm was necessary for survival; it was also viewed as a time of training to acquire the skills necessary to the adult of the time. Starting with adolescence, the child was thought of as an adult to some extent, worked like one, and given latitude to make decisions in social activities as long as they did not interfere with the work obligations. The adolescent period of the child was an explorative period in which the young person decided whether he or she would join the church and accept its order. The child had his own space in the family group, suffered some from the ancient projections of inherent badness, but lived in a positive environment in which he was allowed to grow, subject to the constraints of economic necessities, into a self-willed individual. This self-will was tempered somewhat by his training that life was purposeful, work-related, and religiously oriented.

5

Parents

The parents are the most important part of the nurture system of childrearing. Even though their effects on the personality and character of their young are defined and limited by the genetic make-up of the child, they can help him reach his potential by taking his individual strengths and weaknesses into consideration in their parenting efforts. But, just as the child is limited by his genetic make-up, the parent is limited by his reality as a person. An introverted person cannot assume the characteristics of an extrovert for the nurture of his children; neither can a passive personality suddenly become aggressive on a sustained basis. But, despite our reality, we posture as parents; we play the parent role. This role springs from both our reality and from our culturally defined perception of what a good parent should be.

There are no psychological profiles to indicate the reality of the parents of the Dunker subculture. A few general descriptions, primarily of the father, provide insight into his personality and temperament. Some refer to his role as father, some will give a picture of him as a person. This chapter, however, is not about the reality of the parent. It is in part about the child's perception of his parent, determined by the reality plus the role playing.

Four references speak directly to how the child viewed his father. They give an indication of how this perception of his father affected his life. These references will be presented, along with four others that detail specific father-son interactions. In addition, the mother's position, from the limited material available, will be discussed.

Characteristics of the Father
Observations gathered from the general literature indicate

that the Dunker father was not stereotyped. By authority of the scriptures, he was subservient to Christ and his wife to him, yet he spoke of her as his companion, my dear wife, or help mate. He made the children work when they did not want to. He gave them animals as pets, and allowed them the thrill of driving horses when they were only five years old. He took his children's wages until they were twenty-one years old; he gave this money back when the children came of age. He enforced the order of the church upon his children; he defended them against the order when he felt the order was unjust to them. He did not believe the children should go to college; he borrowed money to help them when the children could not provide their own tuition. He had little education, but he carried his own children on horseback across snowy fields to the little elementary school. He served on the important church committees, yet the mother went to church more often than did the father. And when the children reached adulthood they remembered their fathers with respect and wrote idealized letters about their mothers.

The individual father was a combination of the characteristic inherent in these actions. He did not fit any particular mold, though he usually was portrayed as stern and authoritative. Despite this perception of him, the record is clear that he used his authority sparingly, and many displayed a warmth towards their children in subtle ways. This warmth apparently followed family lines and practices.

the Authority of the Father

His authority derived from four areas: one, the scriptures gave this to him as head of the family, suggesting that, as God wielded His authority over the father, he should wield authority over his children. Second, church order required him to be the head of the household. Third, the farm as an economic unit required a manager. This was a matter of survival. The children came under this managerial authority since they were an integral part of the work force. Fourth, the custom of the day required the children to be under the father until they reached majority. The fathers thought this authority to be their natural right and did not hesitate to use it. Nor did they apologize for its use. The use of this authority, its intensity, constancy, and purpose, indicates the status of the child and the attitude that the father had toward him as a person and as an individual. Evidence of this will be noted in subsequent chapters.

The Child's Perception of his Father

The reality of the father and the child's perception of him may be different; the perception is the most important. Four references speak directly to this: D.L. Miller (b. 1846, MD); Jerome Blough (b. 1861, PA); Kermit Eby (b. 1903, IND); E.K. Ziegler (b. 1903, PA).

They respected him a great deal, loved him as their father, feared his wrath, and obeyed his will.[1]

As I think of it now, I really do not know what we were afraid of, because father never whipped us. But he was so, I hardly know what to call it. He was not cross, but he rather impressed as being so. He was authoritative. We never questioned his word. When I wanted a favor from him I did not have the heart to go to him and ask him for it, but would try and coax mother up to ask for me. She was a pretty good intercessor. That continued until I was almost grown.[2]

Dad was head of the family. As head of the family, in the best German tradition, he would sometimes say that, "as long as you put your feet under my table, I'm boss." To this day when I go home, once Dad is out of bed (at 4:30 AM) I seldom fail to follow him because Dad never asked me to live by a double standard. He himself did—and usually better—every task he asked me to do. We shared the pleasant and the unpleasant. And when I worked away from home on threshing days, I was ever conscious of his high standards.[3]

In my growing years, I loved, respected and resented my father. He was rather stern and short-tempered as a parent and insisted on unquestioned obedience. As his eldest child, I bore the brunt of his learning how to be a good father. I began to help with farm chores very early, learned to milk cows by the age of nine, and from then on he gave me more and more responsibilities. By the age of fourteen, I was doing a grown man's work. If I dawdled, or neglected my tasks, Dad became impatient and sometimes exasperated. He believed that sparing the rod would spoil the child, so I got many whippings with a paddle or strap or what ever was handy.[4]

D.L. Miller's father, Abram, was born in 1810 in Pennsylvania;

it can be assumed that the fathers of the others were born twenty-five years earlier than their sons, the latter two in Pennsylvania also, and Eby's father in Indiana. The four sons had the same perception of their fathers: stern and authoritative. Yet all recalled incidents of their youth when a feeling of warmth was demonstrated by their fathers toward them. It is said that authoritative fathers tend to hinder the growth of individuality and independence in their sons, yet Eby was the only one who seemed to retain a dependence on his relationship with his father. This seemingly did not affect his professional career. The procession from 1810 to 1880 supports the contention that the status of the child and, perhaps the culture, changed little in the Dunker world from 1723 to 1900.

Each of these boys, Miller, Blough, and Ziegler, followed predictable careers, considering that none of them cared for farming, the background from which they came. Each was involved at one time or the other in teaching and in religious work, and each seemed to settle into their respective life's work without undue psychological strain. Eby, however, selected a career, after a short stint as a teacher, which threw him into the rough and tumble of union work in the Chicago area in an atmosphere of expedience rather than in the strictly defined life of the rural religious setting in which he was born and reared. His continued dependency on his relationship with his father may have reflected his inability to make the cultural adjustments to the ill-defined world of business and politics, so different from his world of farm and church. But he, as did the others, spent his life in service to mankind, certainly in keeping with the theology to which he had been exposed as a child.

The girls, also, felt the applied authority of their father. Mary Early Davis (b. 1889, VA) recounts this experience which indicated who was in charge of their household.

> Later on in the summer one day my mother decided to go hunting for blackberries. She left Ala and I in Father's care. He thought it was a good time to cut our long hair so she would not have to comb and braid it. But, behold, when she came home and saw what he had done she was quite upset. I do not remember too much about the confab but it was a tense time. I think Ala and I objected also, but he was the boss so we gave in.[5]

The authority of the father continued as long as the children stayed at home. Whether it ended at that point is not clear. This authority was exerted over the children in their work on the farm; it relaxed in the social area as the children entered the teenage years. When they were "set free," they no longer owed their services, either in work or in money, to their father. As a corollary, he no longer owed them board and room. If they elected to stay at the home place, they paid for their room and board with the money they earned. Even though his authority diminished when the children reached the setting-free age, incidents not well documented indicated that his authority was reasserted in their lives in case of catastrophe, such as desertion, illness, and the like.

The five previous references did not tell the reality of the parent. They told of the children's perception of that parent, and Jerome Blough indicates that, as an adult, he wondered why he thought his father so formidable.

The Soft Side of the Father

The Dunker father was not always stern. At times he was warm and human, which was helpful to his children as they formed their life around his example. Paul Haynes Bowman, president of Bridgewater College for many years, wrote an article for the Gospel Messenger in 1933 entitled "As I Knew My Father."[6] This parental image was created in the son:

1. His father's priorities of life were these, in order of importance: Christ, family, church and neighbor.
2. He was the soul of integrity.
3. He talked much of greatness of mind and heart in man.
4. He inspired his children to do worthwhile things.

Bowman's father, Samuel, was born in Tennessee in 1861. James Pritchett, who married a relative of the Bowmans', Rebecca Ann, showed the tender side of himself to his children. This spoke of his character and provided a model for them:

An old mother rabbit crept into the barn when snow was on the ground, which is earlier than little rabbits are born usually, and dug down between the stalls next to the partition between two cow stables. And there she lined a nest with the fur of her own body and deposited her brood.

> Mother, in milking the cows, discovered them. At intervals she and Father took me through the snow and cold up into the barn. He'd reach down, gently bring out the baby rabbits, and show them to me. I can see them yet, cuddled there in Daddy's hand, and that's been more than eighty years ago.[7]

Pritchett's mother came from a long line of Dunkers, but his father was reared a Baptist. The sight of the stern, authoritarian father gently and tenderly handling the little rabbits gave to the son a dimension of his father which would not have been discovered through conversation. Jerome Blough, who feared his father throughout his adolescence, also saw the softer side:

> I remember father would hold me in the evening and sometimes sing to me. Some of those old hymns I still remember.[8]

The Father's Perception of the Child

While reality of the parent and the child's perception of the parent are important factors in the child's personality development and emotional growth, the parent's perception of the child is also important. From this comes a stimulus to the child to establish his own self-worth. Approval of the parent is crucial to the developing child in any mode of childrearing; in the Dunker subculture, where example and a hypersensitive conscience were the chief tools of molding the character of the youth, approval or disapproval was especially important. Many references in several sections speak to this; here are two, one of which illustrates a destructive attitude and one which probably had little effect on the child. This was said of Dan West (b. 1893, OH):

> Dan was a Pied Piper who attracted idealistic youth. His strong, faith, his love for God, for the church, and for persons offered them the solid foundation of belief they were seeking in a world of constant change. He encouraged youths to stand on their own two feet and to argue for their convictions. He trusted them at a time when many adults thought youth had misplaced values. While challenging to other youths, he sometimes produced the uneasy feeling in his own children that they did not live up to his expectations for he often said, "A son should be taller than his Dad."[9]

West was one of the early youth leaders of the church after the denomination had determined that youth programs were necessary for the salvation of the youth and the survival of the church. He became one of the outstanding men in the denomination's history. Note the use of the word "expectation."

Of lesser impact on the child were sentiments expressed by Abram Miller (b. 1810, PA). These were shared by many of the Dunkers of those and later days who thought that the only real work was manual labor and the best place to find this was on the farm. Occupations which required mind rather than muscles provided a "soft" life, not a working life. Bess Royer Bates gives Abram's reaction to his son's interest in books and to his preference for the life of a tradesman:

> His father told him that he would never amount to anything because he did not like the farm.[10]

D.L. Miller did not like the farm, but he liked business and later became a successful businessman, editor, churchman. He was also one of the founders of Mount Morris College. His influence on the people around him, including the young people of the college, was far greater than had he stayed on the farm. There is no evidence that his father's comments represented a general disapproval of the young D.L. as a person.

The Influence of the Grandparents

The generational clustering of the Dunkers allowed the young to be brought up around their grandparents. They influenced the children by passing on to them the culture of two generations back, by moderating the cultural change of the parents, and by providing security. Eby described the work habits of his Grandfather Eby, his meticulously kept farm, and how he lived his Christian beliefs. Of his Grandfather Schwalm, who had an equal influence on the young Eby, he said:

> Grandfather was good and great because he rang true. His life squared.[11]

From these two, he learned many of the values which he carried into his life's work as a labor leader and educator.

William Beahm's grandfather eloquently made his point:

> When William was eight, grandfather found him sitting alone in

the big red barn. There was a full bag hanging there and at the bottom was a corn cob stuffed into a hole in the bag. The bag was filled with clover seed—very precious. William had pulled the cob out and was sitting there transfixed, watching the seed run out in a pile on the floor. Grandfather Bucher didn't say anything. He put the cob back in the hole and picked William up, carried him around to the corner of the barn to a rain barrel and dunked him. William told about it later, he said of course it was three times.[12]

This latter remark refers to the Dunker's belief that baptism, to be valid, had to be three times forward, preferably in running water. Bucher's reaction to his grandson wasting precious clover seed, in contrast with the setting down and explaining method, was direct and fast. It was really not punitive. He was reminded that he had done wrong and he shouldn't do it again. There was probably a good laugh at the supper table over the incident; even Beahm may chuckled after he got over his chagrin.

The Absentee Father

The phenomenon of the absentee father was well known, even in the agricultural subculture of eighteenth and nineteenth century Dunkers. Conditions of the day and the requirements of the free ministry caused many fathers to be absent from the house. It took three or four months to "spy out" new land in the "west" for a prospective homesite. To buy or sell cattle thirty or forty miles away was an overnight trip. Just going into town for weekly or monthly supplies took the whole day. In some instances, the family lived in a settled area, but they had a land claim on the frontier. The father was required by law to spend a number of days on the claim to retain title to it. In other instances, the family lived on a frontier land claim, but the father had to work in a settled area several months out of the year to earn money to buy supplies. In each instance he spent continuous time away from home. Until the late 1800's there were few instances in which employment or travel in the modern sense took the father away for extended periods of time.

The minister of that day was away from home the most of any of the fathers. The trips of ministers like Elder John Kline, who travelled thousands of miles on horseback to unify the scattered Dunker settlements, kept them away from their farm for months at a time. Council meetings, committee meetings, meetings to reconcile differences, funerals, weddings, caused the minister to spend time away from home, often to the detriment of his family and its economic well-being. This was said of Elder John Unstead (b. 1802, PA):

> John Umstead was away from home so much that he almost became a stranger to his family. Once on leaving home he said to his wife of his sickly daughter: "If Sarah dies, bury her."[13]

Elder Umstead believed in the free ministry. He paid all of his travelling expenses, but, being a good businessman, he accumulated a fair amount of wealth so that his family was not deprived. Elder Umstead was born a Mennonite, he used the Friend's patios, and he was a member of the Dunker sect and preached their doctrine. Said to be a blunt man, he served on major committees of the church and was an important figure of the day. Despite this, or perhaps because of this, only Sarah, who did not die young, joined the German Baptist Brethren church. Two other surviving daughters did not become members, even though one married and stayed in the neighborhood. Nothing is said of Umstead's wife and how she accepted her role.

Mary Early Davis (b. 1889, VA) was alone at times:

> They bought a tract of timber in the far side of Negro Mountain which was 7-8 miles to drive. They left home in the dark and came home in the dark in the winter time. Our two little girls sometimes did not see their father for days at a time.[14]

These absences put a heavy burden on the wife. In addition to her work, she had to assume the responsibility for the total operation of the farm. Usually, there was a hired hand, a live-in relative, or a good size son to do the manual labor, but the wife had the business decisions to make.

Faulty Parenting

Interaction between a parent and the child provides examples of specific dynamics, normal and abnormal. Most of these found in literature are about a famous father and his child, or about a child who has grown to be a famous adult and his not so prominent father. While these do provide examples of psychological interaction, it cannot be assumed that they occur in the relationship of the average parent and his child. In the following four examples of Dunker father-son relationships, this flaw is present. Each of the men, though not of immense achievement, did advance more than the average man of the sect, proved by their presence in the literature if for no other reason. Only one of these relationships, Bower, approached the normative; the others were unhealthy. That they were not destructive is evidenced by the success which each of the sons enjoyed in his own life. These cases span the period under study: Mack around 1735; Bower around 1810; Miller around 1850; and Flory at the turn of the century. Each represents a variation of faulty parenting.

The first, Alexander Mack, Jr. (b. 1712, Germany) shows the most pathology:

> During this time, young Mack was very closely associated with his father and enjoyed the unusual advantage of this conversation and wise counsel. The death of his father in 1735 cast a deep gloom over the young man. His spirit became restless. The mystical influences with which he had been surrounded all his life were beginning to exercise their power over him. The prudent counsel of his father was now wanting.[15]

The subject was born in Germany in 1712, the son of the founder of the sect which would become known as the German Baptist Brethren. He came to America with his parents in 1729. Mack, Sr., was an educated man, steeped in theology, and fortified with faith that his views were as close to the truth as God's word was presently revealed. In addition, he had the presence to command the respect of people and for them to accept him as their leader. Such a man undoubtedly developed a firm hold on his son's mind and caused the son to be subordinate to him. In any generation, the death of the father, leaving the son as the generation closest to eternity, has a profound effect on the sense of security of the son. Mack, Jr. reacted to this loss of security with a deep depression which sent him searching for a lifestyle to fill this void and a religious expression to lift him out of his depression. Several years after his father died, he entered the cloistered community of Ephrata. After a short stay there, he joined the Eckerlin brothers in their adventure in establishing a similar settlement on the New River in western Virginia. He left the community on the New River to return to his old neighborhood around Germantown where he

PLATE 12. A pioneer couple among the Brethren of southern West Virginia

Do you A.B take the woman ~~you~~
whose hand you now hold to be
your lawfull wedded wife & do
you promise to be to her a faithfull
& affectionate husband & forsaking
all others to cleve to her so long as
you both shall live
Do you C.D. take the Man whose
hand you now hold &c (as above)

By virtue of the authority vested
in me as a minister of the gospel
I pronounce you husband & wife
& what god has joined together
let not man put asunder
          prayer

PLATE 13. Excerpt from the marriage ceremony of Elder Abram L. Conner

made his living as a weaver of stockings. Giving up his Sabbatarian views, he returned to the religion of his father. As the bishop of the Germantown congregation, he became a leader in the denomination, wrote some poetry, and, because he was a prolific writer of letters, left many historical details and insights into the sect and its people of that time. This letter writing may have indicated a difficulty in establishing interpersonal relationships. While John S. Flory's account of the adjustment of young Mack to his father's death is not completely substantiated, supporting the statements suggest that the account is plausible and that Mack was not prepared by his father to assume an independent adult role at the time of the father's death.

Alexander Mack, Jr. gives the picture of the son who conformed to his father's values with the life that they called for because of the presence of his father. He neither completely internalized those values nor developed convictions that sprang from them. After a period of turmoil, this was accomplished.

Jacob Bower was born in Pennsylvania in 1786 and migrated to Kentucky as a young man. Jacob's father follwed him, settling a short distance from his son. Jacob and his wife went to visit him.

> But when the time arived that we must lieve for hom, I felt unusally solemn. My father accompanied us about four miles to a large creek, and now the time came that we must take the parting hand. I put on as chearful a countinance, and said. Well, father, come and lit us take a parting dram, perhaps it may be the last time we shall ever drink together. I dont want to drink a drop, said he, I have something to say to you, Jacob. Well Father, said I, what is it? "I want you to promise me," said he, "that you will serve God and to keep out of bad company." Well, Father I will, said I. Farewell, Farewell. I started to go across the creek, which was about thirty yards across, and as my horse stepped out of the water to rise the bank instantly my promise staired me in the face. Although he had given me the same council, and in the same words, perhaps and hundred times before. Yet it never produced such an impression on my mind as now. To serve God and keep out of bad company wrung in my ears all day long, I had promised my father and God heard it, that I would do it, but alas how can I, and he expects that I will do it. I began to feel in a way quite different from what I had ever done before---.[16]

Bower had been exposed to his father's values and, to a certain extent, they had influenced his life. But he was independent enough of his father that he followed his own inclinations, which included the keeping of "bad company." Unlike Mack, he was able to break the hold which the father had placed on him as a child. Whether his wayward life was a result of rebellion, or whether it represented a stage in the development of his system of values is not clear. Nevertheless, several months after the above incident in 1811, he began the search for salvation as promised in the New Testament. This seach was initiated not only by his promise to his father but also by the great earthquake of that year which apparently scared many people into reevaluating life's priorities. Bower determined that he would lead his life according to the primitive Christians. In deciding which form of baptism was the correct one, he chose trine immersion forward because he thought it was the right way or "his father would not have been baptized that way." Because the Dunker minister would not be making the rounds for three weeks, he was baptized into the Baptist church and preached in it for many years.

Three points stand out. First, Bower's realization that he might never see his father again impressed on him that he was now responsible for his own life and would not have his father's influence as a brake against violating the internalized values given to him as a child. Second, his father's views were respected, if not always followed by him, shown by the acceptance of trine immersion as the correct form of baptism. And, third, parents of that day, just as in this day, blame bad company for the transgression of their children. It is hard to admit that children seek out company who share their perceptions of the proper way to behave and to conduct their lives.

Jacob Miller (b. 1828, PA), son of Elder Andrew Miller and possibly a descendant of one of the earliest leaders, Peter Miller, was a bright and energetic young person who was trained in English and in classical literature under a Catholic teacher, Professor Harris of Bedford, Pennsylvania. After completing his training, he taught school at New Enterprise, Pennsylvania. In 1848 he married Eleanor Arnold and, in 1849, he and she were baptized into the German Baptist Brethren church by the eminent Dunker churchman, James Quinter. Though married and settled in life, he thought there were greater opportunities in the West.

In the summer of 1851, his great uncle, George Butterbaugh, of Illinois offered him great inducements to go west, and Jacob had already sold his personal effects, intending to go west, and grow up with the country, but his father took it so hard that the young man's heart failed him, and he relented.[17]

Mack's father had effective control over his son; the exact mechanism is not described. Bower influenced his son, but he had little or no control over him. Miller controlled his son by using "emotional blackmail" in a process called reversion. In this mode of parenting, the parent reverses roles—he becomes the child and the son acts as the father. This mechanism is a perversion of the true role of a parent, that of helping the child grow and develop emotionally to adult status. In this relationship, the needs of the parent are paramount and the needs of the child receive scant consideration. Andrew Miller's remarks, made after the funeral of his son, reflect this role reversion: 1) he was obedient to me as a child, and 2) he caused to happen a large funeral (which made me proud). In a later paragraph, his father tells how much he missed him at the next two preaching appointments. These remarks reflected the feelings of the father, none for his son as a person. A normative relationship would have produced remarks such as these: He had so much to offer the world; I am sorry for his widow; or, it is a shame that he could not have gone West as he wanted to.

Roland Flory, who served in the church as a minister for many years, remembers this about his father:

Throughout all the years my memories wander back to my childhood days. Little time has been spent during these many years in the community of my youth, but the influence for good of my father still lives on with me. He was a friend to all, young and old alike, whether they were of like religious faith or Catholic neighbors. In fact, when his earthly body was laid to rest, a Catholic friend prepared the obituary for the funeral services. On a recent trip to my old community, some forty years after father's departure, this remark was made by a man who knew my father as a youth, "Surely if anyone gets to heaven, he will be found there."[18]

This would seem like a usual relationship between father and son; however, Flory did not mention specific acts or interactions in summing up his relations with his father. Rather, he spoke of his father in the context of the neighborhood, his popularity in the community. Perhaps this was the legacy of the minister-father to his children; he was a friend to all, then a father to his children.

Women in the Dunker Community

Men were the leaders or perceived to be the leaders in the German Baptist Brethren Church. Therefore, more has been written about them than about women. Just as the children were the "silent partners in the church," the women did not occupy a visible position even though it would be misleading to deny their influence. Consequently, there is little hard data that can be used to define their position in the eyes of the children. There is even less to describe their personal characteristics, how they thought, their temperament, or their relationships with their husbands and children. Prior to 1900, what is written about the Dunker women is so idealized that instruction in the true nature of the women is absent. This is demonstrated in Inez Long's "Faces Among the Faithful."[19] The outstanding women in the church prior to 1900 are described in generalities, while the story concerns mostly the accomplishments of their husbands. It might be argued, with some logic, that this tells the story of the women of that day—they were homemakers while their husbands did the more visible work in the family, business, and church. It might be argued that theirs was a supportive role rather than one of equal participation in the substantive issues.

But although we might not be able to document this, those who have known these old sisters of the church find it very difficult to believe that they were not equal partners, in substance if not in role, in most of the issues that faced the family. Two references speak to this. Kermit Eby tells of the annual visit by the deacons, prior to the Love Feast, to find out whether the family was in peace and harmony with the church:

> My father was one of the deacons; so he was usually out on a visitation trip with his partner, Dave Holmes, when Eli Wenger and Delbert Markham stopped at our house. We knew about what time to expect them; so mother had washed our faces. My sisters and I had put on clean clothes. If the hired man were a member of the church, he joined the family circle. Mother met the deacons at the door, greeted them, and invited them to be seated. For several minutes all sat still and silent. Eli Wenger was short and fat and

slow-spoken, Delbert Markham was old and stooped, his gray beard scraggly and unkempt. Both men were none too happy at their task. For forty years two sharp-tongue and efficient deaconesses had told them what to say—and now they were alone.[20]

Minor Miller (b. 1889, VA) had an assertive mother:

When my father and I reached home Mother had plenty to say, and she had plenty to say for weeks and months after that Friday night. She did not attend the meeting because it was still "a man's world."[21]

Tongue power has been used since woman discovered that she was not as strong physically as man; again, knowing these old sisters, it is not probable that tongue power was used extensively by them. At the risk of being accused of idealization, the following reference represents the more usual relationship in the decision-making process: Ernest Wampler's wife wanted him and her to volunteer for foreign mission work. Wampler (b. 1895, VA) was not sure whether this was his calling, but finally he made up his mind.

One evening as I went home for supper, I decided I would ask Vida (his wife) about going, or volunteering for the mission field. On arriving home that evening I spoke to her as I passed through the kitchen, went on in to the living room where our little daughter, Sara Anna, of about seven months, was sleeping in her crib. I sat down and called out to Vida and said, "I have decided to follow your wish and volunteer for mission work." She came into the room, kissed me and said, "You make me very happy."[22]

Status of Women in the Church Order

There is a conflict between the statements that man is the head of the woman and the basic belief of the Dunkers that all were equal in the eyes of God. They wrestled with this. Believing in equality, they tried to make the women's role as equal as the current mores would allow, but when the final word was reached all equality disappeared—it was still a man's world.

Elder Henry Kurtz compiled and translated from German the minutes of the AM's up to 1867 with notes when needed to explain some of the actions and conclusions. His words provide insight into the status of the women of the church in the church order. In one area of the order involving the women, there was

disagreement—the serving of the bread and cup during communion. The men, on their side of the table, took the bread and cup
and passed it along the line of participants. For the women, the
administrator carried the bread and the cup, ministering to each
sister individually. Numerous queries were addressed to the
various councils seeking to require the same procedure for
women as for men in this important ordinance of the church.
Elder Kurtz adds this note to the answer given to the 1857 query
concerning the matter:

> There is scarcely any church or society, beside our own, where the
> rights and privileges of the female sex are better regarded. Not to
> speak of those chuches whose principles were established in the
> dark ages, when woman was considered as an inferior being, and
> even manhood groaned under the tyrannical sway of popes and
> priests. With us, the sisters are on a perfect equality with the
> brethren. The youngest sister's voice counts one, and the oldest
> bishop's vote does not count more, in any ordinary question before
> the church, or in a choice for ministers of deacons. In all things,
> rights and privileges, there is no difference between the male and
> female portion of the membership, and the only exception is the
> service of the church, from which the sisters are exempted by the
> gospel, though the wives of ministers and deacons are also
> presented to the church, and charged to be helpers to their
> husbands in their service.[23]

> Enough has been recorded to show that at the beginning, and at
> least for fifty-four years, in the early church the sisters each one
> passed the cup and broke the communion.[24]

Shirley Holmes observes:

> Women were given fairly equal status in the life of the congrega-
> tion even during the early years. They were admonished just as the
> men were for sins and asked to leave the church just as often.
> Women were given responsibilities as deacons and solicitors for
> various projects.[25]

In 1910, the Bridgewater, Virginia church allowed the sisters to
receive communion in the same way as the brothers. At the next
meeting, this was recorded:

> On motion of a sister it was decided not to use the liberty granted at
> our last conference by which sisters are allowed to break the bread

of communion but to adhere to the usual practice of the minister breaking the bread to the sisters.[26]

This supports Elder Kurtz's thesis that there was a reason of usefulness for serving the sisters in a way different from the brothers.

The church faced some difficult questions when they disciplined the male members. Since the wife was "yoked" to the husband, did the penalty also apply to the wife? If the husband was avoided, was the wife also? Did the wife have to avoid the husband? Could the wife of a man who was expelled from membership still belong to the church? There is a body of decisions relating to these; this query sums up the attempts at equity in answering these questions:

> A.M. 1804 Art. 1   Yet the sisters, who are bound in such matter by the urging of their husbands, and would gladly be relieved from it, but cannot without the consent of their husbands, they should be held less guilty. (refers to keeping taverns and selling liquor)[27]

It was within the context of these references that the mother assumed her role in the Dunker subculture.

The Mother in the Dynamics of the Family

Children need strong parental guidance and control. The Dunker father provided this to the extreme when compared to present-day standards, making it necessary for a "safety valve" to be in the home to blunt the impact of the sometimes overly dogmatic stances of the father. There had to be an intercessor. The Dunker mother served in the capacity, as have mothers down through the ages. The one area that seemed to require this intercession frequently was in education. Most of the fathers permitted their children to go to public school. In their view, education beyond public school was either useless or sinful. Since the teenager owed his services to his father until the age of "setting free," the mother oft-times had to persuade the father to release him from this obligation so that he could attend "Normal School." There are numerous instances of this where the mother either helped the son secure his father's permission or helped the son raise the money to get an advanced education.

One instance of mother intercession involved feeding her

children more often than the father permitted. To make the food supply last through the winter, the father decreed that they should be fed only twice a day. But the mother gave the children an extra helping of cereal. As the account told, the mother was fearful that the father would notice the rapid disappearance of cereal. This apparently escaped his attention, demonstrating the subtlety in the family dynamics and relationships of the Dunkers. The father certainly knew that his wife was feeding the children the third meal, because anyone who watched the budget as carefully as did this father also watched the inventory. A hard, domineering man who had ego problems would have stopped her. The Dunker man laid down the law and then enforced it compassionately because of his feelings for his wife and children. This interpretation may be an idealization; it probably is not.

Evidence of Equality of Sexes

In some societies, a college education was considered proper and necessary for the boys, but not for the girls, who needed to know only the skills of the housewife. But when education was finally accepted by the German Baptist Brethren, it was accepted for both the girls and the boys. Bridgewater College, a Dunker-affiliated school, was founded in 1880 and was the first coeducational college in Virginia. This southern college had an open admission policy towards races and had a few black students before this became a common occurrence in Virginia.

Anna Blough Williams wrote a short description of her grandmother, Lovina Conner, which tells of family life in Pennsylvania and Virginia in the later 1800's and early 1900's. Note that the boys cooked "as well as the girls," again an illustration that the Dunkers strove toward equality of the sexes:

LOVINA KINSEL CONNER

Lovina Kinsel was born in 1847 in Schuylkill Co., Pa., the daughter of Samuel and Eve Kinsel. I believe she was the oldest, but I am not absolutely sure of this. She had three sisters and at least two brothers who grew up and raised families. The farm where she grew up was near Pine Grove, Pa. and near the Strouphauer Church of the Brethren which the family attended and where her parents are buried. As a young girl she left home and worked as a tailoress in Pottstown for several years before she was married.

In 1870 she married Abraham Landis Conner and went to live in the house where he was born near Royerford, Pa. This house is still standing, a typical Pennsylvania farmhouse, three stories above a full basement. His mother had died about the time they were married and, since he was the youngest child, I assume that was the reason they went there to live. He later bought this farm from his father and they lived there until they moved to Virginia in 1885. At that time, he sold the farm to his nephew, Jesse Conner Ziegler. Edward was born in this house when his parents were living there helping his grandfather operate the farm before it was sold to a Mennonite family.

Nine children were born to Abraham and Lovina, five boys and four girls, all but the youngest before they moved to Virginia. One daughter died as a small child. Raising a family of that size required a great deal of work. My mother said that twice a week they baked countless loaves of bread and at least twenty pies at a baking. All the clothes were made at home, and, since she had worked in a tailor shop she made the suits for her husband and sons as well as all the other clothing required for such a family. My mother's wedding dress is one of the few pieces that have survived to show how beautifully she sewed. The boys were taught to cook and help with the housework as well as the girls. My mother said several of her brothers could cook as good a meal as any of the girls.

Besides taking care of her family she was interested in the church and all of its activities. She assisted her husband who was a minister in any way that she could. This sometimes meant taking all responsibility for the family and the farm when he would be away overnight to preach or attend meetings. I remember the ruler she kept just for marking off the bread into strips before baking it. When she could no longer do it my mother took over the job, using the same little ruler. My mother than taught Elva Kline and Crystal Wakeman to bake the communion bread. I don't know whether she passed the little ruler on to them.

After the death of her husband in 1918, she lived with us until her death in 1920. Her health was not good then as she had asthma for many years, but she could still do some hand sewing and enjoyed reading.[28]

Abram Conner was progressive in his church and in his work. Apparently, Lovina Conner was also progressive, because she, as a young girl of eighteen, left home and worked as a tailoress for several years. This was not in keeping with the custom of the times in the sect and represents a break with the cultural pattern.

Faulty Parenting by the Mother

Several instances of faulty parenting by fathers have been given. Two rather blatant cases were found which indicated that the mother was also guilty of this. That of Sarah Richter Major is more appropriate to another chapter. Another account, however, fits the aim of this chapter because it gives the perception of the mother by her son. The son's feeling are expressed in her obituary published in the church-approved magazine, *The Gospel Visitor*. In addition to his reaction, the account tells something of the faith and character of the Dunker mother:

> Died in Montgomery Co., Pa., on the 13th of July, Sister Price, consort of Daniel Price. The following extract is taken for a letter to us from br. C.H. Price, son of the deceased.
>
> In her extreme suffering, she "endured." She did not exhibit any marks of impatience, nor was there one murmur heard from the commencement to the end. She was triumphant. She told me her hope in God was strong. In the morning in which she died, she had a spell, and we all thought she was gone, but she came back again, oh says she, how sorry I am that I had to come back, I felt so happy. Br. Ja. Reiner came into the room and she says, Br., "I shall no more sit under your voice." He told her she would soon sit under a sweeter sound. She told him she was near her journey's end, and would not wish to get well any more, as her hopes were bright, and she had no fear of meeting her goal. (The writer switches to himself.) Dear Bro., I have a strong hope, but Oh! my dear mother, I feel that the loss of my mother will bring me to my grave. I am fast wasting away. I am dead to the world, and desire no earthly enjoyment. The only place I want to go is to my dear mother's grave, and weep there till all my tears are exhausted. She was the only comfort in the world, the only one to lean upon—I know not where to go to mourn and weep for her as long as I am a pilgrim here. (After another paragraph he ends stating that Bro. Ja. Reiner spoke to the satisfaction of all on "Blessed are the dead who die in the Lord, etc.")[29]

This was written by Caleb H. Price and was published in the October issue of the Gospel Visitor, about five months after the death of Price's mother. The many hundreds of obituaries examined are more in the style and content of the first part of the account in which the faith and courage of the terminal patient are shown by happy anticipation of soon being with Jesus. The survivor usually mentioned that the death was a triumph and a reward for "the pilgrim who has completed his earthly journey." The survivors rejoiced that the journey was complete, the pain and suffering over. In contrast, this account indicates that Price was left an emotional cripple. In view of the usual belief that the person had gone to his reward and that this letter was written perhaps four months after the death of his mother, this would not seem part of a normal grief reaction but rather an example of an abnormal symbiosis. Usually, this is due to the failure of the mother (and/or father) to allow the child to grow and mature on the usual track, brought about by the need of the mother or father to use the child to fill deficits in his or her own personality.

But other stories present a more wholesome attitude of the mother to those around her.

This story, told about a Dunker mother born in Virginia in 1884, sums up the caring position that the mother had in the family:

> I will always remember this picture of my mother. One evening after supper, she left the house to pick some blackberries in the far corner of the field. Soon, the cat saw her and followed after her, to be joined by the dog, later the rooster, and as she went into the field, the cow and then the horse joined the procession. And there was my mother, going through the field to pick blackberries with the cat, dog, rooster, cow, and horse following after her.[30]

So what was the typical Dunker mother like in the years prior to 1900? We would like to know more, but hard data are not there. Was she more than the faithful helpmate? Less than the idealization of "sacred memory"? More will be learned about her as discipline, training and value transference are considered.

Summary

The Dunker father was the head of the household in fact and in perception. His children saw him as stern and authoritative, feared and respected him, but also experienced instances of warmth and caring. He expected his children to be obedient in work and behavior and at times commented on their shortcomings. The father-minister was called away by the duties of his office; other fathers were absent from the home because of economic circumstances. The mother had both childrearing and managerial responsibilities. She was equal in substance in family and church life. Both were guilty of faulty parenting. True descriptions of the Dunker mother are scarce; idealized accounts are plentiful.

6

Family

The family had the most influence on the Dunker young, serving as the cradle into which the infant was born and the training ground for the pre-adolescent. To some extent, it contained the youths during their turbulent adolescent years. The family, in an essentially unchanged form, maintained its role as the agency responsible for the care, nurture, and religious upbringing of the children well into the twentieth century. In the later period, through, there was sharing of responsibility with the church and public school system. During this period, the family seemed less effective in retaining the youth for membership in the German Baptist Brethren Church. This was perceived as a developing weakness in the family structure.

Characteristics of the Dunker Family

In the typical Dunker family during the period of this study, the father was the head; the mother was his faithful supporter; and the children were economic assets, viewed with love and sentimentality. It functioned as an economic unit throughout the period for the support of its members rather than for lineage reasons. Functionally, the family was capable of the adaptations necessitated by changing economic and social conditions.

The Dunkers espoused the married life. There is no evidence that the single life had any appeal for them, but it did not carry a stigma. The young people selected their mates, although at times the advice and consent of the elder of the church were required. The ceremony was held at the home of the bride. It was festive, religious, and the infare (belling or serenading), though forbidden by church order, was held. After a wedding trip to visit relatives, the young couple settled in the area in which one of them was raised and, with the help of their parents, started their own life.

Except for temporary or unusual circumstances, there is no evidence that the Dunkers adopted the practice of a large group of blood relatives living under the same roof after they came to America. It was quite common, however, for an uncle, aunt, an elderly grandparent, or an orphaned child to become part of the family, forming a modified extended family. Temporary shelter was given in times of crisis or relocation. But the privacy of the family was the rule, made possible by the abundance of land and building material in colonial America.

What was the Dunker family? Dove has this to say:

> The Brethren family of the early days was a unique institution. Located generally in the open country, Brethren homes were more or less isolated from the larger culture centers for the most part, and developed an independence and unity all its own ... Each member of the family was a part of an industrial, social, moral, and religious organization, the functions of which were closely inter-woven. Dominated principally by a religious faith with strong insistence upon the simple life, the family often exercised a stern and puritanic discipline upon its members.[1]

Dove was partially right. There is no evidence, however, that the Dunker family was unique. Its characteristics were shared by many other frontier families with the "stern and puritanic discipline." But all Dunker families did not fit his description. Elder John Kline, on one of his preaching tours in western Virginia, described a family on the other end of the economic spectrum:

> Monday, April 13, 1835   We found some of the members in very poor condition. One sister, in particular, moved my feelings deeply. Her husband is somewhat dissipated and does not provide for his family as he should. She is the mother of three small children, and judging from their present appearance, they have undergone a good deal of suffering for want of food and clothing. None of them have any shoes; and the thin coverings they have on are so patched and darned that one can hardly tell the kind of goods they were originally made of.[2]

It is safe to say that the Dunker family covered the economic spectrum just as did other similar groups, although the work ethic and plain living probably made them better off than the average frontier farm family of the day. Accounts suggest that they, because of their farming practices, produced more than others on the same quality land. None of this speaks to uniqueness. If the Dunker family could be called unique by stretching a point, it was in degree, emphasis, and constancy in their daily lives. This is difficult to prove. There was one constant characteristic of their life, however. They were rural, and the references which follow are from this background.

Size of Family

The family was large, as were most families of that time, by today's standard. Disapproval of birth control and the need for help on the labor-intensive farm seemed to be the principal causes. The biblical admonition to "be fruitful and multiply" was also noted. Thirty families at random were examined from material prior to 1900, revealing an average of seven children per family, ranging from three to twenty-three. Approximately seventy-five percent of the children survived.[3] Dove guessed that there were five people in the typical family by 1920.[4] Ziegler states that there were 6.5 children in 1880, 7.9 in the families of 1900, and 5.1 in 1920.[5]

A host of factors may influence family size. For the Dunkers, the rising level of education may have affected it; the movement of the members to the cities before 1900 did not, because in the three generations studied by Ziegler approximately ninety percent of the families lived on the farm, reaffirming that the culture of the Dunkers remained predominantly rural well up into the twentieth century.

Early Death of Parents

The Dunker family often lost the father or the mother before the children were raised. Life on the frontier was primitive and many dangers in the environment took a toll of both mothers and fathers. But the mother had to face an even greater danger than the father: childbirth. Infection and other complications of delivery caused many women to die before their time. Because of this, some men had as many as five wives and had children by each one. This mixing of generations posed problems: the third or fourth wife could be the same age as the oldest child by the first wife. This query was brought before the AM:

Y.M. 1854 Art. 16   Is it allowed by the Gospel for a sister, after her
husband is dead, to be married to her stepson? Considered, not to
be allowed according to the following passages 1 Cor. 5:1; Lev.
18:8.

Churches should be watchful to purge out such leaven from
among them.[6]

Despite early deaths and generation mixing, happy, fruitful
marriages producing many children were the rule. This account,
concerning Daniel Barnhart (b. 1791, VA), was given in Memoriam
in the *Pilgrim* in 1875:

His (Daniel Barnhart) first wife was Eve Bowman. Daniel and Eve
had born unto them two sons and nine daughters, one died when a
child, but the rest grew up to be men and women. Eve was born in
1768 (sic) and died January 22nd 1833 in the 39th year of her age.
Daniel then being left with a large family, after a time, feeling the
need of one to see to the wants and cares of his children, took unto
him a second wife, namely Catherine Brubaker, who was born in
the year 1808. They had born unto them nine sons and two
daughters, one of whom died when a child. By his first wife he
raised eight daughters and two sons, and by his second wife raised
eight sons and two daughters. In the year of 1867, early in the
Spring, Catherine, his second wife, was taken ill and died Sunday
morning, August 4th, 1867. (Daniel died two years later.)[7]

Another couple was more fortunate:

At the time of this meeting, Brother Daniel Miller's family was
young, and most of them were at home, eighteen in all; and all by
children of one mother.[8]

Functions of the Family

The experiences of childhood mold the child and determine
to a great extent what the adult will be. The adult, by the values
learned in his formative years, determines the content and flavor
of the society of his time. This process was important to the
sectarian Dunkers. By attempting to shield the outside world from
the child and by exposing the child to the values held sacred by
them, they continued their sectarian existence with a constancy
of practice over a sustained period of time. The church order
placed the responsibility for the religious training on the family.
With this responsibility, and with the nature of farm life providing

its own value system, the family was the funnel through which the Dunker child passed on his way to adulthood, acquiring the values and philosophy of a stylized and purposeful way of life. Four functions can be identified in the workings of the family: economic, support, religious, and value transference.

The Family as an Economic Unit

The Dunker family existed to provide the daily necessities of life. It engaged in subsistence farming in the purest form; excess money was rare. Each member of the family had a job to do as part of this unit, and the success of the unit depended greatly on how well each did his job. The children became part of the work force at about five years of age and worked until they were "set free," somewhere between sixteen and twenty-one years of age. Kermit Eby described the children as economic assets. This they were. They were an essential part of the farm work-force where more than one pair of hands were required to do the work, and hired farm hands were in short supply. When work on the home farm was caught up, the children, if old enough, were hired out to the neighbors. Money from this went to the father to provide additional support for the family. For their work, the children were fed, clothed, and given the education that existed in their particular locality; in addition, they were trained in the basic skills of farming which they could use as adults.

Skills other than agricultural were present among the Dunkers. Elder John Kline, along with his preaching and farming, practiced medicine. On his ministering trips, he gathered medicinal herbs for use then and when he returned home. Many of the Dunker women were midwives. Whether this was a commercial occupation or a neighborly service is not stated. A few were physicians. Apparently one Dunker physician's practice was not very prosperous; he advertised. Some of his fellow church members did not like this, because a query was sent to the AM asking whether the meeting approved of a physician boosting his reputation by saying he was a member of the German Baptist Brethren Church. The meeting did not approve of that type of advertisement.

The Family as a Support Unit

The Dunker family was a support unit—the personal relationships within the family structure provided emotional support to each member of the family. This was different in degree only from other rural families of other denominations. The role of each member was well-defined. The father headed the family, yet he depended on the wife for sympathy and understanding in difficult times and for her help in making a living. This excerpt from the diary of J.J. Emmert (b. 1833, MD) suggests a very close and supportive relationship. His letter was written in 1870 in Illinois:

> My wife stands by me while I write, but now she had retired for the night. Eddie is still at the table. Those two and unworthy self compose the family.[9]

When the father was away from home preaching, working, or spying out new land, the wife ran the farm. In correspondence, the wife was mentioned as "help mate." "House mother" or "house mate" was occasionally used. George Whitmer (b. 1878) used the more frequent term, "companion."*

> My companion, having had an urgent call to come to South Bend, Indiana, to see her old father, John Studebaker.[10]

The use of "companion" is an expression of the devout Dunker's belief that life is a necessary journey that one must take to reach Heaven. His wife is his companion on this journey. The wife referred to her mate as "husband," "my husband," or "my dear husband." A reasonable explanation for the use of the term "help mate" relates to her role on the farm and the help that this gave the man in his role as provider and as leader in the church.

How did the man support his wife emotionally? On the surface, it would appear that the husband thought of himself first, but this was not true, despite the fact that it was a man's world. The following indicate that concern was shown for the wife and her desires. The B.E. Plaine family moved to Iowa from Maryland in 1866.:

---

* Other idioms were used: "broke up" appears to be equivalent to the modern term, "bankrupt;" "great" seems to be a generic term for anything above average; and "undone" (He is undone.) suggests an emotional upheaval.

Hannah seems to think she will never feel at home here. I still hope
that when we fix up a little that mother will be better contented.[11]

E.K. Ziegler stated:

I never heard him utter an unkind word to my gentle mother in the
fifty-seven years of their married life.[12]

In the J.J. Emmert Diary:

My dear wife suffered extremely for 3 hours with her sore breast.

My dear wife has still an open running breast, very painful at
times.[13]

Alexander Mack, Jr., son of the founder of the sect, had an
unusually warm friendship with another elder, John Preisz (Price)
of the neighboring congregation of Indian Creek (in Pennsylvania), and many letters were sent back and forth between them
over the years. These letters spoke to the church issues of the day
and to the affairs of their families. In this letter, Mack is apparently
responding to a note of sympathy from Price over the misfortunes
of two of Mack's children. This letter was dated February 14, 1776.
The first paragraph is in greeting and is omitted:

I can therefore not very well avoid telling you a bit about the
present situation of my children. It is true, my Hannah had thought
at first that her sin was not so great because they had been engaged
never to leave each other, and both she and her husband (Adam
Weaver) indeed intend to prove this. However, she realizes her error
and recognizes her misdeed. She wants me to ask you especially
for your forgiveness as she has always held a special love for you,
because she believed that you feared the Lord. She would be
especially grateful if you prayed to the Lord for her that he might
have mercy on her in her condition and request, for she does not
want to remain behind completely.

My Sarah thinks that she has done quite well, because she has
rejected many and finally accepted the one she loves. She has
indeed been spared the kind of shame my Hannah bears. Her
husband is Jacob Ziegler, a tanner, who lives not far from you. She
has been excluded from the kiss (of love) and the communion for
three reasons. First, because she married outside of the brotherhood; secondly, because (the marriage) was performed with a

> license; and thirdly, because her husband had not quite completed
> (his apprenticeship) and his master knew nothing about (the
> marriage). My Hannah has been disciplined even more severely, so
> that we do not even eat with her---.
>
> As far as I am concerned, I publicly asked the brethren whether
> they had anything against me but they testified that they were
> satisfied with me and really did not wish to place any blame on
> me.
>
> Yet before God I cannot declare myself entirely blameless even
> though I did certainly think I had used great diligence and sent
> many sighs to the Eternal Love for these two poor children---.[14]

The offense of Hannah appears to relate to pregnancy.
However, Brumbaugh lists their first child as being born nine and
one-half months after marriage. So this might relate to detected
fornication, punishable by avoidance into the early 1900's.[15]

In addition to the support factor, this letter is instructive in
two other areas: church discipline and family dynamics. Sarah
was disciplined by being "put back," that is, two of the privileges
of membership were withdrawn. Hannah was placed in full
avoidance for a more serious offense, and even her family was not
permitted to eat with her. There was some doubt whether it was
proper for her to send greetings to Elder Price. And, in keeping
with the responsibility of the father to rear his children properly,
Mack subjected himself to the judgment of the church and was
found blameless.

The children's deviations from the family norm shamed the
father. However, he blamed himself rather than his daughters. Of
significance is the fact that the mother is not mentioned, speaking
again to the status of the father as head of the house. Apparently,
with the authority went the responsibility. He did not renounce
his daughters but experienced the hope that things would work
out. Mack ends his letter with "My dear wife and children send
their kind greetings as far as it is possible and acceptable."

The effect of group approval as part of the support mechanism is also demonstrated. Hannah wanted the forgiveness of
Elder Price, even though he was not a relative. But he was a friend
and a senior member of the brotherhood and his opinion was
important to the young Hannah.

The extended family was also part of the support system.

Uncles, aunts, and cousins often lived in a neighborhood cluster and were available for daily or weekly contact. This cluster living also provided an economic advantage. The average daily work load was geared to the help available, usually consisting of the father, older children, and perhaps a hired hand. At harvest time, extra help was required, and the presence of family members provided the cooperative force which was needed to harvest the wheat and corn, butcher the hogs, or perhaps build a barn. Although this activity was primarily economic, the social contact during these times was part of the sustenance which bound and maintained the families.

It has been noted that families of the church were persuaded to locate close to other Dunkers. Many fathers helped their children get started in life.

> My parents had bought an additional farm close by and after the oldest son was married they arranged for Jacob and Allie to settle on the farm—we assume at a reasonable cost. When the second son was married they arranged for him to buy a portion of the original farm and helped him finance a house (exactly like theirs). They also helped the daughters and their husbands finance homes. By the time the last three of us were growing up they decided that they would give each of us $3000 to start life with. The younger boys worked away from home for room and board and a small monthly salary, but the salary was collected by Papa and applied to their $3000.[16]

There were a number of accounts such as this which suggests that keeping the children within the family network after maturity was a common practice.

The presence of the children provided emotional support to the parents; ultimately, it provided a caring support as the parents grew older. Kermit Eby had an unusually successful professional life and lived in eight different places. He maintained his ties with his parents until they died, returning to the home place two weeks every summer. Despite the success and security that his professional achievements gave him, the home farm was the place where he felt the best:

> Dad's home—the brick house, the red barn, the pine trees in the front yard, the woods—give me a sense of security which I've never experienced anywhere else[17]

The family support system took different forms; providing help for the children was not unique to the Dunkers. Demos describes this among the Puritans of the seventeenth century. He ascribes to it: 1) An extension of the moral and legal obligations to care for the children in their minority. 2) This, along with inheritance, provided control over behavior and selection of mates. 3) It tended to keep the family together. 4) It was not an attempt to perpetuate a patriarchal system. Levy noted the reasons for this economic practice among the Quakers of the seventeenth and eighteenth century: 1) Lack of jobs for the young. 2) To keep the children away from the "worldly" cities. 3) The observation that prosperity of a family increased the likelihood that its members would follow the Quaker doctrine. Senior members of the Church of the Brethren thought it preserved the farm work-force.[18]

Another function of the family as a support system is to keep a proper emotional tone among its members. To maintain this state, the air must be kept clear of problems, personal or otherwise. Children do not tolerate strained feelings between members of a family, particularly if the father or mother is angry with the child. Samuel Glick used family devotions to air problems and concerns:

> When I was small, Mother told us how Grandpa Glick had his family gather together each evening in the living room for devotions. They would talk about anything that was troubling any of them and then he would read a chapter out of the Bible and they would all kneel and each one would pray.[19]

There are several references that indicated that the evening meal was the air-clearing time, when the problems were "taken to the table." Myron Miller, son of Minor Miller (b. 1888, VA), recalls that this was the practice in their home, and that the children used this practice as a threat: "If you do that I'll tell Dad at supper time."[20] This method of reconciliation would not meet with the approval of the present-day psychologists and the gastroenterologists (stomach specialists), both of whom recommend quietness and tranquility at meal time, one for the sake of the mind and the other for the sake of the digestive process. Despite these shortcomings, this method has at least two features to recommend it: It deals with the transgression promptly and on a group basis, so that the person at fault has the support of the other children in the moment of trial. That the breach of the family code of conduct was discussed and settled in a family setting, as opposed to a one-on-one basis, unified the family.

Family as a Unit for Religious Instruction

The Dunker family was a unit for religious instruction because of: 1) the practice of formal congregational worship in homes; 2) the daily life being patterned after the scriptures; 3) the inability to attend congregational worship on a regular basis; and 4) the non-existence of Sunday Schools. After meeting houses were permitted by church order, services were held monthly or sometimes twice a month, even into the twentieth century.

Therefore, the home was the only constant, acceptable place to receive the spiritual blessing of formal worship. These religious exercises included Bible reading, grace after meals, and the family altar. Bible reading was encouraged, and, with a poor supply of newspapers, magazines, and books was a ready source of stimulation for the eager young mind. However, illiteracy was prevalent among the Dunkers, as among all frontier people, so Bible reading was not as extensive as one would think. In the generation of 1880, forty-seven percent of the fathers read the Bible, and this improved only to fifty-four percent in the 1900 generation. Grace at meals was more prevalent, and has remained so: 1880—ninety-four percent; 1900—seventy-five percent; and in 1920—seventy-six percent.[21]

The mothers did read the Bible to their children, improving on the religious exposure related to the statistics above. They also said prayers as they tucked their children into bed, and it was their duty to lead family worship when the father was away.

Family worship was usually held in the evening, although some held it in the morning. Supper over and the children ready for bed, father finished his after-supper nap. All gathered in the living room where a selection, or selections, of Scripture was read with the children sitting quietly. After father finished his reading and offered a prayer, the family went sleepily to bed. Discussion or other group interaction was not a usual part of the occasion. Some held family altar daily; others at less frequent intervals during the week. In the generation of 1880, eighty-two percent held family altar regularly; 1900—twenty-five percent; and 1920—twenty-two percent.[22] Why did this family practice all but disappear?

> We had it (family worship) at night. Father would sit around and read until he would get sleepy. None of us children were permitted to go to bed until we had family worhip. We would get sleepy and lie down and go to sleep. Then when father was ready to go to bed we would all be waked up for family worship. Father would read and pray. Several times he went to sleep while praying. I got so disgusted with it that we never had it in our home.[23]

"Perhaps it was this formalism and lack of planning with consideration for the children fifty years ago that caused the last two generations to turn from it."[24] This was Ziegler's conclusion as to why families turned away from family altar. He may have been right; however, he wrote this around 1940 when it was believed that children could do no wrong and parents could do no right. There were certainly additional factors.

The family accepted responsibility for religious training for many years. Among the Dunkers, religious training outside of the home was suspect. However, when the Dunker parents began to take their children to Sunday Schools of other denominations, the sect reluctantly approved this form of religious instruction. Even so, it took the schism of 1881, when the conservatives withdrew, to finally make this a wholly acceptable part of the sect program. There was the stipulation, of course, that they be conducted in the "gospel order." Relinquishing part of the responsibility for religious training to an agency outside of the home was the first or second major adjustment the family made to societal change. At about the same time, the Dunkers allowed the influx of youth reading-material into their homes which, though religious, directed the minds of their children to an authority other than their parents—the printed word. The decrease in family altar more or less followed in inverse order the acceptance of Sunday Schools.

Sunday Schools represented a threat from the outside, one in which it was perceived that the children would be taught to play and to socialize rather than to study the Bible in a serious way. The rejection of Sunday Schools, therefore, was a protective measure; the acceptance of them was a reaction to the conditions of the day. Still the Dunkers continued to protect their children. One brother recalls that he was sent to a country school because his family did not want him exposed to the children of a city school (this "city" was a country village). The Midland, Virginia church, around 1890, decided in council that their members should not invite neighboring children into their homes for parties.

Despite the inevitable changes, the home still exerted the major religious influence on the children. Dr. J.M. Henry (b. 1880, VA) remembered:

> The morning before these lines were written the writer took a walk over the old homestead where so many precious memories of his boyhood cluster. The old familiar places were visited, the old spring house on the hillside where father sat and talked with his sons about a Galilean who sat by a well and told of living water. Then at another spot where the hay wagon turned over and I ran at the risk of my life to help him, but no spot was more precious than the hearthstone where father entertained so many ministers of the gospel and had family worship. Memories of other years hold fast.[25]

The Family as a Unit for Value Transference

The Dunker family was a unit in which values were transferred from the parents to the children. All facets of family life were involved in this process, not just the conversations of the parents, but they way they lived and the way they carried out their daily duties. Of particular importance is what they expected of their children. Lester Flory's account of his childhood is a powerful expression of the value transferring function of the family and is representative of many of the Dunker families of that day. Although a few paragrahs are omitted, the account is essentially unedited; his manner of speech with its intensity and positiveness of tone is as informative as are his words.

> I want to say that when I was a boy just coming into this world about 1905 I growed up in a home that was a Christian home. We believed in obedience, in Christian work, and in doing things that we were told.

> When I was about five years old I know one time that I didn't do what I was supposed to do. I didn't listen to my parents and I got a good spanking. I think it learnt me to be what I ought to been. It learnt me to listen, obey, and this is what we were taught to do. We used to work, we all had a job.

I know when I was about seven years old I had to carry in the wood in the evening. We had a box on the porch and a box in the kitchen we filled with wood and I know that when I didn't do it they wanted to know why. We didn't just do what we wanted to do, when we wanted to do it, we done it when they told us and if we didn't we got punished for it. And when I got a little older my father had sheep, had cattle, chickens, hogs. We had sheep and we had them penned in a pen for the winter time. My little brother and myself went down in the pen and went catching the sheep. My father came along and caught us. My younger brother he rolled over the fence and my Dad gave him a couple licks with a paddle and he went on out a-hollering. Of course, I went over the fence the other way and run around the barn and went and hid. Of course he found me later on. Believe me I sure got a good spanking. He got a switch and he give it to me not only for running the sheep, but for running away and hiding. I got two in the one time. So we had these things to kind of keep us straight and to keep us remembering that we was supposed to do what our parents told us.

And when along about six, seven, or eight years old we got so that they taking us along to the field and we picked up corn. We'd pick it up out of a pile when they had shucked it and we'd pick it up into a basket or a tub. My older brothers or father would load it on the wagon and we'd pick up another tub. So when we'd get a load on and bring it in to the house and unload it in the corncrib. Well we done that when we was small and I never will forget one fall when they went to sow wheat my father and two older brothers was working on the wheat drill getting it ready to go to the field with and sow wheat, and they was oiling it, greasing it and getting it freed up. I was around there and I picked up a oil can and begin to squirt it along a hand saw and that was laying there and my Daddy picked up a board and fanned my setter good because I was wasting oil. Said he'd learn me not to waste oil. I'd do what I was supposed to do.

A little later when I got a little bigger, about seven or eight years old, I thought I was big and I went with my Mother to the barn. She done the milking and I thought I'd milk one of the cows. She milked two cows. So I got to milking one and she would come around and finish mine. But I soon learnt how to milk. By the time I got to where I could do it, then she just turned it all over to me and I had the whole thing to do and I done it—milking, feed the cows, put them, turned em out, and my younger brother he fed the chickens and do the eggs. My older brother would take care of the cattle and the horses. Well then when I got a little older about nine, ten we had to go to the corn field in the morning. We'd get up and do the feeding, eat our breakfast, be in the corn field by daylight and shuck corn.

PLATE 14. A Brethren minister and his wife on a pastoral visiting trip

PLATE 15. Teachers in a Brethren mission school in Greene County, Virginia—1920's

We'd set out there and shuck corn until time to go to school and then we'd run in the house and wash and change our clothes and get ready to go to school and we had 2 1/2 miles to walk to school and we walked everyday 2 1/2 miles to and from school.

School taken in at 9:00 o'clock and we was supposed to be there. We had time to get there when we left the cornfield and we better not fool around and be late either. And school let out at 4:00 o'clock and we would get out of school and we had just a certain time to make the 2 miles and a half because we had work waiting for us at home. And if we played along the road and fooled and didn't get home when we was supposed to they soon reminded us with a little switch that we was supposed to be there at a certain time and made us remember after that that we should come right on home —we had work to do and we was supposed to do it.

And we growed up and got bigger we always had a little more to do, more work put on us. I know by the time I was a right good size, probably twelve years old, I don't know just exactly, but somewheres around that, my father give me a job to do and told me to do it before he came back—he was going away. Some boys came along and wanted to go down to the creek and go swimming. "Oh, we can get down and come back, you can do that when you come back."

So I went down to the creek, went swimming with them. Well, when boys get to playing and swimming they forget the time and we forgot it and it was late when we got back. My father come before I got any work done, so he wanted to know what happened. Wanted to know where I was at. He knew I'd been swimming. And he got a good old switch and he really switched me for fair you well. I tell you I got one of the awfulest whippings I ever got in my life. But it learnt me that I'd do what he told me and I'd do it when he'd tell me. Any other time that was all right, but we had to do our work.

We went to church every Sunday, every thing that there was. One time I got to going out a little on Sunday and (Sunday) night I was with some other young people, I thought I'd have a little fun and wouldn't go home and go to church. So I didn't go. Well, Dad wanted to know at the breakfast table "Where was you at? Where was you last night?" I said "Well, to see so and so and with so and so. They didn't want to come to church, so we just didn't come." "All right," he said, "from now on you'll stay here, won't go to where, won't go away at all for sixty days, two months." I drove a horse and buggy, at the time we didn't have automobiles, but he said you won't get a horse nor buggy for two months. That was my punishment for not going to church. But we got put to work, we done the work and we done what they told us, when they told us.

When we had Christmas, we didn't have Christmas like we have today. I know there were several years we had a bench right along the back of our table where us boys eat on and we lined our caps on this bench when we went to bed. When we got up in the morning and come down our caps had a apple, an orange, a chocolate drop and maybe two pieces of candy and that was our Christmas. I never will forget one time when I was about twelve or fourteen years old I got a little red wagon to carry wood, carry wood in the evening and I thought that was really something. I guess I could have carried more wood than I could have hauled on that little red wagon, but I thought I was really doing something. And that was the way we had our entertainment and fun when we was boys.

We'd go out in the field and thin this corn, had to pull out all but two stalks in the hill. I never will forget one day I thinned about twenty acres of corn and when I got done my Dad walked around over a little bit and found four or five hills with three stalks or more in it and he told me to go out there and start right at one side and go over the whole field just to get them few stalks. But that was the punishment I had. I hated it and I sure didn't do that again. But this wasn't a bad job sometimes because if it was a little wet everybody would get their shoes off and go out in the cornfield and thin corn and it didn't take but a few hours to go over a field when there were five or six of you.

For our fun in the winter time we went "Belsnicklin" which was something like Trick or Treat. We dressed up as Santa or in other costumes. We did not do any tricking, we went to the homes around our neighborhood. The people would ask us in, then try to guess who we were. Them days most people had cider at Christmas so they would serve cider and cookies. We would stay a while and talk then go to the next house. It was a lot of fun. The people liked visitors to come.

I think myself that I've had a pretty good life. I tell you it's a lot different from what the boys have these day. We did work and we did have work to do. You didn't gripe about it, you just went on and done it and was satisfied. You realized that you was doing it to benefit somebody. You didn't do things because you wanted to get paid. You done them because you liked to help. And we'd go out and help other people when they needed help, they was in trouble or had something to happen that was out of the ordinary. We'd do for them and we never thought about pay. Helped many person, many a time and din't think about any pay for it. We liked to do it and we liked to help people, like to do things for people. We would get a lot of enjoyment out of being bunched together and doing things. We didn't mind the work. It was one of the things that we kind of praised ourself in and we'd get joy by it. We'd get enjoyment of work. We'd work and try to see which one could do the most not which one could get by without doing anything, we didn't think about that. We made a game of work. We tried to see which one could do the most, which one could pick up the most corn. When we were filling silo we didn't bother with what we were doing, or how much we were doing. It didn't interest us at all, we just wanted to get it done.

We did what our parents told us and we obeyed them and we were taught not to do anything to anybody elses stuff, it belonged to them and we were to leave it alone. We never destroyed anything that belonged to anybody else. Tried not to do anything wrong to anybody. My parents always told us if we couldn't do anything good for anybody not to do anything. We just didn't.[26]

Lester's father was Elder S.H. Flory, from the Shenandoah Valley; his mother was Fannie Kerlin. Both were birthright German Baptist Brethren and were life-long members. They had eight children, seven of whom reached maturity. Elder Flory was a successful businessman as a farmer and auctioneer; he was just as successful as a churchman and minister. Neither he nor "Aunt Fannie" was educated beyond the public schools of the day.

Some of the values held by the Flory family are apparent: obedience, work ethic, frugality, responsibility, preciseness, life guided by Christian principles, and mutual aid. His story tells of the characteristics of a Dunker family, its life and setting, which caused these values to be passed on to the children: obedience to the parents; adherence to the family norms; work structure of the farm; the constancy of the environment; and appropriate punishment to the individual when the values held by the family were violated or ignored. He gives no instances where punishment was for an offense which did not relate to the central themes of the family; corporal punishment was used more than in others, but its use indicates that disobedience to the parents was the most serious offense. His careless work in the corn field was remedied by doing it right the second time, not by spanking. He was not punished for staying out with the gang, but he had the privilege of pleasurable activities withdrawn when he did not go to church. A major factor in his life, which he mentions in different ways, is striking: positive expectation. He was expected to do his work; he was expected to behave; he was expected to go to church. There was no "expect to do this, but." He was offered no alternatives and allowed no excuses for not doing what was expected of him. This exceedingly positive attitude was common in the Dunker family of that day, an intangible around the tangible, and, in numerous studies since then, has been shown to be an effective molder of a child's behavioral pattern.

The Flory children were still allowed to be children. They were allowed to play after the work was finished, to participate in group activities, to participate in the recreational customs of the day, and they were regarded as children, evidenced by the work given them. Flory thinned corn when quite young. Milking cows required some strength, technique, and judgment. He was first trained in this by his mother, and, when he showed her that he had mastered the task, it was given to him as his responsibility. Jobs, age- and size-related, were delegated to the children, a clear indication that the Dunkers viewed their children as developing individuals with the limitations of that stage of their life. This may not seem noteworthy to the reader, yet just several decades before this, very young children were working in the textile factories of New England and roaming the streets of New York as little adults, not children. The Dunker children entered the work force of the farm at a young age, but it was a member of the cooperative force, the family, and under the supervision of the parents and the older siblings. It was part of a training process which related not only to present needs but also to the future individual needs of the child. To the Flory children, this respect and regard by their parents continued into their late teens as they were helped to enter the vocation of their choice.

The Minister's Family

Almost all of the Dunkers were farmers. One group, however, deserves special mention—the farmer-minister—because it is from these families that the future leaders of the denomination could be expected and, indeed, were produced. This group is not as small as one would expect. The minister was elected by the congregation for his lifetime, and the designation went with him as he moved from area to area. A congregation could have only one elder presiding, usually the oldest. If a presiding elder moved to another congregation, he lost his presiding role but he retained his eldership. Therefore, a congregation could have several elders. In some, because of the movements of families and because of the "calling" of new ministers, there were as many as ten ministers. All of them were involved in some way in the leadership of that and surrounding congregations. Of course, the converse occurred; some groups were left unattended when their only minister moved away.

These men were generally the more intellectual of the church population with qualities of leadership; they had helpful wives and generally secure families; but many of their children became angered and bitter at the church. Why? It was said to be economic.

The German Baptist Brethren did not pay their ministers until the second or third decade of the twentieth century. This was based on scriptural considerations and church history which biased the members against the paid ministry.

Not all of the free ministers could make enough to provide for their families. Some wives and children became bitter and the children's attitude toward their fathers and toward the church was strained becasue they felt that they were being penalized while other members of the church were not. As children of ministers, one would expect them to become the leaders of the future. How many of these children were lost to the church because of this bitterness is not known, but a number did remain in the church and became effective leaders. The free ministers served mostly without complaint:

> During my life, I never had a salary in the ministry. Ella and I, we ate with the chickens a few years.[27]

H.C. Early (b. 1855, VA) was called to the ministry after marriage, which was unusual in those days. He had married a Baptist girl who felt that a farmer's life was hard enough; to add to the burden by being a minister, she thought, was excessive. Elder Early was interested in medicine as a life's work: "The profession looked fascinating. These men made more money than I did and did not work as hard beside the good they did in relieving suffering and distress and helping people back to health and hope." Despite this and the pleas of his wife, he decided to enter the ministry. He later said: "I had looked forward to the ministry and although I knew that for me it meant a life of sacrifice and hardship, I was glad to accept it when the time came." "From the standpoint of a businessman, it was a costly decision" (to go into the ministry). His ministry took him away from home, often to the detriment of his family. This apparently bothered him, because in later years he mused: "Isn't it easily possible for the preacher to lose his own family in the hope of serving others?"[28]

J.H. Longenecker's life of service included both the free ministry and the paid ministry. The "paid ministry" deserves to be put in quotes because the pay was hardly any in the earlier days and not a great deal in the later days. Even with the salary, it took the help of the wife to support most ministers' families. Longenecker (b. 1852, PA) was faithful to his calling:

> He was a living demonstration of consecration to his task for he literally left all to follow Christ. He lived in the days of the free ministry and while his services were given freely to the church, he paid a tremendous price to do it. He was always ready to respond to the call of need. Whether in time of seeding or harvest, his farm waited until he did the work of the Lord. Many times in evangelistic meetings, he received less remuneration for his services than he had to pay a farm hand to take his place at home. Many churches paid the evangelist a dollar a day for meetings but would not include any remuneration for the ministry on the Lord's day. His family bore a heavy responsibility during his absence and missed his companionship and counsel. His farm was neglected and he suffered heavy financial reverses. Even after he left the farm and devoted all his time to the work of the church, he received very modest remuneration for his faithful service.[29]

The plight of some of the preachers' families seems well expressed in Maggie Moomaw's account of her husband in the free ministry and the effect that it had on her and the members of the family:

> In Gospel Messenger No. 6, page 82 (1901), an article from Bro. S.Z. Sharp, "Frontier Mission Work," brings to my mind vividly my experience as a minister's and elder's wife. My husband was elected to the ministry in the West and it has been my lot to be on the frontier most of our time. Years ago while we were young and when the Indians were plenty, husband would have to go and leave

me alone with two or three children. We had only a shanty to live in, with a piece of carpet for a door. I had to spend the time as best I could, often in fear of being killed. He would be gone for three or four days, and sometimes a week at a time, preaching to save souls. Sometimes the cow or the horses would get away, as we had no fences in early days. I would have to call on my neighbors to hunt them, or go myself. When winter came husband had managed to build a rude sod house covered with brush, then a layer of hay, and sod on top. This constituted our dwelling for five years. I did very well in winter, as we had but little rain; but when spring and summer came we would get a good drenching, sometimes two or three times a week. I could have stood it all very well if husband could have been at home.

I remember one winter I was very sick, and husband had to stay at home with me, and the appointments were neglected and the church began to think something was wrong, and some of the members even said Brother J. was neglecting his calling. Then in winter I was often in dread of those awful blizzards, when husband was gone, fearing that he would be lost and frozen to death. In the summer he would often have to go and leave the wheat on the ground, while others could get theirs in stock. Sometimes the hack tongue or wheel would be broken. Husband would come home with a cottonwood pole for a tongue, or a wheel held up by a pole. Then there was a blacksmith bill to pay. Finally we got behind, had to mortgage the farm, then crops failed. The farm had to be sold to comply with the Scripture, "Owe no man anything," Rom. 13:8. So we had to move and start anew. Finally the oldest children could help, and it went a little better; but then, too, the boys had to hire out to make ends meet. The consequence was they got in rough society, and to-day part of them are out of the church, and we have to say with the poet, "Where is my boy tonight?" It is all right for fathers to go, but I think there is need of some teaching along the line of the duties of members and the church to the minister. In reading Brother B.E. Kesler's "Analysis of Index of Gospel Messenger," I thought there might be something written to good advantage on duties of members to their minister. None but the minister's wife knows the privations that have to be gone through with. Now we are old, and if it was not for our boys I cannot tell what would become of us. We would be a charge to the church, I presume.

I am glad that the Brethren are doing more thinking along this line than in former years. Some of the Brethren used to think as they were taught, that if fifty cents was given to the minister it would spoil him. There have been many good ministers spoiled because they were not assisted in time of need. When they begin to fall behind financially some are ready to say, "He is a good preacher, but no manager financially. See, he is getting in debt badly." Whose fault is it that council must be attended, that funerals must be preached, and then the Communion attended: Then too, some unfaithful member gets into trouble. Then there must be a church meeting. The minister's duty is to be sure and be there; but some lay-members cannot go. They have hay down and wheat in the field that must be looked after and they think they can't possibly go. Brethren and sisters, let us do more teaching along this line, so ministers' wives will have no reason to feel that the church has not done her duty to her ministers.[30]

The free ministry gave way to the part-time, partially-paid service, and then to the full-time ministry. John Jacob Ernest (b. 1876, NEB) became a member of the church at the age of seventeen, and he was elected to the ministry in 1901 at the age of twenty-five. At some time in his career he became a part-time paid minister:

My father (John J. Ernest) drew part salary and worked part of the time. Many times produce was brought instead of money. I remember one winter a farmer who had grown cabbage brought a spring wagon load of them for his share of the salary. We children who had wanted other things grew awfully tired of cabbages that winter. But, father was always appreciative of what others could give.

Father worked hard in the fields all day and then would come in and sit up half the night studying a Bible lesson. Once he took a month's preaching trip around the Carthage, Missouri direction and mother had to go to the barn with a lantern to tend newly born pigs and other livestock, leaving the children in the house alone.[31]

The writer of this account remembers the deprivation which the children felt as they ate those cabbages. He also remembered being left alone because his father was away doing for others, perhaps deserting him in his young mind. Why did the children become bitter? Was it economic? Was it the actual absence of the father, or was it the time given to the church which, of necessity, detracted from the involvement of the father with his children? There are no specific references to answer these questions.

But the farmer-minister was not the only absentee father. As the Dunkers moved to the cities, in some cases the city to them, and into occupations other than farming, the family-nurturing

PLATE 16. Jesse & Hannah (Horning) Ziegler
Standing: **Mayme Horning (niece of Hannah); Warren Ziegler; Harry Ziegler**
Seated in front: **Samuel Ziegler**
Seated on Jesse's lap: **Howard Ziegler**   **Taken about 1891**

PLATE 17. Feeding the chickens—part of a Brethren mother's day

farm life was missed. The children of some saw little of their father, not because of the demands of the free or paid ministry, but from the demands of the occupation. Kermit Eby remembered his time with his father on the farm, and felt guilt because he could not or did not spend either the quantity or the quality of time with his children that he had received from his father:

> I, too, have sons and I must confess that the hours I have spent with them are fewer than those Dad and I had together. Many are the times when it seemed to me that giving so much of oneself to one's fellow workers was unfair to one's family.[32]

Eby's remarks, made in 1960, sound very much like those of H.C. Early, made in 1900.

One cannot infer that the Dunker father on the farm was more interested in his children than was the Dunker father who entered a profession. The operation of the farm required, demanded, that the parents and children work closely together, thus providing the interaction which was not possible in the city family. Here again, childrearing is defined and conditioned by economics.

While many ministers' families suffered under the handicaps of the free ministry, others survived nicely and produced leaders for the denomination. Abram Conner served without pay for forty years while running a prosperous farm and several other businesses. He used his children as "economic assets;" he did not believe in education beyond high school; he gave each of his children five hundred dollars when they reached majority; and all of his children remained in the church.

One gets the impression from the many accounts that the bitterness toward the office of free ministry was proportional to the poverty which it caused the family. Despite the lack of specific references, there appears to be more to it than that. Certainly, the demands of the free ministry reduced the time available for the minister-father to spend with his children, making a proper relationship difficult to establish. Probably, neither poverty nor absence was the major cause of the feeling of anger which seemed to be in some of the children.

It is possible that the attitude of the father towards his children caused this anger. Eby and Early, sixty years apart in different worlds, alluded to this. When the father's attention is consumed by his "calling," be it the ministry, business, or a profession, the child is relegated to second rank, creating a psychological distance between him and his father. The minister-father did not believe that his children were of secondary importance (or did he?), but perhaps the child perceived it to be. This feeling of being neglected and rejected stirred unacceptable emotions in the child (it would be sinful for a Christian child to despise this godly man who was giving his life to the church)—so he transferred his anger to an acceptable object, the economics of the family, blaming the ministry rather than the person.

These dual feelings are seen in the letters of William Beahm in his college years. William was upset at the lack of money in the family; he was also very angry at his minister-father, I.N.H. Beahm, for being away preaching rather than at home providing for his family. He did not repress his feelings toward this man who, at that time, was one of the most outstanding in the brotherhood. His letters express frustration, bitterness, and disrespect as he worried about the financial state of the family. At one point, he concluded rather sadly that he never knew his father. These letters, expressing the author's feelings so freely, provide an excellent case to study the relationship conditioned by the ministry, between a son and his father.[33]

The Dynamics of the Dunker Family

One gets the impression that the nuclear family of the Dunkers changed little, both in form and dynamics, over the period of this study. It has been stated that the family structure weakened after 1850 in the response to, or because of, the changes which came about due to the maturing of the society of America and the advent of the industrial age. But this may be a misreading of what actually happened. Usual signs of family disintegration such as widespread divorce, juvenile delinquency, or behavioral aberrations, either of adults or of children, did not appear. What did appear were deviations from the established order of the church involving the superficial requirements of dress and lifestyle.

The farm economy was changing, however. This caused the isolated and self-sufficient farm of previous years to become more like the commercial farm of the next century. Children were still needed as unpaid hands. Hired help was not in plentiful supply;

neither was excess cash with which to pay them. But productivity and commerce increased, providing more contact with the outside world as well as opportunities for work away from the home farm. Therefore, the economic ties, which had bound the Dunker young to the family for more than a century, loosened and permitted more options for the children. But the ties of personal relationship remained the same, perhaps even stronger than in the early Dunker experience. The father retained his role as the authority figure of the family; the mother her role as the homemaker, supporter, intercessor, and behind-the-scenes force; and the children were used less as economic assets, but cherished just as much. The church shared the life of the members more with outside interests; it offered support in the instruction of the young in religious matters; but it did not intrude into the functions of the family.

Loosening of family ties, so described because the members of the family, particularly the children, interacted more with the "outside world," seemed an expression not of change but of adaptation. In this adaptation, there is no evidence that the family structure was damaged. Had there been damage, more evidence of basic discord would be found. Also, there is little evidence that the family failed in its duty as a transmitter of values, the essential ones at least. Those aspects of Dunker life which were spurious to the meaning of Luke 6:45 such as the garb, lightning rods, life insurance, and musical instruments in church went the way one would expect for practices that did not have a firm foundation in the theology of the group. But those founded in the core meaning of Luke 6:45, the love of God and the faith in the redemptive power of Jesus, persisted. These were the basis for the purposeful life espoused by the Dunkers and were passed from generation to generation, even into the twentieth century.

Therefore, it is difficult to hold that the family ties loosened after 1850. Rather, the looseness was in the family structure, and part of the family dynamics. As economic pressure decreased, and as other options for vocations presented themselves, the family accommodated itself to these changes. In the same light, the status of the younger children did not change around 1850 when schools, Sunday Schools, and periodicals entered the sectarian life of the Dunkers. New opportunities arose, and the status of the children of the sect permitted them to take advantage of these.

The adaptation of the family to the conditions of the late nineteenth century indicated that the religious individualism of Pietism, constrained for a while by the Anabaptist devices designed to preserve community, had been translated into a secular individualism strong enough to assert itself when alternatives to the life on the subsistence farm became available. This adaptation was made possible by the relationship between the members of the family. It did not indicate weakness of the family structure; rather, it indicated that the relationship between parent and child had achieved the delicate balance between interdependency and dependency. This relationship let the child go when he was ready.

Summary

The Dunker family was nuclear in form with the members dependent on each other for survival. The father was the head of the family by ethnic custom and religious command, and he exercised a distant authority as he directed the members' lives. A self-contained economic unit, it also gave emotional support to its members; provided religious instruction to the children; and, with its locus in rural areas, was a means by which values were transferred from one generation to the next. Although not unique, the dynamics of the family provided space in which the children could grow. It also provided the flexibility of control that allowed the children to leave for their independent life. Finally, these dynamics permitted an adaptation to the changing outside world that served the needs of its members.

7

Value Transference

The continued existence of societal groups depends in a large part on their conservation of the value system of the group with its attendant traditions and mores. Though values cannot remain the same in the continuum of history, the rate of change can vary. This rate of change, while a function of the economic and political forces, may be dependent upon the methods by which the values of the parents are transferred to the children, the values of one generation transferred to the next. What methods did the Dunkers use?

While searching for areas where they could both physically survive and preserve their identity, the Dunkers faced a particularly difficult task. This search spread their members across the United States in a pattern that eventually made them vulnerable to the larger population's culture. Their Germanic language, rural lifestyle, clumping of families, and the order all served as the containment for their subculture. Labeling the "outside world activities" as sinful further protected them. Lacking the full commitment to community as a theological imperative, they used sparingly the two most effective tools—excommunication and limited education—to preserve their way of life; rather, the order and their value-transmitting methods were relied on to pass the customs and beliefs from generation to generation. That the group existed in sectarian form at least one hundred and fifty years, perhaps longer, indicates that these mechanisms were generally effective in the face of limited challenge. But as the pace and magnitude of societal change impacted on the Dunkers after 1850, these mechanisms showed vulnerability; the evolvement of the sect into a church mode began and progressed rapidly.

The Dunkers transferred the values of their religious and

cultural life (these were so closely intertwined that it may be artificial to separate them) to their children through instruction, example, and, while not listed as one of the value-transferring mechanisms, through occupation. Before considering these, the role of the Bible should be mentioned again.

The Bible as a Guide to Childrearing

There are major differences between the Old and New Testaments, though similar themes are common to both. Pertinent to childrearing are the themes of God's authority over his people and the theological imperatives of love between individuals. Punitiveness in these relationships is expressed more strongly in the Old Testament.

As a society that acknowledged the Bible as their guide in all areas of life, the Dunkers drew on some of the passages to form the basis for their relationships with the children. The general theme of obedience was quite strong; the theme of love and caring was evident; but the punitive aspects of the Old Testament were lacking. Rather, the love and caring of the New Testament seemed to predominate, not surprising, of course, when one considers that the German Baptist Brethren Church professed that its theological basis was the New Testament.

As a church of adult baptism there are few scriptural references in the minutes of the AM's of the brotherhood relating to children. The three referred to the most are these:

Deuteronomy 6:5-7   And thou shalt love the Lord thy God with all thine heart, and with all thy soul, and with all thy might. And these words, which I command thee this day, shall be in thine heart. And thou shalt teach them diligently unto thy children, and shalt talk of them when thou sittest in thine house, and when thou walkest by the way, and when thou liest down, and when thou risest up.

1 Peter 5:2   Feed the flock of God which is among you, taking the oversight thereof, not by constraint, but willingly; not for filthy lucre, but of a ready mind.

Ephesians 6:4   And ye fathers, provoke not your children to wrath but bring them up in the nurture and admonition of the Lord.

These scriptures were selected because they were mentioned most often. They show the basis for the God-given authority of the father over his children; for the love of the individual as a member of God's group to whom care and nurture was due; and for the direct responsibility of the father to rear his children according to the teachings of the New Testament, all three with an individual-biased connotation.

Other scriptures by inference contributed to the perception of the Dunker child, mostly with a benign effect. In the sectarian system where conformity was essential to the survival of group identity, it is easy to think that the children were trained as soldiers are trained, putting aside the welfare of the child for the group's welfare. This was not so with the Dunkers. Though they were economic assets under the control of the father and though they were required to give their services to him up to a specific age, the children's training related to the needs of the family to survive, not to build up wealth and power for the father. Of equal importance was the need of the child to be trained so that he or she could function as an adult. The responsibility of the parents to do this is implicitly expressed in the scriptures quoted above, and the evidence suggests that the Dunker parents recognized this duty. Elder John Kline said that a widow's children needed someone to train them to labor, and the Dunker mother had her daughter's wedding delayed for a year so that the daughter could learn to do those things in the house and on the farm that a good wife should do. Children learn best within their field of interest. Several times it is stated that the children were given a choice of work so that their aptitudes and desires could be matched with the suitable job on the farm.

Occupation in Transferring Values

The scriptures provided the basis for the Dunker parents' attitude towards their children and gave to them the responsibility for their growth and nurture, but the economic setting prescribed the chief method of value transference. This was the farm, and the method was participatory example as opposed to demonstrative. The farm was labor-intensive and required coordinated work by all members of the family. The father and mother were the coordinators; they were also the lead laborers who worked with the children, providing many hours of exposure where their actions, reactions, and attitudes could influence the growing child. Tied to this participatory example were the various instructions that were necessary to teach them how to handle the chores of the day. Along with these instructions came explanations of why this was done instead of that, or how to handle dangerous situations. Often, these instructions and explanations contained principles larger than the immediate solution. One Dunker youth remembers his father explaining that it was safer to walk close behind a horse than to pass behind him at the maximum distance. Close to the horse, his hooves and legs will propel you. Two or three feet behind the horse, the kick may kill you, because the horse can extend his legs with the full force of his body behind them. Seemingly an insignificant trivia, this taught the Dunker youth to examine what seemed obvious and to question the usual.

Instruction alone was used, as will be noted in a number of the references where the child remembered the conversations that he or she had with their parents. It is assumed, without proof, that these were average conversations of social interaction rather than a didactic exercise, but each child received enough from them to remember the contents. J.M. Henry heard conversation about "living water." A number of the references relate to the talk of the role model members of the sect. Children learn through hearing worthwhile adult talk, from parents or from others. But it cannot be represented that the Dunkers used this as conscious mechanism to teach their children. It is safe to assume, however, that they were aware of the value of the adult conversation on the young because the culture did prize the learned mind as long as it did not contain the frivolities and heresies of the "outside world."

It was the responsibility of the parents to train their children "to labor" since this was the only way in which the Dunker youth of those days could earn a living as an adult. Not only was the primary value of a marketplace skill learned during these training periods, but also secondary values accompanied these. It was said of Jacob Longenecker (b. 1852, PA):

> From his grandfather, he learned the use of woodworking tools. This may have laid the foundation for his preciseness and methodical way of life that was so characteristic of his long life and so evident in all he did.[1]

Kermit Eby was brought up in his father's home, but he was

influenced by his grandfathers who lived nearby. Eby was required to gather eggs when he was big enough and, when older, he graduated to feeding the cows and the pigs. He could milk a cow at the age of seven and occasionally drove the team of horses at that age. Several years older, a boy rode the horse to guide it along a row of corn which allowed the father the free use of both hands to handle the double shovel corn plow. Working with his parents and grandparents, he was readily available for their instruction and object example:

> My Teachers were Father and Grandfather. Like so many of their kind, they were hard-working and perfectionist disciplinarians. Sometimes I rebelled and shirked the tasks as they grew ever more arduous. Once I planted all the seed corn in one spot—seed corn that I was supposed to use for replanting. Of course, it came up and gave me away.

> As I arrived at my adolescence, Dad and I marched side by side at haying and harvest. I was the oldest son, and Dad was twenty when I was born, so that I grew up in his most active and driving years. Mine was the task of keeping up. Often enough, sweat-blinded and tired, I rebelled against the single-minded determination to get in three loads of hay before dinner and ten before supper, or to get the wheat shocked before dark in order to escape threatening rain. But most of all, I hated to cut corn by hand. One hundred shocks a day was Dad's norm. And only by fierce and dogged concentration could it be reached.

> Now as I look back on those years there are certain impressions which stand out, and certainly many which determined my own attitude as a father.[2]

Ten loads of hay in a day—maybe. A hundred shocks of corn in a day is a whole lot of corn. But Eby gets the idea across: his father showed him how to work and set the standards by which the work should be done. Instead of giving his son a job and going off to something easier, he worked with his son according to those standards. His grandfather also contributed to his training and to his value development:

> My memories of Grandfather are mixed and varied. When I was five, he gave me an orphan lamb, which I desperately wanted. When he gave it to me, he said, "Kermit, this is your lamb. Love it, and take care of it," and to my young mother he said, "Lizzie, he

must always take care of it, never you."

Later when I was in my teens and big enough to go threshing he taught me the same lesson even more graphically. We were threshing some smutty oats. Clean-up time had come, and dirt and smut were almost strangling me. I stepped back and permitted one of the neighbors to do double duty in the dust. Grandfather saw me, stepped up and asked for my shovel, and took my place. I stood there, awkward and alone. After the job was finished, Grandfather stepped back and said, "A man always helps clean up." Many times in later years, when I had to listen to the "belly-achers" who complained about hypocrites in the church, corruption in politics, or racketeers and communists in labor, I remembered Grandfather's "A man always helps to clean up."[3]

Examples of Character in Value Transference

The Dunker fathers, by example, taught values of character to their children, giving them a glimpse of the innermost but seldom-revealed spirit. That the two incidents to be presented were remembered many years later showed the impact that these revelations had on the children. In the first of these incidents, the son saw a depth of feeling which he did not know existed. Robert E. Mohler (b. 1886, NEB) lived with his family in a sod hut in Nebraska where the going was tough for those of business acumen; for those like Mohler's father who could never seem to get ahead financially, the going was very tough and discouraging. Mohler was critical of and impatient with his father, because his father could not make enough money to get him the things that other boys in the neighborhood had. In all other respects, he had a delightful relationship with him which reached some maturity of understanding after this incident. He and his sister were enrolled in McPherson College in 1906, planning to return for the fall semester. But the drought was severe and there was no crops to harvest, so there was no money to pay the tuition:

My father and I had made a trip to town in the lumber wagon. As we were ready to start home he climbed into the wagon and seated himself beside me, and as he did so he reached his hand into his pocket and pulled out a roll of bills amounting to $100.00 which he handed to me with the remark, "Now you and Mary can return to college." It was near impossible for me to realize just what had happened and I was indeed reluctant to accept the gift when my father added, "Take this money and go back to college but don't tell your mother or Mary how you got it." I was well aware that no such secret could be kept from the rest of the family but I accepted the money.

It was not uncommon for most of my father's livestock and farm equipment to be mortgaged, and this was most likely true in a drought year such as the one we were then experiencing. My father owned one horse of which he was especially proud. This horse was affectionately known as "old Bill" and he was truly quite a horse and valuable to us. He was large, strong, and seemingly could and would willingly work any place at any and all times. For fear that he might lose this horse my father always refused to allow him to be placed as surety for a loan. The story ends, as I presume you have already guessed—my father had mortgaged, and had done this in order that I could go back to college. I do not recall that I at this time so much as said "thank you" to my father for this act, neither do I recall that I ever did thank him. Regardless of any neglect or carelessness on my part, I now declare that this act was never forgotten. At no time when going was hard and I might have had some thought of quitting was I not brought back to a determination to go on as I thought of the confidence that my father had in me and of his desire that I remain in school. I would indeed be an ungrateful son who would not respond with his best to a father who had so nearly given his last dollar for him.[4]

Mrs. J.Z. Gilbert also got a glimpse of the unrevealed father:

My father had rented a farm to a certain man who proved to be an unreliable tenant. The farm soon showed signs of neglect, but father hesitated to refuse the man further chance to improve. However, after two or three years something had to be done, and so father told the man that he wanted to secure another renter. Instantly the fellow flew into a rage and gave vent to language unfit to print. Throughout his abusive talk father sat and listened, never saying a word in reply. After this man's anger has subsided father got into his buggy and drove home. A few days later he related the circumstances to me. The thought that my father had been thus unjustly treated stirred my whole being, and I rose to the occasion of ridding my system of some of my indignation. And then on looking into father's calm face I noted his sad smile as he said quietly, "If I had known it would make you so angry, daughter, I wouldn't have told you."

The matter was dropped immediately and was never again referred to. But the contact I made that day with the great soul of my father gave me a new vision of him. Had he left me an inheritance of houses and lands, such possessions could never have been to me the blessing I have realized through the years whenever I recall the time I learned from a living example that "he that is slow to anger is better than the mighty; and he that ruleth his spirit than he that taketh a city."[5]

Instances such as these give a glimpse of the noble and selfless side of the parent; they give an ideal, a beacon to guide the young as they grow into adulthood. This, perhaps, is the highest function of parenthood.

Imitation and Identification in Value Transference

In addition to instruction and example, identification and imitation are mechanisms of value transference. Retrospectively, the use of these and their place in the character building of the Dunker young are difficult to document or even to assess. Imitation is a conscious copying of another person and this was not mentioned in any of the accounts of the lives studied. Identification is a mechanism which operates below the conscious level and contributes in a much more subtle way to one person assuming the values and characteristics of another. Since most of the people represented in the references rejected, to some extent, their parents' way of life by entering another occupation, it is unlikely that the mechanism of identification was used very often by them. Kermit Eby may have identified with his father; J.M. Henry may have also. When these mechanisms were used, they most likely were used by those children who stayed on the farm and lived the same life as their parents.

Isolated Experiences in Value Transference

Acquiring an education is said to consist of a series of learning experiences. The experiences listed below stood out in the memories of the old Dunkers. The children did not learn skills from these; they gained a sense of importance, self-worth, approval from the adults in their environment, and, in several instances, a direction for their life from a chance remark at an opportune time.

Jerome Blough (b. 1861, PA) remembered:

---often, they (the older men) put their hands on my head, and said I was a brave little boy. That always made me feel good.[6]

This certainly influenced Ruel Pritchett (b. 1884, TN):

One time when Uncle George (Bowman) got off the mule, he reached up and I fell down into his arms and stood by. He laid his hands on my head, gave me a little prayer, and quietly said something that shot me from toe to toe. "Ruel, I want you to be a preacher some day"[7]

Ernest Wampler (b. 1881, VA) said:

One religious experience which meant more to me than anything else was a time when I had left my work in the cornfield in order to play along the creek trying to catch a fish. Upon going to the house tired and hungry that evening, my brothers and sisters jumped on me about my laziness and uselessness on the farm. Mother came past me stroking me lightly with her hand and said, "Well, some day I hope Ernest will make a fisher of men." Later, when telling a Chinese fellow-pastor of this story he said, "You had a wise mother."

I always attended Sunday School and church services, for that was just a must in our home. But the thing which meant most to me in my church activities was the young peoples' society which gave us young people the opportunity to participate in religious life. Here we could sing, recite poems, and prepare talks on Biblical teachings. I remember one time when I had presented one of these topics to the audience, the Elder of the church came to me and complimented me on my talk. I have always remembered his encouraging words. He did more than he thought in helping to keep a boy, still searching for God's way for his life, going on in that search.[8]

Brother Burkhart had an uplifting childhood experience:

One unusual incident in the boyhood of Brother Burkhart had much to do in after-life in determining his life activities. His aged grandmother made her home at their place one winter, and as her sight was poor, she had her little grandson daily reading the Bible to her while she was engaged in her knitting. In this way he not only acquired a thorough knowledge of the Scriptures, but, by faithful reading, his mind became so occupied by thoughts of God and Heaven and good people, that he felt called of the Lord to give him his young heart, and had it been as common then as now for children to unite with the church, he would have been baptized. But in those days there were no Sunday Schools and only grown people belonged to the church so Joseph had to quench the Spirit's call. As a reader for his grandmother, she always called him her "little preacher" and told him he certainly would sometime become an ambassador for God.[9]

Children need and respond to positive remarks and attitudes of the adults in their lives. It is from these that the children establish the tone for their emotional lives and develop the confidence in themselves necessary to fulfill the promise of their own talents. The opposite is true; derogatory remarks by adults who mean something to the children put a gloom on the emotional life of the children and create self-doubts. Most often, this works to the detriment of the child. Occasionally, it stirs the child to work harder to prove his worth, but, even when this happens, the child still remembers and carries some bitterness with him for the rest of his life. Robert Mohler remembered the unfeeling remarks of his uncles:

> There was still another situation in my Nebraska experience that I have never been able to completely forget. This was brought about by the fact that while living there I was always associated with folks who were more prosperous than my parents. I was continually being reminded of this handicap, the least of those reminding me were none other than two of my uncles by whom I was often faced with such remarks as, "I will give that kid a job when he grows up, if he amounts to anything." By moving to Michigan, I was completely freed from this depressing thought.[10]

Behavior Modification in Value Transference

Behavior modification is a method used extensively in training the mentally retarded. Stated simply, approved behavior is rewarded and inappropriate behavior is not rewarded and sometimes carries a punishment. This method works with those of limited intellectual capacity as it does with animals, but has questionable worth in the average child. To rear a child to believe that he should be rewarded for proper behavior gives him the idea that life is a transaction. The Dunkers seemed not to follow this method of childrearing as a general rule. Rather, they established that certain behavior was acceptable and that was it. Life was not a series of transactions. Modes of behavior were not negotiable. Children were expected to follow family values in their work and in relationships, and their conscience was honed to the point where an aching conscience was the punishment and their parents' approval was the reward. As they grew older, they sought also a way of life that they felt met with God's approval.

Some families, however, did use behavior modification.

Samuel Weimer, in his eight points of raising children, said that he provided his children with good reading material and that "we also gave them inducements to read the Bible."[11] He raised his children in the last half of the nineteenth century.

The carrot was extended to Nancy J. Snider (b. 1829, IND):

> Her mother once offered her a new dress if she could verify her statement of ability to spin, in one day, a "dozen of flax." The result was that she easily did the work and got the dress.[12]

Models in Value Transference

The close working relations with the children on the Dunker farm caused example to be the prime mechanism of value transference. This term carries the sense of one specific act or a series of specific acts as the medium through which these values are imparted to the young. The term "model," though it includes example, has a much broader connotation, one in which the totality of the person becomes the example. These references imply that these persons served as models to J.E. Miller, Edward K. Ziegler, and Robert E. Mohler, respectively:

> And then I thought of myself at the age of 10, when J.H. Moore began coming into my father's home, and what what meant to my life.[13]

> Her appreciation of beauty and God's created world rubbed off on all of us children. Perhaps my own great interest in birds and flowers, in books and music I owe very directly to her, though the love of reading comes more powerfully from my father.[14]

> My father loved music and good literature. It was his supreme joy to find a book that he could read aloud to his family. No single factor of my early life stands out more prominent in my memory than that of his reading aloud to the family and discussing with us the things that he had read.[15]

Perhaps, because there were fewer people around in the neighborhood, each family knew the members of other families well, their strong points and their weak points. Values became personified. This man was the strongest, that man was the meanest, this woman kept the neatest house, while the other was the best cook. That fellow down the road was shrewd and you didn't want to get involved in a business deal with him because he would cheat you. The children tended to associate those values with those persons. The German Baptist Brethren, with their system of elders and visiting ministers, provided the Dunker young with models with whom they could identify, as J.E. Miller seemed to have done with J.H. Moore and J. Henry did with the visiting ministers. This method of building the value system of the young seems less of a factor as the country has become urban. But in the Dunker subculture, exemplary adults did influence the lives of the children in their rural habitat.

Maturing Effects of Rural Life

Perhaps the most difficult state to reach and one which has been defined in various terms, maturity came early to the youth on the farm and particularly on the frontier farm where work and responsibility were the norm. Adolescent delaying activities were nonexistent. The selection of tasks, the opportunity to work alone, and the lack of someone to pick up the slack forced the young worker to grow into the demands of the job.

When a six-year-old and a twelve-year-old were sent to carry water from the pump or well, the older boy carried the bigger bucket. This allowed the younger boy to do his assigned task without feeling shamed. As this younger boy grew older, a bigger bucket was given to him in keeping with his increased size and strength. More responsibility was given as the children grew older. The parents judged whether the child's capabilities had been exceeded and made adjustments, not only from a caring stand-point, but also from a practical standpoint—if he could not do the job, someone else had to do it. The child, then, grew with the knowledge that he was competent in some areas, that he had actually done the work, and that he could carry the task through from start to finish. This met one definition of maturity: the capability of completing a task.

Farm tasks provided the opportunity to develop another facet of the mature person: the capability to exercise good judgment. The six-year-old learned quickly that if he filled his bucket too full of water, it slopped out onto his pants as he carried it; in addition, the load was very heavy. If he put a lesser amount of water in the bucket, the load was lighter but he had to make more trips to fill the watering trough. Self-interest caused him to strike the medium where the trips and the load equaled the least work.

PLATE 18. Horse and buggy was the transportation of the day.

PLATE 19. A fashionably dressed young lady from a Dunker family—1895

In this way good independent judgment developed.

Young people live in the present. Two days from now it is ages away. They find it very difficult to observe another criterium of maturity—the ability to forego immediate pleasure for future gain. The growth of crops and animals on the farm provided the experiences which trained them in this precept. The freshly tilled garden, with its rows of corn, cabbage, beets and onions were, through successive planting seasons, a means by which it was shown that the work to plant a garden translated into food for the winter table. Though not a pleasant thought, cute little pigs would eventually be ham and sausage, and the affectionate, wobbly calf provided delicious milk in several years, or, in the worst case, veal.

The farm taught that unpleasantness could be turned into the pleasant, or that both could be gotten from the same situation. Snow, which chilled the hands when on the wood pile, made very good snow balls at the school yard; rain, which soaked through to the skin when bringing in the cows, produced puddles where dams could be built and boats could be sailed. The farm taught that, at times, one had to endure the unpleasant to gain the pleasant, certainly a maturing concept. Huckleberries were delicious, but, when they were picked, one got chiggers, little mites that burrowed into the skin and produced intense itching. Fried chicken, even the wings and necks, was the delight of a Sunday dinner, but that chicken had to be killed. To see a chicken flop around after its head had been cut off was not pleasant to the child. Sometimes, there was no pleasantry. Occasionally, a horse had to be put away or the old dog had to be mercifully killed; to the tenderhearted child this was a traumatic experience, but it taught the child to face up to unpleasant, difficult situations.

The farm taught accountability for the commission or omission of acts, the hardest but most necessary lesson that the young must learn. It was great to stay up late for a box social; the cows still had to be milked at the same time the next morning. One who was reared on the farm can never forget the abdominal pain which came from eating green apples or the bitter, puckered-up feeling that come from eating persimmons before they were fully ripe. The hornet's nest was an inviting target for a boy with a rock. He threw the rock at the nest, and then he found out whether or not he could outrun a bunch of angry hornets. If he couldn't, his accountability was established. Acts of omission had to be rectified. To leave the pasture gate open was unforgiveable; chasing the cows back into the pasture was hard work. Running cows to the milk barn was not permitted. If the boy or girl did not observe this rule, they spent extra time trying to get the cows to let their milk down.

The farm and its economic system, which demanded hard work, punctuality, perseverance, frugality, and equanimity, was the matrix in which life concepts as listed above were learned. In addition, an appreciation of nature was gained. To an extent greater than other occupations, the farm provided tasks which could be given to the very young with the expectation that they would be done at an age when the child was still under the absolute control of the parents. By the time the children reached adolescence when rebellion became possible, they had been conditioned so that less parental authority and guidance were necessary. Dan West's (b. 1893, OH) son, Joel, began his conditioning early:

> At the age of five, Joel, was assigned the task of sorting nails, his contribution to a building project that involved tearing down walls and rearranging partitions. A lot of nails were scattered around. It was Joel's job to decide whether they could be rebent, or whether they were just too far gone and could be eliminated. Such frugality was often a nuisance to the West children but later the wise use of money and materials became part of their philosophy.[16]

Assigning this task to Joel is illustrative of the Dunker approach to childrearing. The job of reclaiming nails conveyed a value, that of frugality. Some families would not have gone to the trouble to sort out the old nails; instead they would buy new, straight nails. Second, the job had no life or death connotation. If Joel missed a few, so what? Therefore, he could succeed at this task despite his age. Third, sorting those nails made him feel part of the family, a contributing member at that. And fourth, he began the process of developing his judgment by doing a man's job. While little Joel made many trips over to his Dad to see whether he should keep this nail or throw away that nail, Joel was basically working on his own, a situation that was sure to lead him into the way of the mature. And if the child's inclinations and work demands could be matched, the way to maturity was a bit more pleasant.

Work Experience in Value Transference

The farm was not run like a military outfit, with duties assigned regardless of the desires of the children, even though the ages and strength of the child had to be matched with the demands of the task. Since there were a limited number of hands available, perfect matching according to wants could not always be carried out. Parents discovered that they got better and more enthusiastic work if the children were allowed to do the chore which was least distasteful to them. Mary Early Davis' account of her family's work experience illustrates this. These sentences are excerpted from her description of her life:

> Fortunately, a few of us liked to sew and Ella and I made much of the clothing that was needed.
>
> Milking cows was one job I detested, espcially when I had the kicking cow to manage. She knew I was afraid of her which made the job more difficult. One week two of us would do the milking and other outside chores and the other two would do the housekeeping. The next week we would change. I was always glad when I could clean and cook and wash dishes.
>
> We always had a good garden and we all worked in it. After supper 3 or 4 including our mother to portion off a certain part to each to hoe and weed. We worked diligently until it was finished.[17]

General statements were found to describe the work experience of the Dunker youth; specific statements such as those from Mary Early Davis were rare, so to postulate that the Early family's way of portioning out the work to the children represents the practice of the sect has to be based on bits and pieces of information. But different accounts suggest that the child in the Dunker family had to do the pleasant and the unpleasant, but they were given as much choice of tasks as was consistent with getting the work done. This is further evidence that the children in the Dunker family, while certainly under the authority and control of the parents, were viewed as individuals from an early age; were treated as such, consistent with their age and the requirements of the farm; and that this continued as they grew to adulthood.

The children were required to work, some more than they

liked. J.H. Moore (b. 1846, VA) was one of these:

> During the week days there was plenty of work on the farm to keep
> a boy busy, and sometimes a little too busy to his liking. It is said
> that "all work and no play makes Jack a dull boy." I would change
> that a bit and say that "all work on the farm and no recreation
> makes Jack a discontented boy." The most that people knew about
> boys in the backwoods, was to feed, clothe, and keep them busy, if
> possible, and let them grow.[18]

But the environment provided training to Moore which
apparently was more to his liking. His family had moved west
when he was small where the land was wilder than his Virginia
birthplace. He tells of fighting prairie fires through backfiring, and
he especially remembered the snakes:

> Well, I got my hand in at fighting snakes and in this way developed
> an early disposition to master the forces opposing me. After all,
> fighting snakes was not such a bad training for a boy.[19]

Moore was not hurt by his early training. He became a leader
among the German Baptist Brethren and lived into the 1920's,
where he became a reactionary force that opposed the newer
concepts of childrearing, ones that advocated more freedom and
self-choice for the children with more recreational and secular
exposure. His statement paralleled an earlier one: the men of that
day knew more about raising hogs than they did about raising
boys. This, of course, is a catchy statement without much basis in
fact. Each generation has to rear the next generation within their
prevailing environment, from their own background, and with the
thought of preparing that generation to survive in the same
environment. Except in times of rapid change and except for
children with exceptional potential, this system has worked very
well. History has had few periods of rapid change and the
exceptional child has been able to break away from his upbringing into the area to which he has been drawn. The Dunker's first
one hundred and twenty-five years in America was a period of
little change, and the children needed to be trained essentially to
live as did their parents. When the time of opportunities arrived,
the motivated children were able to pursue their own interests:

> Teaching was the only approved occupation that offered escape

from the dull treadmill of farm-life drudgery for the brighter boys and girls. Many of the more independent, progressive ones entered neighboring normal schools and became graduates.[20]

But there is more. The frontier environment demanded "rugged individualism." What better way to train a child for this life than to teach him skills and let him grow? A child with the verbal ability of the average present-day teenager would find the life on the prairie very lonely. The capacity to be happy with oneself was a prime requirement for those days, and the farm upbringing, where the children worked independently at an early age, helped develop this capacity. While they may not have used "modern methods" of childrearing, the references indicate that they knew the minds of the young. In this instance, T. Richardson Gray's father knew what it meant for the boy to emulate him in a grown-up task:

> How proud I felt at the age of five or six years when, standing with my father in the deep wagon box and holding the lines, I drove the big team of horses! What boy can ever forget such a thrill?[21]

And Dunker parents knew that their demands were for the ultimate good of the child, though E.K. Ziegler (b. 1903, PA), did not recognize this at the time:

> Though I sometimes rebelled against the incessant work on the farm, I now know that the stern discipline and sense of urgency in feed time and harvest helped me to form invaluable habits of self-discipline and a deep appreciation of work well done.[22]

The Dunker family lived in close interaction in their rural environment. The child was with the parents in work, in worship, in social affairs, and in whatever recreational functions there were. He saw his father deal with the banker and with the other farmers as they bargained for livestock, land, or grain. He was exposed to the ethical decisions that these transactions occasionally caused his father to make and to the aggravations that they posed. How his father handled these problems, the basis for the ethical decisions, and the "spirit" in which these were made were readily apparent to the child and provided a basis for the development of his own reactions. The one fault which has been ascribed to the Dunker father in his training of the child is that he made decisions alone without involving his children, resulting in a delayed development of this capacity in the young adults. In today's world this would be a grave fault; in the Dunker world before 1900 this was not a serious indictment. There they lived in clusters where the extended family was available to help the young man in his decision-making as he started his own family. The uniform practies of the scattered Dunkers provided this help to the young person, even if he moved away from his family into another area.

Although hemmed in by the dictates of the order, the Dunker youths were prepared by their training to compete in the marketplace of a comparable economic setting. Thoroughness, reliability, promptness, capacity to face the unpleasant, assumption of responsibility, honesty—these values prized by the larger community made them acceptable to the non-Dunker world and helped them compete, actually with some advantage.* Well indoctrinated at an early age, the Dunkers used these as part of their being, thus giving a constancy to their performance.

Religious Training of the Children

Economically, the methods of imparting cultural values worked well for the Dunkers. However, the method of transferring core religious values became suspect. It had served them well for almost one hundred and fifty years, evidenced by the growth and persistence of the sectarian form. But after 1850 the changing industrial environment and the introduction of school, papers, and periodicals brought them into closer contact with the outside world and the mind-awakening which that caused. D.W. Bittinger highlighted the problem in 1944:

> When I was a lad I sometimes asked my father, "Why do we have a love feast?" or "Why shall we be baptized?" My good father usually replied very earnestly, "Because the Bible says so" or "because Jesus commands it."

This may have meant that father thought his small son would not

---

* There are no references to support this statement; however, from a general reading of the literature concerning the German Baptist Brethren, from the absence of extreme poverty in the sect and from oral tradition, the statement appears to be justified.

understand more meaningful reasons than that, or it may have
mant that father, along with many others of his generation were
satisfied with that answer. He and his generation were people of
the Book and when one could point to chapter and verse, why go
further? That was reason enough.

And it is if one wanted to stop there. But father testified later that
stopping there had caused him to miss the best part of it. Knowing
chapter and verse had made him a loyal, even an argumentative,
defender of Brethrenism. But when he later attempted to answer
his child's question, "Why did Jesus command it?" there had been
opened for him the heart of the scriptures, he said.[23]

It is remembered that the Dunkers, from around 1780 until
1850, were semi-literate. Even after 1850 the level of education
rose slowly, and the thought that a common school education was
all that was needed persisted well up into the 1900's. Because of
this low educational level, it is thought that the cognitive ability of
the Dunkers to understand the Bible was extremely limited.
Therefore, they memorized and quoted it, usually with a literal
interpretation. It was in this context that Bittinger described his
father and how he taught his children about the scriptures. This
way of teaching the children about the scriptural values worked
well as long as the Dunkers remained a sectarian society with
little contact with people of different views. But as the children
associated with those from other subcultures, doubts developed
and questions were asked. Bittinger's father was unable to answer
those questions. The Dunkers had to find another way to teach
their children about the Bible.

As these changes occurred among the Dunkers, the world
outside of their sectarian existence was changing: children were
coming into their own. While laws safeguarding and promoting
the welfare of children would not be formulated until several
decades later, other forces were at work in the interest of the child.
States were passing enabling legislation for a public school
system, and the various political subdivisions started elementary
schools. Many books were published in France and in England
exalting the child and pointing out their sorry treatment at the
hands of the adults and in the social and business system. Among
these was Victor Hugo's *Les Miserables* in 1862. The lay press
turned out an increasingly large number of children's periodicals:
1865—70; 1870—1200; 1885—2200.[24] Two hundred and fifty

children's books were published each year from 1865 to 1881.[25] The schools in existence assumed more and more the responsibility of character development with its moral concerns. Each of the two hundred and forty-five textbooks used in the Connecticut schools in 1846 showed a content directed towards moral training.[26] Why this awakening to the plight and to the welfare of the children? On a world-wide basis, Holt thought that it was due to fears of depopulation with the resultant economic and military weaknesses and to increased humanitarianism.[27] In the United States, we can surmise that it was due to the traditional factor of economics. There was an excess of land based on population and a high proportion of it tillable. The developing industrial capacity of the country required non-agrarian skills that were acquired through education. Business competency required even more education. In an environment of plenty, children have flourished. The adults, relieved of threats to their existence, were able to turn their minds to the children.

The changing status of the child was reflected in his place and importance in the medical world. Diseases commonly affecting children had been written about since the early days of Egypt, but doctors took care of the sick children just as they did the adults, that is, as a little adult. It was not until the sixteenth century that Phayre wrote what is thought of as the first English book on pediatrics. Not until several centuries later did physicians narrow their interests to children; in the United States, pediatrics became a separate discipline in the 1850's. In 1855, the first hospital solely for children was established—the Children's Hospital of Philadelphia[28]—and in 1860, Abraham Jacobi was appointed to the first chair for the diseases of children.[29] This was created at the Medical College of New York. He and J. Lewis Smith were the only two practitioners in America at that time who confined themselves primarily to children. The specialty grew over the next decades and evolved from one which was concerned only with the diseased state to that of the child advocate concerning itself with the total child. In 1880, the American Medical Association established a Pediatric Section which has continued to this day.

While the mainstream culture in the United States experienced a change in attitude about the children and their place in society, changes were occurring within the Dunker world, some paralleling and some in reaction to the changes in the outside world. The world was growing up around the frontier Dunkers and the cities beckoned both young and old. The young wanted education; other occupations became more appealing than the farm; and the accoutrements of the surrounding society tempted the tastes of the prim sectarians. Church order came under a strain that was to lead to a three-way schism. And, after a hiatus of seventy-five years, Dunker printing was revived, which was to be the catalyst for many additional developments and was to change the way that scriptural values were taught to the children.

The old ways of passing the religious beliefs of the German Baptist Brethren to their children, family altar, Bible reading, discussion, and expository preaching, all in a single view learning mode, did not work in the emerging social order of the late nineteenth century America. The sectarian cocoon was opening; unlike some of the other sects, it could not be kept closed. Why this was so, and the full gamut of changes that occurred, is the beginning of the study of childrearing practices in the Church of the Brethren after 1900. But it is appropriate to consider briefly the three adjustments that the church made before 1900.

Sunday Schools, Periodicals, and Church-Related Colleges

First, church order accepted the concept of Sunday Schools. Note the time element between the two queries:

Y.M. 1838 Art. 10   Whether it be right for members to take part in Sunday Schools, Class Meetings, and the like? Considered, most advisable to take no part in such things.[30]

Y.M. 1857 Art. 11   How is it considered for brethren to have Sabbath-Schools, conducted by brethren? Ans. Inasmuch as we are commanded to bring up our children in the nurture and admonition of the Lord, we know of no scripture which condemns Sabbath-Schools if conducted in gospel order, and if they are made the means of teaching scholars a knowledge of the scriptures.[31]

In 1862, a query asked it if would be all right to go to Sunday School celebrations. The answer: Sunday School, yes; celebrations, no. The old Elders were still skeptical of what would be taught at the Sunday Schools, and they wanted to be sure that the atmosphere would be in keeping with the gospel order. In their efforts to ensure this gospel order, apparently they continued, for a while, the adult format.

For people who understood the young well enough to let them hold the lines of the big team of horses, to overlook a burned cedar tree, and to ride miles for dawdling boys and then not spank them, the Dunkers had a difficult time adjusting their teaching methods from an adult level to a child's level:

> The Sunday-School was among the first organized in the District (Northeastern Ohio). The date of the organization was not preserved. Elder Alpheus Dickey, now of Oregon, was the first suprintendent and Samuel Beeghly, now of California, the assistant. These directed the work of the Sunday-School for a number of years. No Sunday-School helps were used the first ten years. Chapters were read from the New Testament. In fact, this Sunday-School in all its history prides itself in having a good, up-to-date school. The first Children's Day exercises were in 1882. Sister William Shidler read an essay on "Influence"; Sister Joseph Beeghly, an essay on "Friendship"; Sister Kate Shidler an essay on "Sunday-School." Several speeches were made by the brethren, among whom D.N. Workman, from the Dickey Church, gave an interesting talk. The song book used in those days was entitled "Imperial Harmony."[32]

In the Mississenawa Church in Indiana, Children's Meetings were held twice a year following Love Feast. In 1892, at these meetings, children were to listen and to answer questions asked them. Perhaps it was this method of instruction that caused the class to silently disappear through the window as their teacher bowed his head in prayer.

Despite the fact that the Dunkers taught their children from tasks that were age- and size-related, indicating that they were quite aware of the limitations and abilities of children, their mindset where religion was concerned did not relate to the children's ability to comprehend. This was slow in correcting itself, because in 1919, A.C. Wieand had this to say:

> At least two or three mornings a week, in the family worship, ought to be adapted to the children. Without this they are likely to feel that they obtain nothing from it, that it is not for them, and they have no interest in it. On these occasions the Bible lesson should be selected from the stories of the Bible which will especially interest the children. A few of the harder words should be paraphrased into language which the children will understand. There ought to be in

some cases, a pause to explain, to ask questions, and to answer their inquiries. Special pains should be taken to give vivid expression to the reading, so as to make it intelligible to the children, and bring it within their comprehension.[33]

The Sunday School movement continued, despite the pedogogic problems, and began to augment the family as the means of providing Biblical training for the children.

In the second adjustment, the sect accepted children's periodicals. From the description given by Kaylor, these were written in children's style and content. It is doubtful whether the editors of those periodicals felt free to include controversial or avant garde material, because there was an element among the Dunkers that distrusted written media and would have immediately protested.

Third, the Dunkers very reluctantly agreed to establish church-related colleges. They did this because the young were going to the state schools, which were usually in areas of few Dunkers, and thus escaped the influence of their faith at an important time in their lives. As was their practice, the elders reacted to the reality of the situation and decided that, since the young people were going to school, the brotherhood should endorse colleges. At least they could go to school in a Christian environment. They were so distrustful of higher education that the college heads felt it best not to offer classes in religion at first, even though the campus life was strictly controlled and religious exercises such as compulsory chapel were part of college life.

The sect as a body religious made adjustments, but this was not enough. The parents within that body had to alter their perception of the adolescent and adopt a different relationship with him. However, these adjustments occurred for the most part after 1900.

Parents and Their Adjustment to Change

Acceptance of higher education, however reluctantly, exposed the youth to the surrounding ways of living, causing some problems to the parents who wished to keep their children true to the values and mores of the ancient brethren. When the children worked on the farm during their adolescence, the environment provided the control over them. Parental authority was there but did not have to be used extensively. As the population built up, contact with the neighborhood exposed the Dunker youth to temptations heretofore not faced. A tough stance was required for the parents to control their children in these situations. Ruel Pritchett (b. 1884, TN) received this parental guidance:

> My mother and father protected me. I never ran headlong into immoral situations. They steered me away from poke suppers and wild games and dances.[34]

This indicates that these parents not only had the authority over their son but also were willing to use it to help him grapple with the adolescent attractions. This is a function of the effective parents—to make an objective determination as to what is best for their child, and then to use their authority to see that this happens. Of course, this should serve the child in his development rather than fill a deficit in the parents' personality. The current designation of this attitude is called "tough love;" many parents of that era, not only Dunkers, had that attitude even though they did not know the designation.

On the other hand, at times children need silence and understanding more than they need commands and solutions. Since this is to help the child, it, too, is a proper technique. Mrs. Gilbert remembers such an incident in her life:

> My earliest recollection of a mirror remains very vivid to me. I was quite small when I climbed upon the table that stood just under a mirror, and the child I saw in it was so real to me that I cried broken-heartedly because no one would get the little girl out of the glass that I might play with her. No amount of explanation seemed to satisfy, for to my mind this was entirely possible if only someone would try.
>
> No harsh words were spoken, not a threat was made as to results if I did not quit crying, but my wise mother simply took me by the hand and together we went to call on a neighbor. There the little girl in the mirror was soon forgotten. Through the years since then I have often seen my mother in that mirror, and the example in child-raising has been a happy memory to me and a benediction to our children.[35]

The little girl in the mirror story is empathetic childrearing at its best. The mother did not make the daughter feel stupid; she understood that little girls and their crisis are as short-lived as they are frequent, and she used a tactic which took advantage of the fleeting involvements so characteristic of the young. The mother put herself in the child's place, understood the reaction of the child, and then, with her adult wisdom, found a solution which served the child. Had the mother spanked the child for getting up on the table and then sent her to her room until she quit crying for the girl in the mirror and laughed about the incident in front of the other children, she would have served herself—not the daughter. The Pritchett story shows empathy on the part of the parents, but not as subtle. They were dealing with a teenager. They understood how the young reacted to temptations. They "steered" him away from those temptations, which denotes some subtlety; most likely though, they simply told him he couldn't go to those poke parties unless it was with a group from the church. They used their adult wisdom and experience to give him the guidance that he needed and were not afraid that they would hurt his feeling or cause him to think less of them. Kermit Eby's mother was equally firm.

Eby's mother taught him to sit still and quiet during the worship service, an instruction which also taught values of reverence, obedience, and self-discipline. On occasions, the little Eby would forget and make noises or other distractions. His mother then had to decide whether to use the "enforcer" of the value transfer process—discipline. This will be considered in the next chapter.

Summary

The Dunker parents worked side by side with their children on the farm. Through their actions and conversation, many of the values of the sect were passed to the next generation. The setting and content of the rural life aided the parents as they followed the admonitions of Ephesians 6:4 and Deuteronomy 6:5-7 and the requirements of the order to bring up their children to love God and obey His commands. The demands of the life on the farm trained the children to succeed as adults in the work-world of the rural America of that day, adding vocational skills to traits of character demanded by the order. This inclusion at an early age in the adult economy prompted early maturity. In addition to example as a method of molding the lives of the Dunker children, adults in their subculture acted as role models who had a significant impact. Learning experiences in this relationship were frequent and had a profound effect on many of the children. In the later part of the period of study, organization began to play a more important part in the lives of the children as Sunday Schools and periodicals were permitted. The total training procedure of the Dunker child was carried out in a predictable environment where positive expectation was a central component of the parents' authority. As the twentieth century approached, both the sect as an organization and the parents within that body began the difficult transition from their world of farm and church to one where the influences of the outside world played more heavily on their children's lives.

8

Discipline

The discipline of children through the ages reflects their status in the societies of those days and tells of their parents' regard for them. This regard for the children was culturally determined, influenced to a large extent by factors unrelated to the children. Among these were the various supernatural beliefs prevalent from time to time, generally working against the child. Child sacrifice, the fire of Molok, the killing of the first-born were not themselves directed toward the child, but were carried out in the context of the beliefs of the adults of the times. The child was an instrument of solution, not necessarily an object of denigration. His status improved when Christianity displaced the prevailing religions of the areas which would become the western world. With this improved status, he was no longer sacrificed to mollify the gods; instead the child was seen as the means to meet the problems of depopulation, agricultural production, military defense or aggression, and other socio-economic concerns of the day. This required conservation of the child rather than destruction.

When the church decided that the child at the time of conception had a soul, Christian beliefs were added to the other two major factors—economics and maternal influence—and provided a powerful ally against the forces which would use him for their own means. These were the impersonal state; the selfish adult; the mercenary trader; the unfeeling employer; and, pertinent to this discussion, the fears, foibles, and demands for ego-fulfillment and enhancement by the parents. It was from this recognition of the worth of the child by the church that he gradually became accepted as an individual. Despite some aberrations, it was from this status that severe, punitive discipline was discarded. Discipline as constructive correction took its place. That is not to say that the influence of the church was all positive; some of the worst discipline was derived from religious beliefs, such as "beat the devil out of the child" and "control his inborn evil and tendency to self-will." But the basis was laid. The world needed time to discard the remnants of projective superstitions that were in the early church.

The constructive approach has been slow in evolving, marred by continued inhuman treatment of children in some countries. But the Biblically-oriented Dunkers used the corrective form of discipline from the beginning of the sect. They used "spare the rod and spoil the child" as a slogan, but it was more rhetorical than substantive.

In assessing methods of discipline two important points should be considered: impact on the child's emotional state and the appropriateness for the time and place. In consideration of the first it is important whether the child secures quick release from the parent's displeasure, or whether the displeasure continues for a protracted period. Does the child perceive that the parent is angry at what was done or at the doer? Is the punishment fair in the eyes of the child? How quickly does the method of discipline return the child to the full graces of the family? The Dunkers used punishment that triggered these questions and, in some instances, the wrong answers resulted. But there were many correct answers. It has been seen that the air-clearing exercise of bringing complaints to the supper table resulted in immediately restoring the child to the family. So did the practice of doing essentially the same thing at family worship. The infrequency of lengthy punishment, such as the restriction placed upon his child by Samuel Flory, indicates that transgressions were dealt with promptly and completely. For the most part, then, the designed measures of discipline were quick, offense-related, and the child was restored to a good standing in the family without a period of alienation. These measures were not used often or on a regular basis. Their primary method of discipline grew out of the Dunker lifestyle and beliefs; it related to life on the subsistence farm.

In consideration of the second part, the student of childrearing must consider whether the forms of discipline are appropriate to the demands of the life of that age. Part of army training in the Second World War was to stress this as it related to the military.

The sergeant pointed out that if one is told to duck in a snowball battle and doesn't, the worst thing that can happen is to be hit by a snowball; in battle, one might get his head blown off. A severe sunburn in civilian life causes the loss of a day's work; the punishment, the loss of a day's pay. In the army, a severe sunburn incapacitates the soldier; his absence might cause the loss of a buddy's life; therefore, the punishment was severe, a courtmartial. The running of a farm which barely provided enough food to last through the winter; the care of the cattle; the gathering of fuel, all of these were important to the farm family beyond what they seem to the casual reader today. Their lives depended on the orderly and timely tending to these jobs. For this reason alone, the necessity of the obedience of the child was important. And to the devout, the necessity to follow the Biblical road to salvation required authority that could extract obedience as the children were trained.

Finally, the references which tell of the attitude of the Dunker parents towards their children may be better understood in the framework of de Mause's psychogenic theory of childrearing.[1]

Modes of Childrearing: Projection, Reversion, and Empathy

Of these three modes which he postulates, projection, reversion, and empathy, the most primitive is projection. In this the fears, weaknesses, or desires of the parent are placed in the child as a means of ridding the parent of those thoughts. A present-day manifestation of this mode is seen in the pubertal girl who is brought to the physician by the mother, fearing that her daughter will become sexually promiscuous. The physician immediately notices that the thirteen-year-old is dressed like a girl ten years older. The mother points to this "look" as evidence that her daughter is on the verge of becoming a hussy. Of course, no thirteen-year-old girl can be dressed in this way without the help of the mother. The mother has a suppressed sexuality which she projects into the child by giving the child the physical attire to play the role of a hussy. Then she panics at the thought that the girl will live that role.

The second mode described by de Mause is "reversion" in which the child becomes the parent to the parent. Many children have the capability to assume this role; the pathology is when the parent permits or demands the child to do so. The previous reference to Jacob Miller, who did not go to the West because the father took it so hard, illustrates this mode. This is seen in the adoptive family of today. The reason for adoption is "to give the child a good home." They lavish love on the child and expect it to reciprocate with the love that they did not get from their parents. But when dirty diapers, incessant demands, and midnight vigils result, the parent feels rejected just as he did when he was rejected by his own parents.

The third mode of childrearing is the most desirable one and requires the most mature personality in the parent. This is called "empathetic." In this mode, the parents are able to see the child as an immature person with limited capabilities and many needs. Their response to these needs is from a basis of selfless love. They are able to view the child with sufficient objectivity to make decisions that will accrue to the benefit of the child, not fill their own personality deficits or meet their own emotional needs. They are able to understand the infant and the older child as a growing person with characteristics appropriate to their age.

However, no parent relates to his children within one of the three modes; the Dunkers were no exception. From time to time, evidence of any of the three may be present. Which one predominates is the most important factor. Elizabeth Kiser, in an 1855 letter to a relative, shows a mixture of modes:

> "I said in the commencement of my letter that we were all well—well we are with the exception of sore eyes. Sis's are sore but I am in hopes they won't be sore long. I think they look better today than they did yesterday and Susan Virginia is well and hearty except burns. She has two or three burns on both hands. She is not afraid of the stove as soon as one burn is well there is another some other place.
>
> Jinny is awake I have her setting on a chair eating pop corn to keep her employed. She wants my pen and ink and paper so that I can scarcely write."[2]

One might attribute the burns to the attitude that experience is the best teacher. Even if this was so, that the mother tolerated her little toddler burning herself on the stove suggests that the projective mode was present in that instance. The mother projected her own feelings of unworthiness and guilt into the child, and these were removed through the pain and suffering of her child. However, in the later scene, feeding pop-corn to keep a toddler employed is an adult way of handling the nuisance of interruption. Minimizing the disruptive acts of the infant, child, or youth assumes different importance at different ages.

Control, Authority, and Age

The two important ages in rearing a child are the first five years and the teenage years. The first period is crucial, because parental authority is established, the acculturation process is begun, and internal controls are established. On the other hand, the converse of these happens; parental authority may be misapplied, rebellion to the family values may begin, and this rebellion may disrupt the system of internal controls. Therefore, misapplication of the principles of childrearing during the five critical years by the sectarians most certainly would thwart their aim of continuing the values of the sect in the next generations. In this same context, how and what principles were used determined to some extent the adult outcome.

The Hutterites entrusted the training of their children to their schools. The Dunkers did not have a systematic method. Rather, the children were reared within the matrix of the family, governed by essentially the same factors that governed the rest of the family. Of the many facets of training to discipline, obedience was prized and insisted upon more than any other. They did not hesitate to expose their children to that which goes with obedience—the state of deprivation. The demands of the farm superseded the desires of the young and conditioned them early to do what was necessary, then what they wanted to do. As the child grew older, obedience became part of his expected pattern of living. Since this pattern was dictated by the work style rather than by parental commands, the instances of confrontation were lessened.

It is confrontation, the daily contest of wills, that has the potential to produce alienation and rebellion. The constancy and predictability of farm life blunted the usual clashes between parent and child, and those that did occur could be resolved quickly with logic that even the young child could understand. In those few instances where logic failed, a more direct approach was permitted. In a number of cases, such as Pritchett's burning cedar, the act was ignored, a technique at times more effective than confrontation.

Since there was no institutional protocol to follow, the discipline of the children varied with the rank of birth, just as it does in the present time. The older child has a father who is younger, more immature, more ambitious, and usually in poorer economic circumstances. Therefore, this child is controlled, worked more, and expectations of him are greater. The father of the younger child has matured, mellowed, and is in better economic circumstances, so this child is given more advantages and is subjected to fewer controls. So it was with the Dunkers. E.K. Ziegler (b. 1903, PA) seemed resentful of this:

> I often protested that, though he disciplined me severely, my brother Jesse, ten years younger, never was whipped.[3]

Forty years earlier, in Southern Iowa, a member of the church remembered:

> Being the youngest in a family with several boys, he was permitted to spend considerable time in the schools of the day, and was not necessarily disciplined to hard work in childhood as were the older ones.[4]

The Rod, the Child, and Discipline

Though the intensity of discipline in the family diminished as the number of children increased, even the youngest was expected to conform to the family values and to do the necessary work on the farm. Their performance was the responsibility of the father, who, from the German tradition, Biblical injunction, and the prevailing custom of the day, was the head of the family. He had the last word in disciplinary matters. He accomplished this more through perceived authority rather than through actively punishing the children. He did not whip as much as did the mother, and she did not whip often. Only Flory and Ziegler mentioned that they were whipped by their fathers. Several references pointedly said that their father never whipped them. The mother did use the birch or hickory when it seemed indicated, perhaps because the children were under her feet when they got under her skin and were more available. But she also used perceived authority, remembered by J.H. Moore (b. 1846, VA):

A stern look from my mother and a vigorous reprimand gave me to understand that this was not the way for a boy to talk.[5]

The mothers had their breaking point and resorted to the rod when this point was reached. E.K. Ziegler remembers his mother's endpoint of tolerance:

Mother was always quiet and gentle, but our antics sometimes exasperated her to the point that she would threaten to spank us with a paddle.

Once, when the sound and the fury were too much for mother to endure, she tethered me to the big pear tree in the back yard by a ten foot length of clothesline.[6]

Threatening to use the paddle was considered good form by the Dunkers. It was likened to the threat of power by a head of state to avoid the use of this power in war. Needless to say, the threat was real; the Dunker mother was no paper tiger. She spanked and, at times, the spanking was hard. Several other references said that the mother threatened to tell the father of the antics of the children. This did not seem a prevalent response.

This account by Kermit Eby gives the best picture of the emotional content of the disciplinary process of the Dunker family. The circumstances contained two of the most cherished values of the group: obedience and reverence. It was customary for the children to attend worhip services. Eby occasionally did not sit still during that long hour. Here is his account of what happened:

"But it must not be forgotten that the basic emphasis at Baugo was religious. The Brethren believed that life was real, God ever present, and sin something to be trodden underfoot. Children were to be brought up in the nurture and admonition of the Lord. As babies, we sat on our mother's lap—that is, until the inevitable younger brother or sister crowded us off; after that we sat next to Mother, and believe me, we were supposed to sit still and listen to the minister. If we disobeyed our mother's admonitions she faced a grave decision—either to permit us to go on being noisy thus disturbing the service, or to take us "out back" and thereby confess she had failed to teach us to sit still. Usually Mother took the second alternative and we were taken "out back", far enough so that our howling would not disturb the congregation, our posteriors were turned toward heaven, and we were thoroughly spanked; and as we were spanked, Mother reminded us that the church was the house of God, the minister His servant, and, furthermore, if we wanted some more of the same we knew exactly how to get it. Consequently, we soon learned to sit still. We didn't want to go "out back" again. Mother, I learned, always spanked hardest when she was embarrassed, and by the time we were five or six years old we were pretty well broken in and ready for our first Sunday School class."[7]

Teenage and School Discipline

The Dunker children were disciplined in different ways, occasionally punitive, but these measures seemed confined to the younger period of the child's life. How were the teenagers disciplined? Only one instance is mentioned: Flory's father restricted him to the farm for sixty days. Yet these are the years when the young men and women try their boundaries and their parents' patience and authority. This lack of reference indicates that it was not the practice of the Dunkers to actively control their adolescent children; generations now living, reared by parents born prior to 1900, confirm this. This was due to the culturally-determined perception that the child assumed somewhat the adult status when he reached the teenage years, and it was made possible by the internal controls already in place at that age. But the parents were not the only ones who monitored the conduct of the children. When they went to school they came under the authority of the teachers.

School teachers carried much more authority in the 1800's than they do in the present time. Since this discipline was carried out with full knowledge of the parents, it gives an insight into the Dunkers' attitude toward what was proper and permissible in that they accepted it for their own children. L. W. Shultz (b. 1890, Ind.) recalls:

> "In elementary school, many types of punishment were endured by students. Standing on tip-toe with one's nose in a ring on the blackboard, sitting on a sharp three cornered or three edged stick of wood, whipped by a long leather strap, and even physical blows on the face.[8]

Shultz tells of the direct ways that school children were punished. There were, however, more creative ways, as the following accounts show. D.L. Miller's biographer records some of his school experiences which, one will note, did not suggest that the stress on obedience at home hindered him in his social activities at school:

> "But his school days were not all spent in standing at the head of his classes. He had his share of trouble and mischief which was punished in the usual way. The hickory was used in those days, as he can well remember. But there was one punishment that made a deeper impression on him than any whippings ever did. He tells of it as follows:

> One day, a few of us boys caught a frog in a neighboring brook and butchered it. The teacher heard of it and had the five of us seated together on one of the slab benches. He had us roll our trousers about our knees. The he stood in front of us, knife and whetstones in hand. As he sharpened his knife, he told us how the frog we butchered suffered pain, and he wanted us to know just how the poor little thing suffered when we cut his legs off. I do not think there was a boy in the lot but that felt assured he was going to lose a leg. There was weeping and mourning in concert. When the exhibition was over, and we escaped with our legs, we were a happy lot. I learned a lesson then that I never forgot. Teachers used the rods in those days freely, but the rod never gave me a lesson as did the teacher with his knife and whetstone.[9]

Positive Expectation

The farm life was an instrument of value transference in that it provided a constant environment with demands which had to be met. This had a maturing effect on the child. There had to be, however, a force which caused the children to take up the farm tasks and to finish them in an acceptable way. This was not physical force, though the threat of physical force was present. And this behavior was not the result of bribery. Yet, there was an effective method used by the Dunker parents, one illustrated in these next accounts. Note the obedience theme in Wampler's account where he could not remember ever doing anything his parents specifically told him not to do.

The major training method is set forth in the accounts of Ernest Wampler and Charles Bonsack, respectively:

> With such instructions and examples we were made to realize that God was the Father we were learning to obey. The teachings and

commandments of the New Testament were to be followed. This principle was the basis for the authority of our parents. Generally speaking we did. I do not remember ever doing anything that my parents specifically told me not to do. Yet, I did many things that displeased them, for which my mother punished me. I do not remember ever being spanked by my father. God's laws and commandments were of first importance in our home. We were told that God was the creator of everything and that we were made not to question His ways and laws.[10]

The children understood clearly what their mother's wishes were in regard to the family duties. There were tasks for each one and they were distributed in areas—at the chicken house, in the dairy, in the woodshed, in the garden, and in the house. If anyone came to the supper table delinquent in completed tasks the fact usually became known. In such a case, one learned a new lesson in self-discipline, without many words being spoken. An offender might have emotional disturbance before he closed his eyes in sleep if he remembered that he had failed in his behavior during the day. If anyone had done wrong he was made to feel a sense of regret. A prayer of forgiveness restored him again in renewed understanding of God's love and care and in family favor.[11]

In Bonsack's family, the children knew precisely what was expected of them. In the Wampler family, the children were expected to obey their parents. In the Flory family, the children were expected to do their work and to behave as they should. There was no wavering on this. It was not hoped; the children were not asked; they were not given options; they were expected to conduct their daily life in the way that the family values indicated they should. The children in the Dunker families of that era were reared in an atmosphere of positive expectation, one which admitted no possibility of aberrant behavior and, therefore, gave the children no opening to significantly depart from family values or practices. This was a major component of their childrearing method in directing the lives of the young people "while they were under the control of the father."

Two facets of the Dunker world made this method of influencing the children possible. First, most issues, moral as well as economic, were well defined. There were few options to getting the cows in to milk in the evening or to planting the corn in the spring. When the father told the children that work had to be done, it related to the welfare of the whole family. The children were not "put out" so that someone else benefitted. The second facet was the Dunker parent's belief in the truth and appropriateness of the scriptures as they applied to daily life. They believed this in a literal sense. There was little or no middle ground. So when the children tested their parents, they saw no doubt in the eyes, no wavering of indecision, only firmness.

The imperatives of farm work and the scriptures created an emotional environment for the child where the self-indulgence of the young was quickly brought under control. Thus the child's energies were directed early toward his role as a member of the economic team. Within this team, there was minimal confrontation between parent and child, even though there was no apparent avenue to escape the demands of his parents and of the farm.

The active ingredient of the attitude of positive expectation can be termed moral suasion. In this, the attitude of the parents towards their child is a decisive control mechanism. Disapproval by the parent becomes a disciplinary measure. The close family relationship and the hypersensitive conscience made the Dunker children extremely susceptible to this type of control. E.K. Ziegler said that he would never intentionally hurt his mother; D.L. Miller hurt his mother by going out with his buddies, returning to find her praying and weeping for him. Perhaps a sense of guilt caused him to write a tearful letter years later in which he, in essence, conferred sainthood on her.[12] Kermit Eby wanted the approval of his father and grandfather. Hannah Mack was sensitive to John Price's regard for her. The extended family and other church members, who had a similar relationship with the child, contributed to an environment from which the child received approval. Much was expected of the child. The degree to which he met those expectations, shown by the approval of the adults in his life, established his self-worth. One's conscience was very active in this process.

The Good and Bad of Moral Suasion and Positive Expectation

These forces, expectations and moral coercion, had the potential to produce children who were rebellious and who would deliberately engage in activities that would hurt their parents. It also had the potential to produce children who were in an emotional straight-jacket and who were deprived, therefore, of initiative and of intellectual curiosity. To what extent this happened is not known, since these cases generally would not be represented in biographical date of outstanding leaders. Some of the children, as they grew to the teenage years of self-determination, probably left the order as a defense mechanism. It is reasonable to believe, also, that some would not have the strength of ego to move beyond the protection of the group and its order. There is evidence of this in the individuals who were involved in the church squabbles, but a discussion of these would involve speculative psychology beyond the design of this study.

Despite these potentially crippling psychological results of moral suasion and positive expectation, the references in the next section indicate that the Dunker children were not robbed of the opportunity to explore the things that children delight in and that the teenagers were given sufficient room to test their value system. That this was so relates to the position of the child in the eyes of the parents: 1) he existed in the household as a separate individual whose ego was not intertwined with the parents'; 2) because of this, the parents were able to see the child as age- and capability-related; and 3) the teenager, according to the prevailing culture, assumed the status of an adult, with adult prerogatives, at an earlier age. In addition to these, the adolescent was not bound by the order, which gave him more freedom of activity. Apparently, this adolescent freedom was not designed to acquaint the youth with the world so that he could make an informed decision on baptism. This, though, is inherent in the doctrine of adult baptism.

Imagination, Independence, and Room to Grow

The Dunker young exercised their independence and imagination. The ages are not given when these events occurred, but the children were probably between the ages of five and ten. In the first, L.W. Schultz and his sister cooperated in these misadventures:

> Once Elsie and I murdered a small flock of ducks with hoes. We were pretending they were an army. Once we took a clock to pieces and were never able to get it together again.[13]

Eby and Pritchett, respectively, showed little foresight in their

PLATE 20. Class of 1895—Juniata College, Huntington, Pa.

PLATE 21. William T. Sanger, Ph.D., President of the Medical College of Virginia 1925-1956

rebellion against the arduous tasks of the farm, because they were doomed to be caught:

> Sometimes I rebelled and shirked the tasks as they grew even more arduous. Once I planted all the seed corn in one spot—seed corn that I was supposed to use for replanting. Of course, it came up and gave me away.[14]

> The chief thing my father would not allow on Sundays was fishing. We'd break over and sneak off fishing anyhow and I always caught a fish and the fish'd get me caught, too. I'd hate to throw it back; I'd bring the fish home and there you'd have been fishing on Sunday.[15]

William Beahm (b. 1896, VA) was a thinker and was clever:

> I used to walk backwards through the fresh plowed corn field to the swimming hole so if INH (his father) discovered my tracks, they would be leading away from the creek rather than toward it.[16]

According to Fike, William Beahm was a very bitter young man, shown by the remarks concerning his father's failure to provide a better living for his family. He felt that it was not fair for his father to put so much time in the free ministry to the neglect of his family. Despite this, William entered the ministry, wrote what some consider to be the most erudite theological statement of the church, and taught in its seminary for many years. His talents surfaced early at the old swimming hole.

There is no indication that these young people were disciplined severely for these forbidden acts, even though one involved shirking the important task of planting corn and the other involved direct disobedience. Why was this so? Again, it appears that punitive discipline was not used often in the Dunker household and that the young were given latitude to act as the young will act.

Within this framework, H. Stover Kulp (b. 1894, PA) decided that he wanted more education, even though his father thought that the elementary education was sufficient preparation for the sectarian and agricultural life:

> I remember, he later wrote, while avoiding discussion, I had resolved in my own mind where I would be going. At the end of the

first school day, father learned that I entered the high school. He did
not say much. I imagine that mother had spoken on my behalf.[17]

Though this occurred in the first decade of the 1900's when the
Dunker stand against education had weakened, the authority of
the father had not. Yet young Kulp had the independence to go
against his father's will. In doing so he displayed more independence than one would think existed in the controlled and
constant dynamics of the Dunker family. A footnote to this: Kulp's
father, though financially able, would not give him the money to
go through normal school. He did, however, lend him money at a
point of critical need.

Space for the Children

It is seen that, generally, the Dunkers maintained a distance
from their children which enabled them to see the children as
individuals, separate from the ego of the adults. That the children
were given age-related tasks, that they were shielded from adult
worries, that they were allowed the misadventures of the young
with little or no punishment, and that they were required to be
obedient support this conclusion. The penetrating thinker will
realize that one of the problems of childrearing in the present is
that the children are not thought of as children in many families.
They are co-equal with the parents. In a given day in a
pediatrician's office, a mother will ask a four-year-old whether he
wants an injection; will state that she cannot take the clothes off of
a dissenting two-year-old; will insist that the one-year-old will not
give her the bottle; and will pathetically weep when her ten-
month-old cries while being examined. Once a week, a mother
will ask a ten-year-old whether he wants a boil lanced or a
laceration repaired. Regarding the child as co-equal produces
intertwined egos. Evidence of this is seen frequently. The most
striking sign of intertwined egos of the parent and child is the use
of "we." We have a rash; we have a fever, or we won't eat. Of
particular note is that these are never seen or heard of when the
family is from the nearby Amish community where the culture is
roughly that of the pre-twentieth century Dunkers.

While some will insist that the contemporary actions listed
above represent a respect for the individuality of the child, the
truth is that it represents the failure of the parent to see their child

in an age-related status; it may even represent an inability of the parents to cope with the demands at the age of that child. In effect, the parents who do this may have abandoned their responsibility for the care and nurture of their children by projecting adult capabilities into them. Or they may be covering up a basic rejection of the child by making him part of their own being through the use of "we."

Obedience and Freedom

Obedience demanded of the young was a sign that the Dunkers recognized the dependency of the children on the adult for training and for protection. While this obedience was so inculcated into the superego of the child that it became part of the reactive response of the child when he reached adulthood, the exercise of authority by the parents diminished as the child grew older. It is clear that this authority was used in work matters regardless of age; it is also clear that it was not used as much in social matters as the child entered puberty. With increasing age, the person needed less training and protection and the authority of the parent persisted primarily in the economic field, an area crucial to the survival of the family. Therefore, obedience had two functions: first, to train the young to the Dunker way of life and, second, to enforce the economic contract between the father and his teenager, or, in some cases, young adult.

The freedom of the teenager was not always used in ways consistent with the rules of the order. The comment of the ministers about the wild uncultured boys, undesirable as mates of the Dunker girls, has been given in an earlier reference. Joseph Hostetler (b. 1797, KY) explored the social world:

It was to be supposed that one brought up under such circumstances would readily walk in the way of the righteous. But he was naturally of the very mischievious disposition; at time highly passionate; and "prone to evil as the sparks to fly upward." When, therefore, he grew older and became less in the presence of his parents, he often set at naught all their counsel to walk in the counsel of the ungodly.[18]

Joseph Hostetler joined the church at nineteen; his journey in the counsel of the ungodly had to be prior to that. He later served as an elder in the church in the then western area of the country and upheld the church and its order. Jacob Bower, born ten years earlier into a Dunker family, participated in the social pleasures of the day and in the several "heresies" which were prevalent. Later, he accepted the values of his youth. He joined the Baptist church, where he served faithfully until his death.

Because they were born in the 1700's, Bower and Hostetler were in the period before the secular culture of the European origins had been altered by the order which was derived from the Dunkers' religious beliefs. Yet, fifty years later, the youths were still exploring. D.L. Miller (b. 1841, MD) also searched for the way of life that would suit him, trying the values of his family:

> On coming home from an evening with his associates, he often found his mother praying and weeping for him. Certainly, that sight would do much to keep him in the straight path.[19]

This reference has a different connotation. By 1841, the order was rigid and was enforced with vigor. That Miller, from a stable family of the church, was permitted to mingle freely with those who did not believe like the Dunkers is even stronger evidence that this adolescent freedom was a well-established childrearing practice. But Miller, as did many of the other youths, finally accepted the order.

These stories have another side to them. Why did not the father invoke his authority to control this behavior? Again, it suggests that the teenager was viewed as an adult with the prerogatives of that status and, therefore, was not under the control of his father in the social world. If this was so, the father did not display empathy; this presupposes that he allowed them to search for their own way of life as a deliberate policy, one set for the welfare of the teenager. Rather, it appears that he followed the tradition of the culture. However, the results were essentially the same: the young man had the room in which to test his own inclinations against the order of the church. From the standpoint of conscience and culture, this adolescent freedom allowed him to test the comfort zone of his internalized values.

The Empathetic Capabilities of the Adult
While the references suggest that the Dunker parents' mind-

set allowed the children, within the constraints of the economics of the day, to have considerable freedom of individual expression, two instances of adult discipline more clearly demonstrate the empathetic capabilities of the Dunker man. These, indirectly, tell that this type of relationship was within the Dunker perception of the child. The two adult authority figures did not develop this capability solely from their adult experience—they learned it from the way their fathers related to them. The references illustrate the ability of two men to put the acts of the young into the proper perspective, to maintain a distance from the act so that they could render mature judgments, and to formulate an appropriate response to the transgressors. The appropriate response served the young person, but was formulated out of a need to protect the value system of the adult. It also showed the attitude of positive expectation.

> Always he (D.L. Miller) was their friend. Brother Grant Mahan still remembers those days and wrote some of his recollects of that time: I shall never forget how I first met him and how he became my friend right from the start, trusting me in a way that surprised me then and still does when I think about it.

> He knew when to speak to the boys and what to say to them. In writing about these things one must necessarily write about himself, for Brother Miller was not given to telling one boy what he said to another. And one lesson he gave three of us boys because of what we did in the dining room has remained with me. It was holiday time and we were full of fun and mischief. But he did not reprimand us before the roomful of other boys and girls. He waited until he saw the three of us together outside, and then he came up to talk to us. Even then he did not reprimand us, but simply asked us whether we thought we had acted as we should. That got us all in a way that nothing else could, and it helped us more than a dozen lectures and reprimands would have.[20]

D.L. Miller was a member of the administrative staff of Mt. Morris College, and he was responsible for the conduct of the students. The rules at Mt. Morris were strict, and conduct that breached those rules usually resulted in a severe disciplinary action. Professor Miller, in his early forties at this time, displayed remarkable empathy with the young students as their tendencies conflicted with the established order of the college. The student finishes his remarks:

And whether it was one boy or a few boys or all the boys, he talked to them in the same way. He appealed to what was best in them, and they responded much better than they would have to the man who would have taken a different and harsher method of correction. He was kind to us, but we always knew that he did not condone serious offenses; there was never any compromise with wrong. He was the warm friend of the young all his life, and more than one young man and young woman owe much to his inspiration and help. Some of us are no longer young, but we still cherish his memory and are thankful that he came into our lives when he did.[21]

In dealing with his wayward students, he appealed to their consciences and he appealed to their sense of values, two items of their makeup with which he was familiar. He had come from the same background as they and had participated in as much mischief as they would before maturity tempered his spirit. He also knew the independence and the stubbornness that the constant battle against the elements bred into them. And finally, because of their limited horizons, he knew what basic preparation they needed for their future occupation and life. This knowledge of their superego and their value system, his understanding of why they behaved the way they did (because he had done similar things as a youth), and his faith in their worthiness allowed him to appeal to them, arousing their conscience a bit, to correct their behavior. He also had the maturity and the positive attitude which, instead of causing him to become threatening and punitive, allowed him to handle the matter so that they, in fact, punished themselves.

The next incident, already referred to, illustrates empathy between father and son. This is more subtle, but it shows an adult making a decision based on what was good for the boy and not necessarily what the father would like to have done. The story has more significance if Tennessee of that time was like Virginia. In Virginia, cedars were too scarce to be wasted—they were all needed for fence posts. Ruel Pritchett (b. 1884, TN) still remembered the incident:

One night a number of us boys was out late strolling home from a corn shucking, and we came by my Father's upper field. Where we boys had to separate, we clumb up on the rail fence and set and talked a while. It was a dark night and no moon.

Father had some nice young cedars trimmed up, high as your head to the first limb; and then they bunched way out. The prize tree was right next to us. The field was full of sage grass—that's grass that shoots up as big as wheat and dies and looks dead. It was well along in the fall of the year and the grass was dry. We boys thought of an experiment: We jumped over, wring off the sage grass, got up on the fence, clumb the tree and stuffed that cedar full of the grass, all up in there just loads of it. Then we struck a match to it. Oh, it burnt vehemently. The moonless night wasn't dark anymore. You could see the time of day by your watch a hundred yards distant. It was a wonderful leaping light. Cedar'll burn if it get primed; the sage grass got burnt off, and there stood the stub trunk just sticking straight up, ghostlike, way on up, and not a limb on it.

Of course, Father, he discovered the remains, and he says, "Ruel, what in the world's happened to my cedar tree?" "I don't know pappy, unless the lightning struck it." He was guessing at the reason purty close, but he didn't whip us.[22]

He was not disciplined for burning a tree which might have yielded two or three fence posts. Why? Since Pritchett had been to a corn shucking, he must have been over ten years old, and physical punishment is difficult to administer to older children. However, Lester Flory's father restricted him to the farm at that age.

The Hypersensitive Conscience and Guilt

Dunker children were disciplined, but punitive discipline seemed to be administered infrequently, particularly after the age of five years. As Kermit Eby remembered, several trips "out back," and the child, by that age, was pretty well broken to sit still for preaching. The control established at the earlier age kept them in line as they grew older. Projection and reversion were used—one father spanked his six-week-old baby—but a surprising amount of empathy was shown to the children in this strict sectarian environment. Why was this so? Certainly the cultural progress (psychogenic growth?) of the Dunkers was not ahead of the surrounding people's. It may be that, since the farm and its requirements embraced most of the values held by the parents and since farm life was part of the method of childrearing, parents did not have to resort to the projective mechanism as much. Although the Dunkers studied, quoted, and obeyed the Old Testament, they attempted to live by the New Testament. Perhaps the love theme of the New Testament increased their ability to empathize with their children.

The physical entity of the farm provided space in which the children grew and developed; the natural hazards of the environment promoted self-reliance; the demands of the work developed discipline in the children; and the authority of the father and the influence of church order were available as further means of control of the children. But these were not enough to allow the principle of positive expectation with minimal disciplinary interaction to be effective. More was needed to control the children. This was the hypersensitive conscience with its enforcer, guilt.

The psychoanalytical system developed by Freud has conscience as a tool of one of the three major components of the person's psyche. The Id is the animal, selfish part of the person. The Ego is the person's perception of oneself. The Superego is the value system of the person. There is an interactive process going on between the three components of the psyche which attempts to produce an accommodation of the three elements allowing the individual to be at peace with himself.

The Superego, in Freud's concept, is the value system of the person, but the operative part of the Superego is the conscience. This plays the role of regulator of the actions of the person, sometimes holding the person back, other times urging him forward, sometimes in harmony with the Id and the Ego, at other times in conflict with them. It is not a perfect regulator. It does not always win. When it provides the right regulation, the person feels good. When it cannot do this, the person feels bad.

The conscience is the regulator of behavior based on the value system of the Superego; the cutting edge of this regulator is an affective component of the person's mind and is termed "guilt." Conscience has been called an essentially negative regulator, that is, preventing behavior inappropriate to the person's beliefs, rather than promoting appropriate behavior. It follows then that its tool of regulation, guilt, also has a basically negative effect, not only in preventing behavior that is contrary to the values held but also in its effect on the Ego. Guilt does not make a person feel good; it can only make a person feel uncomfortable to miserable. When the anticipation of guilt works through prevention, the person feels good and the Ego is enhanced. But when the anticipation of guilt is not effective in deterring baser drives, the person feels bad, guilty, because the Superego has been violated and the Ego picture has been damaged.

Guilt is an emotion which functions in everyone. It is a useful part of our emotional homeostatic mechanism, but inappropriate guilt can be destructive to the functional abilities of the individual. Guilt is experienced in direct proportion to the number of "no's" in a person's training and the degree to which the ignoring of those "no's" damages the self-esteem. If these "no's" relate to a divine being, the impact on self-esteem is greater and the guilt is more intense. The guilt-ridden person feels less worthy; he has sinned and he becomes preoccupied with this sinful state, using up emotional energy which could be put to a more productive use.

The Dunkers, with their closed society and their black and white religious and behavioral dogma, were a laboratory setting to produce guilt-ridden, emotional cripples. The issues were so clear that there was little room for rationalization; yet, despite the fact that hypersensitive consciences were developed in the children, there are only a few recorded instances of emotional illness in the literature of that day. Elder John Kline's wife became non-functional when she heard that he died on one of his preaching missions. She did not recover when the rumor proved to be false. Others experienced upheavals which redirected their lives.* But, for the most part, the Dunkers apparently developed a survival mechanism which enabled them to adapt. This mechanism was undoubtedly based in and was an expression of their religious beliefs.

The conscience as a means of control worked for the Dunker parent because the child's idea of his own self-worth was derived almost exclusively from his perception of what his parents and the other adults in his life thought of him. In their isolated environment, peer contribution was negligible. A word, a smile, a frown, a modulation of tone from an adult in his life was enough to cause a reaction in the child through the hypersensitive conscience. Disapproval by the adult hurt, and anticipation of

---

* Of course, the medical profession did not have an extensive list of diagnoses to cover emotional swings. Low blood, vapors, indisposition, and the lay term "troublesome disposition," covered many of the neurotic afflictions that are specifically diagnosed today.

disapproval was cutting enough to curtail or modify behavior which would most certainly result in outright disapproval. This well-developed conscience, based on the value system of the father and the mother, acted as a gyroscope to keep the Dunker child on course. In this setting, positive expectation was not a wishful dream; the course had been well planned and there was every reason to believe that the gyroscope would work.

For the Dunker youths, the absence of guilt and their enhancement in the eyes of their parents were the reward when they stayed within the rules, and the loss of these was the punishment when they strayed outside of the prescribed path. Previous references suggest that the youths were particularly sensitive to the feelings of their mothers and did not want to hurt them, or, just as importantly, fail to live up to what they perceived she thought of them. They wanted to stand tall in the eyes of their father in the work area. Despite these desires, actually they were more than desires, they were emotional needs, the conscience did not always work to perfection. Sometimes it won; sometimes it lost. One of each outcome is presented to illustrate the conscience in action with the corrective power of guilt. The insignificance of the Wampler (b. 1885, VA) transgression in the first reference illustrates the hypersenstive conscience. Guilt was the emotion which spurred each person to attempt to make the Ego whole:

Two things I did of a questionable nature as a child stand out in my memory. I always enjoyed eating black walnuts and one of the big problems was extracting the kernels after they were cracked, generally with rocks. Someone told me that the nails used for putting on horseshoes were good for this task. So I wanted one of those nails. I just felt I must have one for getting out my walnut kernels. One day I got the opportunity for getting my nail. While the smith was in at the anvil shaping the shoes and no one else was around, I just went to the box in which he had his nails, files and knives for shoeing horses, and picked out a nice new nail and put it in my pocket. It was not long, however, until my conscience began to work on me. I had stolen a horseshoe nail. I could not put it back for he would come out and would see me. I do not ever remember using it to pick out walnut kernels, but that botherered my boyhood conscience quite a bit. I know he would have willingly given me one had I asked for one.[23]

Pritchett's experience was more serious:

The third incident in his grade school days occurred just before he graduated from the eighth grade. One night he was out with a gang of boys who visited the school; after rolling a stump up to the window, which was otherwise too high for them to reach, they entered the school and removed the examinations from the teacher's desk. The papers were securely deposited some distance from the school in such a way that they could never have been found. Although the young Ruel "knew it was a mistake," he felt the pressure of the group and was unable to prevent the action. However, he could do something about it, and later that night after the gang had broken up and each had gone to his home, Ruel returned to the area, retrieved the papers, and returned them to the teacher's desk. The teacher, I.N. Humphreys, evidently never realized what had happened, for nothing was ever said. Ruel got off without being discovered by the boys, and it was some fifty years later before he confessed to the last living member of that gang.[24]

Pritchett's regulator failed him the first time around; he succumbed to peer pressure. But when this pressure was removed, guilt took its toll. In reaction, he returned the papers to the teacher's desk, absolving himself of the guilt which he felt for stealing and restoring his perception of himself as an honorable young man. In the eighth grade, he was probably between twelve and fourteen at the time. In Wampler's case his regulator lost, but he was saved through rationalization. Taking the nails damaged his sense of self-worth; using the nails would confirm that he was a thief. So he rationalized that if he did not use those nails, the offense would not be as bad. After describing a similar incident involving a pistol, Wampler remarked that he did not think that his parents found out about either incident, indicating, over fifty years later, that the absolute "sin" of taking the nails was secondary to his concern for what his parents thought of him.

The conscience of the Dunker youths was amenable to the healing influence of rationalization. A young girl out on the prairie wanted to get married. She had a problem. To get the license, she had to be eighteen, and she was only sixteen. So she, in order not to lie, put a slip of paper with the number of eighteen in her shoe and another slip of paper with the number nineteen in her bonnet. When she told the official that she was between eighteen and nineteen, her conscience was clear. This should not be regarded as an example of a hypersensitive conscience.[25]

The hypersensitive conscience can hinder the emotional

development of a child into the adult status, causing the child to seek a place in life where issues have "yes" and "no" answers and where temptations are minimal. These people have difficulty maintaining an emotional balance in a free, fluid environment. They attempt to draw their life and the lives of the members of their family into a tight little cocoon where tolerance is absent and forgiveness hard to come by, obviously a poor environment in which to rear the next generation of children.

But three conditions counterbalance the effect of the sensitive conscience. First, the children must be brought up in an approving environment where they have the opportunity to succeed most of the time. Second, the parents must not make their love and acceptance of the children dependent upon their following the values of the parents, even though the children perceive this to be so. Third, the parents cannot use disapproval too often, even the objective, non-personal, non-threatening type. If these conditions are violated, the use of love as a bargaining agent and criticism as a bludgeon may cause the child to bcome so down on himself that his self-esteem will be damaged. Or he may become inured to the feeling of his parents and thus will escape their control. He may feel unworthy of honors and esteem when he grows up; he may hate the culture that produced him.

The parents usually did not manipulate the conscience of their children; rather, the child knew the rules and what was expected of him. Deviation from these rules activated his guilt mechanism and his conscience restored rightful behavior. If a signal from the parents was needed to stir the child and his conscience, it was very small and slight—a frown, a pained expression, or perhaps, "I'm surprised that you would do that."

One instance was found, however, in which there was manipulation for the mother's benefit. This was in the case of Sarah Richter Major, the first woman preacher of the sect. She sent a letter to her son in Dallas, Ohio, where he attended school. In her letter to him, she describes a Love Feast, which she had just attended, and touchingly mentioned that the young men present reminded her of him. But before that, she laid a heavy load on his conscience to influence his behavior:

> Memory brings you to me as no picture can. I have many and
> serious cares, which press me hard these days of infirmity, but

among them all, you hold your place in my heart. Do not add to my burdens, do not disappoint my hopes, pray with my life-long prayers, that my children may early, and truly be faithful disciples of Jesus our Lord.[26]

We do not know whether this was a routine letter, or whether it was in response to some behavior of her son's that distressed her. The result, in either case, was that she attempted to make him feel responsible for her continuing good health; conversely, were her health to deteriorate, he would also be responsible for that. This is parenting at its near worst; it ranks with the relationship which Mack, Sr. and Andrew Miller had with their respective sons.

The Dunkers, for the most part, used their disciplinary tools in a way that gave to the children a sense of worth and of unconditional love. If the accounts of the Dunker people by outside sources are true, the children grew into self-confident adults, secure and capable in their own environment. However, it was in this context of the Dunker conscience that Eby said to live with a sense of purpose was worse than being an alcoholic, because one could get over alcoholism, but one could never escape the sense of purpose. The ingrained purposeful life guided by the finely tuned conscience was a constant and heavy burden to a few. To many, it was a rewarding way of life.

Summary

The Dunker child was reared in an atmosphere of positive expectation in the stable, predictable farm life. This allowed him to have his own area within the family structure without undue encroachment by his parents. Since he was trained to perform in this structure, discipline as personal confrontation was seldom necessary. The autonomy given the children within the structure and the parents' forbearance when dealing with the antics of the young also lessened confrontation. The mother spanked the toddler infrequently. The teenager was controlled in his economic performance. Minimal control was exerted in his social life. Other than his environment, the prevalent form of control and discipline was through the conscience of the Dunker children. With this, they disciplined themselves. But this hypersensitive conscience, along with the internalized value that each life had a purpose, imposed a motivating, yet constraining, dimension to the life of a Dunker.

9

On Rearing Children

The references presented suggest an approach to child-rearing that served the Dunkers effectively for almost two centuries. It is held that these references support the contentions of this study: 1) that the child was regarded as an individual with his own "space;" 2) that derived from that perception of the child, two major principles of childrearing were utilized; 3) that the father and mother were under theological and cultural pressure to nurture their child in a specific way; 4) and that the Dunker system of childrearing was essentially unchanged over the period of the study. To conclude this study of childrearing among the Dunkers, three areas will be explored: the constancy of the environment over one hundred eighty years that permitted a reasonably uniform and continuous method of rearing the young and the effect that religious and economic changes had on the life of the teenager. The application to the children of the two principles of childrearing will be considered in the last chapter.

The study of the history of the child indicates that two major factors determined the conditions of his existence: economics and maternal status. Added to these were the religious theories and practices of the time. It would follow that these factors would have to be reasonably constant for the Dunkers to have had a uniform system of childrearing over a span of one hundred eighty years.

Economic Setting

In the larger society, historians have noted the difference between the emigrations to the United States for economic reasons and those for religious reasons. The people who left Europe because of persecution for religious beliefs also left in poor economic straits because the persecution either cost them their jobs or ruined their businesses. But, they as a group were more competent than those who emigrated because of famine or unemployment.

The early Dunkers emigrated for religious reasons, not because they did not have the skills to compete for jobs. Naas' letter to his son indicated that the newly arrived Dunkers soon established a prosperous life around Germantown, due in part to their skills as artisans. These skills were critical in the developing economy of the Philadelphia area. And as they moved to the border lands, the artisans' skills were used on their own farms and communities. Elder John Kline of the 1850's was a farmer, preacher, and self-taught physician. A few instances of mid-wifery are recorded. And as the nineteenth century drew to a close, some, such as D.L. Miller, entered the retail business. But the primary flavor of the occupations of the Dunkers was either rural or was carried out in a rural setting.

Dove states that the Dunkers have always been agricultural people.[1] Ziegler's data indicate rural living in his population under study: 1880—94%; 1900—83%; and 1920—92%. Furthermore, almost all of the 1880 generation lived on dirt roads. Of more importance, these people wanted to live in open country. In the 1880 generation, 88% wanted rural life; 12% desired the city. By 1900, 91% wanted rural life and those wanting city life decreased to 9%.[2] As late as 1968, only one-third of the congregations of the Church of the Brethren was in towns of over 2000 people.[3]

This data indicate that the first determinant of the status of the child and therefore of parenting practices, economics, remained rural and reasonably constant from 1723 to 1900. There are two additional indicators to support the thesis. Even after urban congregations were established in the late 1800's, the rural congregations controlled church polity and policy through their numerical and political strength. This contributed to the continuing of the traditional beliefs and practices of the Dunkers. And family size was large and constant during the period of study, indicating not only a rural existence but also a sameness of family life.

Maternal Influence

Until 1860, the mother filled her role in the economy of the farm where she kept house, milked cows, tended to the chickens, and was generally responsible for the care of the garden. After 1860 she was given additional duties outside of the home. Whereas in previous years, these outside duties related primarily to the Love Feast, Sunday School teaching was now added to her responsibilities. After 1880, she also became a member of ladies aid societies, temperance groups, and was sent to the missions field. Despite these added outlets, her position in the home did not change. She was esteemed by her husband; she had the responsibility for her share of the farm work; and she had authority over the children. Shirley Holmes and Elder Kurtz spoke to this in their references. D.L. Miller's mother (b. 1820's) and Lavina Conner (b. 1847) both showed the same involvement with their family as did Mary Early Davis' mother (b. 1870's). Sister Onkst's mother, born in the first decade of the 1800's, displayed almost complete authority over her daughter. And the intercessor role of the mother is scattered in the literature throughout the period of study.

While there is little objective data to establish the constancy of the maternal influence, the existence of the office of deaconess from the beginning of the sect, the one member-one vote practice in the church council meetings, and the embracing of co-education when schools were established indicate an equality between male and female in the Dunker world. This presupposes a strong, constant maternal influence.

Religious Influence

The religious environment of the child of the Dunker sect from 1723 to 1900 also appears to have been relatively constant. This is difficult to assess, though, in a society where the order was strict, but where the permissible level of compliance was low and tolerance for deviation from the order was high. What was in the heart was not always shown by their actions within the order, and the basic attitude comes through to the child. In a system where example was the chief method of value transference, this point is important. Essentially, though, the values of the Dunkers probably did not change; "what is in the heart" remained supreme. The references lend support to this statement. The observation of the outside source on the qualities of the "Meek and Harmless Tunkers" in 1787 is compatible with the the account of life at Baugo by Kermit Eby in 1915. And references dealing with situational ethics in 1816, 1844, 1854, and 1903 say essentially the same: a man's work is his bond and the measure he gives must be "pressed down and running over." Two other accounts, one in the 1920's and the other in the 1950's, indicate that this observance of the scriptures continues.

There were other indications of constancy of applications of religious beliefs. The perception of the father was the same in 1846, 1861, and 1903—stern and authoritative. The oldest child was expected to carry additional responsibilities in the household during the period of study, shown by the references of 1816, 1841, 1877, and 1885. The father had the same attitude towards higher education in the references of 1820, 1879, and 1903. Even instances of faulty parenting spanned the period: 1735, 1810, 1850, 1900. And, of course, the values inherent in the rural life were constant.

The shift in theological interpretation by the average member of the sect from the inerrant scripture mode to that of the "scriptures for our day" did not occur until well after 1900.

Cultural Lag

Material presented in the previous section details the similarity of Dunker life and thought from their early days in America to 1900. To reinforce this, data given by Kett wil be compared with the Dunker experience to illustrate cultural lag, another reason why the childrearing practices remained constant for one hundred eighty years. He states that the Sunday School movement in the outside world was thriving by 1815;[4] the AM gave its imprimatur to this movement in 1857, but it was not until the 1890's that Sunday Schools were widespread among the Dunker churches. Adult-sponsored youth groups were organized in the general population in 1880; these came into being in the Dunker church in the 1920's.[5] Expert guidance was accepted by the American parents around 1904; articles of this type did not appear with regularity in the Dunker media until the 1930's.[6] And Kett indicates that "remote governance" gave way to detailed nurturing of the children around 1850 in the United States, but the Dunkers retained this until 1900 and beyond.[7] Remote governance is an apt term which somewhat describes the relationship between the Dunker parent and child. However, Kett says that this describes a relationship similar to that between the governor and the governed. This relationship is so remote that there are no emotional bonds.[8] At this point, the term fails for the Dunkers. There were certainly emotional bonds between parent and child, but the relationship was distant enough so that there was little ego entanglement.

This lag in adopting the forms and practices of the outside world by the sectarian minds was part of the defense mechanisms which maintained the purity of their subculture. These dates indicate the lag time between the Dunker and the outside culture's progress. However, these relate to what the church was able to do in external programs. They do not tell of the progress of the mind of the average member as he evolved from the sectarian mentality to that of the church mentality. It was his state of mind which affected the child the most, and this state did not change as rapidly as did the external manifestations.

But to be true to the core scripture, Luke 6:45, there could be no lag in matters concerning the person as an individual. The early acceptance of co-education and the continued use of a childrearing method which provided "space" for their children attest to the importance of the person in their view of the Christian life.

The subculture of the Dunkers, then, produced an environment during the period of the study which had as constants, the two major ingredients that historically determined the status of the child. In addition, the religious influence with its accent on the person changed little. And the cultural lag phenomenon, aided by the constraints of the order, worked to keep these elements in place.

A Time of Change

As the order developed towards the end of the eighteenth century, the farm and its related occupations were favored as a means of maintaining group purity because of the simplicity of the existence and the psychological isolation it provided. The rural work form was considered the ideal and perhaps the only work form which would pass the values of the elderly to the young. When this became part of the order around 1800, the economic base of the Dunkers could be considered a designated tool of childrearing. And the child's value as an economic asset increased.

That the child was accorded such a high status in the Dunker world was due in part to his value as an economic asset. After 1900, the non-farm economic aspirations of the adult, causing a corresponding decrease in the value of the child, reduced the child to a less favorable position. The parent who worked in a mill did not need the large, home-grown, unpaid force to help with the support of the family. To the extent that there was no work for the child, he became an economic liability. In addition, as the parent pursued non-farm occupations and left the side of the child whom he formerly trained to labor, he lost a perspective which had made him feel comfortable in his authority over the child. This occurred mostly after 1900.

There were other changes. The order had provided a visible sign of conformity to the ancient rules of the brethren. Therefore, this conformity was a statement for all to see that the family with its children lived in the approved way, a sign that the parents were rearing their children in keeping with scriptural admonition. The loss of this objective criteria as the order disintegrated posed grave questions for the parents. Was the child in a factory suit equal to the child in the garb? Could the interest in reading the Bible be shared with a good novel? Did the child lose some of his sectarian sheen of holiness when he rubbed against the school children from the outside? These were most difficult for the sectarians to answer.

Again, these questions were posed to the Dunkers in the last several decades of the nineteenth century and the answers became more urgent in the first three decades of the twentieth century. Despite the urgency, there is no indication that there was a dramatic change in the parent-child relationship, even with the loss of their signs during the time of this study. Certainly, the Dunkers had not materially changed their perception of the child, and they did not relinquish their responsibility to rear them even though this sharing of responsibilities had begun in the outside world.* Though the parents still felt responsible, more and more,

---

* The period of infanticide, because of the Christian influence, ended after the life of Christ, to be followed by a method of rejection more acceptable to the Christian conscience, physical abandonment. This ended around 1400, followed by a period of ambivalence in which the adults tried to deal with the realities of the child. Can it be that

their children were influenced by agencies over which they had no control. The parents did not understand the response of the children to these outside influences. They had lost the sign of the order. Activities such as dancing had gained respectability as they were incorporated into the programs of the schools. Closer contact developed between the Dunker young and their outside friends. And the better educated young people questioned the farm and church values of their lesser educated parent. This inability to understand the thoughts and activities of the young people led the leaders of the sect to proclaim that a "youth problem" existed and that church programs were necessary to solve these.

Adjustment to Pressures for Change

The society of industrial America did cause the Dunkers to adjust external practices in their care and nurture of the children. Two questions are pertinent to this. Why were they able to keep the proper distance and perspective for almost one hundred eighty years which allowed or enabled them to feel comfortable with their children and confident that the guidance of the parents was sufficient? For completeness, despite repetition, the entire eight reasons will be listed: 1) the concept of the child as an individual and the nuclear family as a sentimental unit had evolved in the German culture from which the Dunkers came; 2) the Pietistic concept of the worth of the individual; 3) absence of dogma calling for the subordination of the individual to organization; 4) economic opportunities which made the child an asset; 5) interpretation of the scriptures which called for the parents to care for and to nurture the child; 6) operation of the farm provided checks and balances for the children, relieving the parents of the need to be on the children's "case" all the time; 7) the farm as an economic unit allowed each individual of that unit to enjoy his or her own space—ego boundaries were

---

the adult was not able to deal with these realities, and, in the 1800's began a period which continues today, emotional abandonment? Putting blame on the parents removes the necessity to face up to the reality of the child's nature; making him co-equal in decision-making takes part of the responsibility for his care from the adult and places it on the child.

observed; 8) the reassuring and visible sign of the order.

And then the next question: Why did they relinquish part of their responsibility for religious training to the church, and then in rapid succession, accept periodicals, high school and college education, extracurricular activities in school, and later, summer camps for the youths? In this, they transferred some of their authority to the Sunday School teacher, the high school teacher, the coach, and the camp counselor. Of even more importance, they relinquished the minds of their children from the example of the parents and from the constant discipline of the farm life.

The objective historian might conclude that, even among people with the religious basis of the Dunkers, the decreased value of the child as an economic asset changed their parents' perception of them: since they were not needed to help the adults as much, they were shunted aside to other agencies. The formula of the ages revisited. And this might have some truth in it. It also might be argued that, psychologically, the Dunker parent of the early era did not have to come to grips with the reality of the child, because the farm environment contained those aspects of the child's nature which seem so troublesome to adults. There may be some truth to this. So one could conclude that their yielding to outside influences represented a weakness in their perception of the child as they were confronted, for the first time, with the child who sought his own self-interests. This is unlikely.

With the possibility that the subjectivity of the birthright Brethren has tainted his reasoning, the author suggests: 1) that the basic orientation of the adult to the child did not change; 2) that release of the child was because of better economics; maltreatment and rejection of the child have usually been in times of poor economic circumstances; 3) that the dynamics of the family allowed this increased scope; 4) that this was consistent with the theology of the group—the purposeful life—when these activities related to personal development; 5) that this was aided by the freedom traditionally given the teenager when he was not needed for family work.

In short, this release of the children to the outside seemed to be an orderly, logical reaction to changing sociological conditions and in keeping with the aims of the Dunkers in their childrearing efforts, not a denigration of the essential child. It is not held, though, that the process was painless or easy, either for

PLATE 22. A missionary couple whose clothes illustrate detail —1906

PLATE 23. The Bull Run Church, Fairfax County, Virginia

the parent or for the child.

Of the infant, child, and teenager, adjustments required by the changing times affected the teenager most.

Three Periods of the Dunker Teenager

While the childrearing environment remained relatively constant over the one hundred eighty years span, the imposition of the order and the emergence of the industrial economy caused the leadership of the Dunkers to alter somewhat the way in which they viewed the teenager and his family.

Kett gives a fascinating account of the history of the adolescent years in his "Rites of Passage."[9] He describes two stages: the preindustrial adolescent and the industrial. Briefly, he reasons that the preindustrial adolescent was viewed as an adult because the farm economy of the day allowed him to participate as an adult. When the industrial era began around 1840, there was no place for the under-sixteen in the industrial setting. So, instead of moving from the partial nurture of the family at age twelve to full production at age fourteen, the young had a period of having no place in the economic, and therefore, social system of the country. He was in limbo. An educational system was developed to provide him with the skills by which he could enter the work force at eighteen or twenty-one. By entering this educational system, his age of dependency was prolonged and, therefore, he assumed a heretofore non-designated status—adolescence. He had developed his adult values by participating in work and in play with adults on a relatively equal basis. In his newly imposed state of prolonged dependency, this relationship was not available to him. In reaction to this, he gathered with others of his age in groups with adult structure but not in adult purpose or discipline—the so-called gangs. Society reacted to this with adult-sponsored activities designed to socialize these semi-dependents with the values of the day.

This evolution was not completed before 1900 in the Dunker subculture. However, there were changes in the perception of the teenager and his relationship with his parents by the sect as an organization. While these changes did not involve the love and sentimentality afforded the teenager, and affected him little otherwise, they did indicate that the process had begun to bring the Dunker young into Kett's flow of events.

In the first period, from 1723 until 1800, the adolescent was viewed as an adult and had the social prerogatives of that age. Control of his behavior by his father was minimal, though he was bound by an economic contract until the age of "setting free." Thus, in this period, the adolescent's status in the family related primarily to economics. In the second period, from 1800 to 1870, an additional factor was introduced into this relationship. The developing order, which had begun with the sect's formation but did not become a major factor in the life of the sect until around 1820, required that the father exert control over the social behavior of his children "while under lawful age." According to this, the activities of the Dunker teenager should be guided somewhat by the rules followed by the adult members of the sect. Therefore, the relationship of the teenager to his parents now contained two areas of control: economic and social. In the third period, 1870 and beyond, this relationship continued, but a third factor was introduced. Now, the father not only had an economic contract with his son with an obligation to monitor his social activities, he also was pressured by the leaders of the sect to view his children as "splendid prospects for the future." This required a more positive effort to help the young people develop their potential in a larger sense, far outside their previous world of church and farm.

Previous references indicate these three periods, while real from the perspective of the sectarian organization, were not as real in the ongoing cultural progress of the Dunkers. The economic contract held constant, but social control was minimal to 1900. And only the groundwork was laid after 1870 to afford larger vistas of life to the farm youth. Though the perceptions by the leaders of the sect had changed, the basic cultural determinant, economics, had not changed enough to cause or permit changes in the parenting practices of the members. Parenthetically, this is an example of a pitfall in the research of childhood— what would seem to be the life of the child is not always the child's experience.

With their society predominantly rural even until 1900, the Dunkers did not have this problem of the semi-dependent teenager, described by Kett, because there was always something for him to do on the Dunker farm. Despite urbanization, even as late as the 1930's, vestiges of the eighteenth and nineteenth

PLATE 24. Class of 1918, Hebron Seminary, Nokesville, Virginia

PLATE 25. Reunion of the Emmanuel Blough family of Pennsylvania—1903

century perception of the teenager as an adult persisted. In one family, a fourteen-year-old boy asked his mother why he did not have rules of conduct like his friends. She said that if, at his age, he did not know the difference between right and wrong, what she said would make no difference. This indicates that she considered him a functional moral unit, an attribute of an adult. But, of course, she still controlled him to a great extent. This control was evident in another family: the teenagers were never specifically forbidden to do anything. Yet, as they remembered, they usually did what their parents wanted them to do.

But after 1900, the leaders of the sect thought that there was a "youth problem." After a decade or so of efforts, the Brethren Young People's Department (BYPD) and the camping program were established in the 1920's.[10] The adult-sponsored and directed programs were not to socialize them to the Protestant-oriented secular values of the day, but to conserve them for membership with its requirements in the now-called Church of the Brethren.

Non-Retention of Children as Members

The way in which the preschooler was trained determined what values would be internalized in the sectarian child. The way in which the teenager related to his family determined to some extent whether these internalized values were sufficiently strong to guide him in a path acceptable to the family values. Generally speaking, if he deviated too far from these values, he was lost to the church as an adult. There were exceptions to this, of course. But many of the Dunker children, despite their training, did not become members.

There were a number of reasons for this. Since it was a believer's church and a person became a member because he wanted to, a positive commitment was needed to make the person take the step. This step was not taken lightly. Therefore, there were many who did not receive the stimulus, either of devout conviction or of psychological trauma, to push them into the commitment. A companion to this reason was the reluctance of some to fully accept the order, or a reluctance to accept the order with less than full commitment. A somewhat contemporary story speaks to this: A young Brethren man had joined but did not attend regularly, apparently because of some disagreement with the rules. He finally transferred his membership to the Methodist church. His aged grandmother, whom one would think would be an argumentative defender of Dunkerism, approved of this. Instead of being hurt and dismayed, she said, "That's all right. If you can't be a good Brethren, be a good Methodist."

Another reason why many of the young did not join the Dunker church in the early period was the isolation of those families who moved away to the better prospects in the virgin lands of the receding West. In many cases, there were too few families to form a congregation, so these, with no proscription against attending services of another denomination, were gradually weaned away. With few families in the area, marriageable mates were found in other denominations, and the couples attended those churches.

One reason for non-retention of members is rarely mentioned: Some people do not feel the need of religious experiences through the organized church. They receive the life values from their parents, they may be in harmony with the ethical and religious values of the church, but they do not feel the need for the constant reinforcement and spiritual nurture which is associated with regular church attendance. There were some of these among the Dunkers in this period, indicated by a number of birthright Dunkers seeking baptism at the age of forty or fifty years.

All of these reasons have been given for the loss of potential members from among the pool of children born to the birthright Dunkers or to long-term converts before 1900. Even the geographic isolation was a factor for the entire period, because many of the states where the Dunkers went to find cheaper and better land were sparsely settled in the early twentieth century. But in the last three decades of the nineteenth century, three additional reasons have been proposed.

First, the continuing and somewhat restrictive order was not well accepted by a percentage of those who, through schools and work, related better to the non-sectarian life. Church council minutes of the 1920's contain instances of sanctions being applied to young ladies who wore fancy hats. Jewelry was still considered evidence of pride. Second, some of the youths, particularly after 1850, who went off to state colleges, tended to identify with other denominations. And, third, the lure of jobs in the cities isolated the young people, not on the frontier, but in the urban areas where the Dunkers were not represented.

The loss of potential members is serious to the growth of any religious organization, church or sect, but to the Dunkers, it was quite serious. They were evangelical during most of the period under discussion, and, in some decades, were very successful in increasing membership by adding members from the outside population. But the strictness of the order as perceived by the potential converts and the prevalence of the "Dutch" dialect held this number down. The children, then, were an even more valuable source of future members. Of even greater importance, these were the conduits through which the cultural values of the "ancient brethren" could most easily be passed from generation to generation. This was self-evident, yet the organized effort to keep this conduit in place did not begin until after 1900.

This free and easy option process was not all bad. A minority group must maintain, to be effective, a distinct identity and a tension with the majority group. It may be that the children who purposefully elected to keep their ties with the "Order of the Ancient Brethren" fitted into this distinct identity, thus maintaining the group for a period longer than had efforts been made to bring in the marginal conformers. In any event, Eby pointed out that the Dunker purpose in life was to make this a better world (of course, along Dunker principles). The children, reared in the Dunker tradition, though stripped of the trappings of the order, carried these values into the world. In this way, part of the Pietistic mission was accomplished.

10

Childrearing

Within a constant environment of economics and maternal influence, the Dunker childrearing practices embraced two principles. The first, respect for the child as an individual, runs strongly through these beliefs: that he was from God with a worth intrinsic to his origin, was born innocent, had capabilities which should be developed, and had a right to freedom of choice in his selection of religion and occupation. The second principle was that the parents were responsible for the physical and spiritual needs of their children through the governance of their family and the conduct of their lives. Parenthetically, it is noted that the emotional needs of the children received scant consideration. This is not surprising because the parent's emotional lives took second rank to the demands of the farm and to the necessity of making a living.

In addition to these basic views of the child, age-related capabilities were recognized. This may not seem significant unless one recognizes that, at that time, the intelligensia of the outside world in America was imputing capabilities and characteristics to the child that he did not have and presumed for themselves the capability to mold character, enhance intelligence, increase performance, all of this in disregard of the true nature and capacity of the child at varying ages. This perception of the malleability of the child reached its height in the second and third decades of the twentieth century. One investigator of advice given by the experts on childrearing characterized the child of that era as the "mechanical child" because, as the experts said, with the proper parental input the child could be made into anything the parents desired. Perhaps a classic example of this is bowel "training." Parents were told to begin this futile exercise at fourteen months despite the fact that the child is not physiologically ready until around two years of age.

Despite the Dunkers' wish to propagate their sect and its way of life, they did not follow the experts' advice of detailed nuturing and guaranteed results. Rather, they continued to view their young as developing individuals who needed nurturing and circumscribed controls. Within these controls was the child's space where he was allowed to grow into a self-determined adult.

The Dunker method of childrearing was based on the two principles given above. To imply, however, that the Dunkers constructed this method to embrace the principles is to ignore the history of children. In it, the children usually fell through the cracks of the adult worlds and where and how they landed depended on factors extraneous to them. This may have been true to some extent in the world of the German Baptist Brethren. Only, in this instance, the outside factors and the cultural and religious beliefs interacted to produce a favorable environment with few cracks. Even though their theology cast the child in a most favorable light, they still had to adjust to economic realities, mainly that they were by background and perhaps temperament suited to the rural life and that this life provided the most opportunities in early America. As successive generations of under-educated, trained-for-the-farm young people came along, this rural life continued as an economic necessity, thus perpetuating the childrearing practices.

Childrearing Methods of the Dunkers

And there is one last question: How did the Dunkers utilize these principles to rear their children? To introduce this, the analogy of the puppy, yard, and house is instructive.

The owner of the puppy that is kept mostly in the fenced-in back yard seldom complains about the antics of the young pet. But if the puppy lives in the house, tales of chewed shoes, messed-up carpets, vomitus, and hair are heard. Why is this? The openness of the back yard contains the natural tendencies of the immature animal. But if the puppy is brought into the inside, which is structured to the wishes of the owner, the puppy's natural and uninhibited tendencies will cause him to run afoul of the rules of the household. Confrontation between the pet and owner results. Contests of wills occur and, in this, there are always winners and losers. Each adapts to the stress of the conflict with behavior that may not be optimal, and relationships deteriorate. It is from this analogy that the Dunker method of childrearing will be presented: their children were reared in the back yard.

The farm was the back yard, giving the space which allowed the natural tendencies of the young to be expressed without minute-by-minute collisions with the rules of the adults. It was within this openness that the parent-child relationships were developed and which made possible the value-transferring mechanisms employed by the Dunkers. The non-verbal and stern demeanor of the typical father, the controlling but compassionate attitude of the mother, the work ethic derived from both religious belief and economic necessity, and the respect for the individual which seemed inherent in those of the Dunker sect rounded out the environment in which the affective and cognitive components of the child developed.

Methods of childrearing can be grouped into two categories. The first, macromethods in which the influences brought to bear are not targeted just to the child, but affect the child as well as the other members of the family. The second, micromethods, is made up of influences or actions which are designed for a specific child, either to persuade the child towards a mode of behavior or in reaction to an act of the child. The Dunkers relied on macromethods primarily with a lesser use of the micromethods.

These are the components of the macromethods available to and used by the Dunkers:

1. Environment—rural isolation with the demands of the farm provided a milieu favorable to the transference of the Dunker way of life. This can be regarded as a designed method of childrearing; the Dunkers selected this life because it provided the values and a protection of those values which they held important. For most of the period, they discouraged other ways of life.

2. Economic—the concept of the simple life, applying to all members of the family, instilled in the children scriptural values relating to pride and priorities and included the more secular values of frugality, conservation of assets, and stewardship of earnings.

3. Church Order—while this did not apply specifically to children until they became members, its presence was always felt as they saw the older people in conversation, garb, and worship.

4. Kinship Grouping—"The all seeing eyes of the sisters" as well as the brothers, many of whom were related to the child, posed a deterrent to actions which were not in keeping with the way that a child of that family group was supposed to act. On the positive side, the approval of relatives and other members of the family was uplifting and reinforced expected behavior. On the negative side, this constant surveillance was chafing to the teenage spirit of adventure and taste for the new or for the forbidden.

5. Perceived Authority of the Parents—in a popular movie, as the division was moving into battle, the colonel said to the general, "Your men fear you more than they do the enemy." The general replied, "Yes, and I hope to God that they continue to do so." Fear caused the soldiers to obey the general without question, a condition necessary to execute the battle plan and win the victory. The general was not so tough and fearsome, but the soldiers perceived him to be so. Much of the same attitude prevailed among the Dunker children. This enabled their parents to maintain effective control based on this perceived authority.

6. Obeisance to the Senior Members of the Sect—approval of the senior members was prized by the children and was particularly effective as a control mechanism because of the generational distance.

7. Example as a means of transferring values was, of course, the major macromethod. This has been discussed in previous chapters.

Although, at times, the macromethod might seem to fit the definition of the micromethod, there is a clear distinction. A member of a local Amish group, whose culture roughly approaches that of the Dunkers of the later 1800's, had children growing into their teenage years. He had worked as a highly skilled carpenter. Nevertheless, he gave up this trade and started into the more risky septic tank business because his children could work with him in that business. As he said, "My children are getting to the age where they need to work with me." His change in occupation related to the children, but it altered the environment for the whole family. Later, he moved to another area and went into chicken growing as his children entered the marrying stage. Undoubtedly, he used specific methods as he "trained his children to labor"; one of the major methods was the changed environment.

These macromethods had this in common: they provided freedom of movement, both of body and mind, yet controlled within the bounds necessary for the material and spiritual welfare of the group. This controlled freedom contrasted with the developing concept of minute control of each and every action of the child, the so-called detailed nurturing.

But, of course, macromethods were not enough; micromethods had to be used on occasions. The Dunkers used these as they brought their children from infancy to adulthood. In the rather detailed accounts of Blough, Eby, Ziegler, and Wampler, however, there are few references to specific actions. Beahm was dunked into the rain barrel; Ziegler was tethered to a tree; Wampler lovingly protected by his mother with her remark that she hoped that he would be a fisherman of men; and Eby and most of the others were occasionally spanked. The absence of reference to specific events indicates that either there was little of this type of interaction or that it was of such a nature and intensity that it made little impression on the child. In terms of its results on the psyche, either would have the same significance.

Of the micromethods, punishment, instruction, and psychic control were mentioned most often.

1. Punishment—spanking as a means of punishment was used by both mother and father; threats of spanking were also used. These did not seem a preferred method, particularly on the part of the father, and by neither as the child grew older.
2. Oral Communications—this was another micromethod used by the Dunkers to train their children. When used, it was more in a conversational, nondirected, perhaps cryptic mode than in a teaching mode. Understanding was not important; doing was.
3. Psychic Control—control of the child by the manipulation of the conscience and the associated guilt was the primary micro-method used by the Dunkers. It was used by both mother and father on children of all ages.

From these micromethods, an implementing principle can be identified in the first and second: preserve the ego boundaries of the child. Because of the lack of repetitive interaction, where the parent was "on the child's case all the time," these boundaries were seldom invaded and provided "space" of his own for the child.

However, psychic control may create problems. This method is intrusive; it can destroy ego boundaries; it can stifle initiative; and it can produce emotional cripples. For the most part, the Dunkers avoided this. If a parent sharpens and strengthens the child's perception of himself as an individual, the child will gain the inner strength and stability to escape this control when he matures. It is in this area that the subtleties of the Dunker childrearing possessed uniqueness which struck a balance between control and ego strength resulting in individual competence as an adult of their time and place. From this method an implementing principle is identified: develop the child's sense of self-worth.

Within these methods was the attitude of positive expectation, so striking, so constant, and so identifiable that it has to be considered a significant part of the Dunker childrearing process.

Escape Mechanism

An oft-stated aim in disciplines dealing with children is that each child should have the opportunity to develop to his fullest potential. An overtone to these statements of aim is that there is, in each child, a potential for brilliance which, if developed, could materially improve the life of our society. This is a lofty position, hard to fault. The realty, though, is that there is only a small percent of the children at the top who, through intellectual attributes, talents, personality, or character, are capable of making a major impact on society. The lower ten percent or so will be economic wards of the world in which they live. The majority of children fall in between these extremes; their contribution will be to provide the economic basis and to continue the values and traditions of the culture into which they were born. This, of course, is a worthy contribution; otherwise, there would be economic anarchy and continuity and stability of values would be lost. So it is important that our training of children prepare them for this role, recognizing that among those children will be some who are more capable. The critical point is whether a system of training has an escape mechanism that will allow those who can achieve the extraordinary to do so.

It is suggested that the Dunkers' approach to rearing children included this escape mechanism. Their purpose was to inculcate the values of their order into the children and that they were effective in this is shown by the existence of the sect for over one hundred and eighty years. But the control that they exerted to keep their children in the "Order of the Ancient Brethren" was loose enough to allow those who could not adapt to the sectarian existence to find their own place in the outside world. Of importance is that there was little alienation when this occurred. This thesis cannot be tested on those born prior to 1850; accounts of their lives are not available. However, a number of Dunkers born after 1850, particularly after 1880, have achieved significant status in the fields of education, science, government, business, and in the higher levels of organized Christianity. Some of these left the sect; others did not. They were indoctrinated to continue the sect, but the escape mechanism was there.

The German Baptist Brethren lived in difficult times: persecution in Europe, ocean crossings, frontier hazards, shifting political and religious doctrines, wars, and the development of industrial America with its concurrent assimilation of diverse groups of immigrants. They survived and prospered despite these obstacles, due no doubt to their work ethic and religious convictions. To these should be added their approach to childrearing. This provided the bridge between generations and continued in these successive generations the values of the Order of the Ancient Brethren.

Footnotes

Chapter 1

1. For detailed accounts of the sect the reader is referred to: Martin G. Brumbaugh, *A History of the Brethren.* (Mount Morris, Illinois: the Brethren Publishing House, 1899); Donald F. Durnbaugh, *European Origins of the Brethren.* (Elgin, Illinois: The Brethren Press, 1958); Donald F. Durnbaugh, *The Brethren in Colonial America.* (Elgin, Illinois: The Brethren Press, 1967); Roger E. Sappington, *The Brethren in the New Nation.* (Elgin, Illinois: The Brethren Press, 1976): and Emmert F. Bittinger, *Heritage and Promise.* (Elgin, Illinois: The Brethren Press), 1970.
2. Philippe Aries, *Centuries of Childhood.* (New York: Alfred A. Knopf, 1962), pp. 154-177.
3. George H. Payne, *The Child in Human Progress.* (New York: The Knickerbocker Press), pp. 277-283.
4. Harold J. Grimm, *The Reformation Era 1500-1650.* (New York: The MacMillan Company, 1954), p. 226.
5. Elmer T. Clarke, *The Small Sects in America.* (Abington-Cokesbury Press, 1937). This text has provided the material for discussion of sect and church. Psychological implications of religion are from Comprehensive Textbook of Psychiatry 11, Alfred M. Freedman, Ed., Baltimore, Maryland. The William and Wilkins Co., 2nd Edition.
6. "Order" is defined in Webster's Seventh New Collegiate Dictionary as a group of people united under the same religious principles. Another meaning, also fitting the Dunkers' use of the word, is "the rule of law or proper authority."
7. J. Carson Miller, *Fifty Years in the Service of the Church.* (The Gospel Messenger, Volume 90, No. 24, June 14, 1941), p. 5.
8. Hillel Schwartz, "Early Anabaptist Ideas About the Nature of Children" The Mennonite Quarterly Review, Volume 47, April 1973. pp. 102-114. Hereafter referred to as Schwartz, "Early Anabaptist Ideas.".
9. Mark Holloway, *Heavens on Earth.* (New York, New York: Dover Publications, Inc., 1966), p. 29.

10. Henry Kurtz, *The Brethren Encyclopedia.* (Columbiana, Ohio, 1867), Printed by W.S. Haven, Pittsburgh, Pennsylvania. See pages 101-104 for decisions of the AM relating to slavery (1782-1863). This is a collection of the minutes of the Yearly Meeting of the Dunkers from 1778 to 1866 with some interpretive notes and miscellaneous documents. Hereafter referred to as Henry Kurtz, *The Brethren Encyclopedia.*
11. Henry Kurtz, *The Brethren Encyclopedia*, pp. 20-23.
12. Henry Kurtz, *The Brethren Encyclopedia*, p. 182.
13. Henry Kurtz, *The Brethren Encyclopedia.* See pages 188 and 189 for decisions of the AM relating to tobacco (1817-1864).
14. Henry Kurtz, *The Brethren Encyclopedia.* To understand the position of avoidance in the sect, read the editorial comments of Kurtz on pp. 25-28.

Chapter 2

1. Henry R. Holsinger, *History of the Tunkers.* (Oakland, California: Pacific Press Publishing Company, 1901), p. 805.
2. Kermit Eby, *For Brethren Only.* (Elgin, Illinois: The Brethren Press, 1958, p. 56. (Kermit Eby was Professor, Department of Social Science, the University of Chicago. Prior to that, he was Director of Education for the CIO. He was an ordained minister in the Church of the Brethren.) Hereafter referred to as Kermit Eby, *For Brethren Only.*
3. Kermit Eby, *For Brethren Only*, p. 56.
4. A letter from W.K. Conner to his brother, in the possession of the author.
5. John S. Flory, *H.C. Early.* (Elgin, Illinois: The Brethren Publishing House, 1943), p. 136.
6. Lawrence W. Schultz, *People and Places.* (Winona Lake, Indiana: Life & Light Press, 1971), p. 16. Hereafter referred to as Lawrence W. Schultz, *People and Places.*
7. Eleanor J. Brumbaugh, *Peter's Mouth.* (The Gospel Messenger, Volume 81, No. 29, July 16, 1932).
8. Jesse H. Ziegler, *The Broken Cup.* (Elgin, Illinois: The Brethren Publishing House, 1942), p. 116. Hereafter referred to as Jesse H. Ziegler, *The Broken Cup.*
9. Henry Kurtz, *The Brethren Encyclopedia*, p. 189.
10. Jesse H. Ziegler, *The Broken Cup*, p. 116.
11. *History of the Church of the Brethren in Illinois by Committee.* (Winona Lake, Indiana: Light & Life Press, 1952), p. 304.
12. Roger E. Sappington, *The Brethren in the New Nation.* (Elgin, Illinois: The Brethren Press, 1976), p. 55.

13. Bess Royer Bates, *Life of D.L. Miller.* (Elgin, Illinois: The Brethren Publishing House, 1924), p. 19.
14. J.H. Moore, *The Boy and the Man.* (Elgin, Illinois: The Brethren Publishing House, 1923), p. 30.
15. *History of the Church of the Brethren, Eastern Pennsylvania 1915-1965,* Advisory Board District Historical Committee. (Printed by Torry and Hacker, Lancaster, Pennsylvania, 1965), p. 248.
16. Elmer Q. Gleim, *Change and Challenge.* (Harrisburg, Pennsylvania: Triangle Press, 1973), p. 345.
17. Kermit Eby, *For Brethren Only,* p. 277.
18. Edward K. Ziegler, *A Tapestry of Grace.* (Elgin, Illinois: The Brethren Press), p. 18. Hereafter referred to as Edward K. Ziegler, *A Tapestry of Grace.*
19. Bess Royer Bates, *Life of D.L. Miller.* (Elgin, Illinois: The Brethren Publishing House, 1924), p. 42.
20. Mary Ann Moyer Kulp, *No Longer Strangers.* (Elgin, Illinois: The Brethren Press, 1924), p. 20.
21. Esther L. Irvine, *Joseph Glick Family Scrapbook.* 1961, pp. 290-291.
22. Ruel B. Pritchett, *On the Ground Floor of Heaven.* (Elgin, Illinois: The Brethren Press, 1980), p. 3. (With Dale Aukermann.) Hereafter referred to as Ruel B. Pritchett, *On the Ground Floor of Heaven.*
23. Edward K. Ziegler, *A Tapestry of Grace,* p. 36.
24. Jerome Blough, Typescript, p. 36.
25. Paul H. Bowman, *Criticism of Modern Youth.* (The Gospel Messenger, Volume 77, No. 3, August 4, 1928), p. 487.
26. The Sabbath Recorder, Volume IV, July 13, 1848, p. 14.
27. Henry Kurtz, *The Brethren Encyclopedia,* pp. 180-181.
28. Mary Early Davis, typescript.
29. Jerome Blough, typescript.
30. H. Austin Cooper, *Two Centuries of Brothersvalley.* (Westminster, Maryland: The Times, Inc., 1962), pp. 219-221. Hereafter referred to as H. Austin Cooper, *Two Centuries of Brothersvalley.*
31. H. Austin Cooper, *Two Centuries of Brothersvalley,* p. 221.
32. Henry Kurtz, *The Brethren Encyclopedia,* p. 119.
33. V.F. Schwalm, *Otho Winger.* (Elgin, Illinois: The Brethren Publishing House, 1952), p. 27.
34. H. Austin Cooper, *Two Centuries of Brothersvalley,* p. 27.
35. Lawrence W. Schultz, *People and Places,* p. 16.
36. Ruel B. Pritchett, *On The Ground Floor to Heaven,* p. 6.

Chapter 3

1. Henry Kurtz, *The Brethren Encyclopedia*, pp. 86-87.
2. When not annotated, references to decisions of the Annual Meeting may be found in Minutes of the Annual Meetings, 1778-1909. (Elgin, Illinois: The Brethren Publishing House), 1909. Published by the General Mission Board, the articles are listed under the year of enactment.
3. The Gospel Visitor Vol. VIII, September, 1858 No. 9, Columbiana, Columbiana County, Ohio, pp. 259-261.

Chapter 4

1. Schwartz, "Early Anabaptist Ideas," p. 108.
2. P.H. Beery, The Gospel Messenger, Volume 16, Old Series, June 19, 1888, p. 371.
3. Schwartz, "Early Anabaptist Ideas." p. 114.
4. Donald F. Durnbaugh, *European Origins of the Brethren.* (Elgin, Illinois: The Brethren Press, 1958), p. 311.
5. Donald F. Durnbaugh (ed.), *The Brethren in Colonial America.* (Elgin, Illinois: The Brethren Press, 1967), pp. 274-275.
6. Jerome Blough, Typescript.
7. Donald F. Durnbaugh (ed.), *The Brethren in Colonial America.* (Elgin, Illinois: The Brethren Press, 1967), pp. 274-275.
8. Donald F. Durnbaugh (ed.), *The Brethren in Colonial America.* (Elgin, Illinois: The Brethren Press, 1967), p. 276.
9. *Our Young Men and Women.* (The Gospel Messenger, Volume 33 Old Series, June 29, 1895), p. 73.
10. Roger E. Sappington, *The Brethren in the New Nation.* (Elgin, Illinois: The Brethren Press, 1976), p. 34.
11. Bess Royer Bates, *Life of D.L. Miller.* (Elgin, Illinois: The Brethren Publishing House, 1924), p. 28.
12. Minor C. Miller, *These Things I Remember.* (Philadelphia, Pennsylvania: Dorrance & Company, 1968), p. 49.
13. Edward K. Ziegler, *Tapestry of Grace*, p. 17.
14. Jerome Blough, Typescript.
15. Minor C. Miller, *These Things I Remember.* (Philadelphia, Pennsylvania: Dorrance & Company, 1968), p. 38.
16. Ruel B. Pritchett, *On the Ground Floor of Heaven.* (Elgin, Illinois: The Brethren Press, 1980), p. 1. (With Dale Aukermann).
17. Roger E. Sappington, *The Brethren in the New Nation.* (Elgin, Illinois: The Brethren Press, 1976), p. 68.
18. Kermit Eby, *For Brethren Only*, p. 217.

19. D.L. Miller and Galen B. Royer, *Some Who Led.* (Elgin, Illinois: The Brethren Publishing House, 1912), pp. 97-98.
20. Otho Winger, *Memories of Manchester.* (Elgin, Illinois: The Elgin Press, 1940), pp. 11-12.
21. Mary Early Davis, Typescript.
22. Minnie S. Buckingham, *Church of the Brethren in Southern Illinois.* (Elgin, Illinois: The Brethren Publishing House, 1950), p. 256.
23. Bess Royer Bates, *Life of D.L. Miller.* (Elgin, Illinois: The Brethren Publishing House, 1924), p. 18.
24. U.F. Schwalm, *Albert Cassel Wieand.* (Elgin, Illinois: The Brethren Press, 1960), p. 15.
25. Ralph G. Rarich, *History of the Mississinewa Church of the Brethren.* (Elgin, Illinois: The Brethren Publishing House, 1917), p. 155.
26. Kermit Eby, *For Brethren Only*, p. 148.
27. Roland F. Flory, *Lest We Forget and Tales of Yester-Years Volume III.* (Orlando, Florida: Golden Rule Press, 1973), p. 185.
28. D.L. Miller and Galen B. Royer, *Some Who Led.* (Elgin, Illinois: The Brethren Publishing House, 1912), p. 121.
29. Lawrence W. Schultz, *People and Places.* p. 34.
30. U.F. Schwalm, *Albert Cassel Wieand.* (Elgin, Illinois: The Brethren Press, 1960), p. 17.
31. Bess Royer Bates, *Life of D.L. Miller*, (Elgin, Illinois: The Brethren Publishing House, 1924), p. 34.
32. H. Spenser Minnich, *Brother Bonsack*, (Elgin, Illinois: The Brethren Publishing House, 1954), p. 22.
33. Lawrence W. Schultz, *People and Places*, p. 15.
34. M.G. Brumbaugh, *A History of the Brethren.* (Mount Morris, Illinois: The Brethren Publishing House, 1899), p. 390.
35. E.J. Onkst, *To Mothers, Wives and Daughters.* (The Gospel Messenger Volume 33, January 15, 1895), p. 39.
36. Jesse H. Ziegler, *The Broken Cup*, p. 137.

Chapter 5

1. Bess Royer Bates, *Life of D.L. Miller.* (Elgin, Illinois: The Brethren Publishing House, 1920), p. 13.
2. Jerome Blough, Typescript.
3. Kermit Eby, *For Brethren Only*, pp. 59-60.
4. Edward K. Ziegler, *A Tapestry of Grace*, pp. 33-34.
5. Mary Early Davis, Typescript.
6. Paul H. Bowman, *As I Knew My Father.* (The Gospel Messenger, Volume 82, No. 19, May 13, 1933).

7. Ruel Pritchett, *On the Ground Floor of Heaven*, p. 81.

8. Jerome Blough, Typescript.

9. Glee Yoder, *Passing on the Gift.* (Elgin, Illinois: The Brethren Press), p. 13.

10. Bess Royer Bates, *Life of D.L. Miller.* (Elgin, Illinois: The Brethren Publishing House, 1924), p. 20.

11. Kermit Eby, *For Brethren Only*, p. 213.

12. Earl Fike, *A Raspberry Seed Under God's Denture.* (Elgin, Illinois: The Brethren Press, 1979), p. 18.

13. *History of the Church of the Brethren of the Eastern District of Pennsylvania 1708-1915.* Committee of the District Conference, S.R. Zug, Chairman (Lancaster, Pennsylvania: The New Era Printing Company, 1915), p. 276.

14. Mary Early Davis, Typescript.

15. John S. Flory, *Literary Activity of the Brethren in the Eighteenth Century.* (Elgin, Illinois: The Brethren Publishing House, 1908), p. 242.

16. Roger Sappington, *The Brethren in the New Nation.* (Elgin, Illinois: The Brethren Press, 1976), p. 36.

17. Austin Cooper, *Two Centuries of Brothersvalley*, p. 257.

18. Roland Flory, *Lest We Forget and Tales of Yester-year*, Vol. 3. (Orlando, Florida: Golden Rule Press, 1973), p. 185.

19. Inez Long, *Faces Among the Faithful.* (Elgin, Illinois: The Brethren Press, 1962).

20. Kermit Eby, *For Brethren Only*, p. 120.

21. Minor Miller, *These Things I Remember.* (Philadelphia, Pennsylvania: Dorrance and Company, 1968), p. 64.

22. Ernest M. Wampler, *Seeing God's Will for Me.* (Verona, Virginia: The McClure Printing Company, Inc., 1969), p. 20.

23. Henry Kurtz, *The Brethren Encyclopedia*, p. 181.

24. Martin G. Brumbaugh, *A History of the German Baptist Brethren.* (Mount Morris, Illinois: The Brethren Publishing House, 1899), p. 543.

25. Shirley F. Holmes, *A History of the Church of the Brethren, Midland, Virginia 1883-1973.* (1974), p. 16.

26. Roger E. Sappington, *The Brethren in Bridgewater.* (Harrisonburg, Virginia: Park View Press, 1978), p. 37.

27. Henry Kurtz, *The Brethren Encyclopedia*, p. 185.

28. Anna B. Williams, Typescript.

29. H. Kurtz and J. Quinter, *The Gospel Visitor*, Vol. VIII No. 10. (October 1858), p. 319.

30. Thelma H. Conner, Oral communication.

Chapter 6

1. Frederick D. Dove, *Cultural Changes in the Church of the Brethren.* (Elgin, Illinois: The Brethren Publishing House, 1932), p. 209.

2. Benjamin Funk, *Life of John Kline.* (Elgin, Illinois: The Brethren Publishing House, 1900), p. 20. Hereafter referred to as Benjamin Funk, *Life of John Kline.*

3. Informal survey by author.

4. Frederick D. Dove, *Cultural Changes in the Church of the Brethren.* p. 213. (On p. 212, he notes that in the early days, twenty children to a father was not remarkable.)

5. Jesse H. Ziegler, *The Broken Cup*, p. 68. (This work will be referred to from time to time. It is a doctoral dissertation whose methodology involves personal interviews and is written with an objectivity unusual among Brethren writers of that day. Some references are taken from the charts; others are computed from his data.)

6. Henry Kurtz, *The Brethren Encyclopedia, 1867.*

7. The Pilgrim, Vol. 6, *Memoriam.* (January 5, 1875), pp. 396-397.

8. Benjamin Funk, *Life of John Kline.* p. 17.

9. J.J. Emmert Diary. Brethren Historical Library. (Elgin, Illinois).

10. Primitive Christian, Vol. 2. Letter to the Editor. (January 15, 1878).

11. Roger E. Sappington, *The Brethren in the New Nation.* (Elgin, Illinois: The Brethren Press), p. 95.

12. Edward K. Ziegler, *A Tapestry of Grace.* p. 34.

13. *J.J. Emmert Diary.* Brethren Historical Library. (Elgin, Illinois).

14. Donald F. Durnbaugh, *The Brethren in Colonial America.* (Elgin, Illinois: The Brethren Press, 1967), pp. 238-239.

15. Martin G. Brumbaugh, *A History of the Brethren.* (Mount Morris, Illinois: The Brethren Publishing House, 1906), p. 265.

16. Samuel Flory Family History. Unpublished typescript.

17. Kermit Eby, *For Brethren Only*, p. 94.

18. John P. Demos, *A Little Commonwealth: Family Life in Plymouth Colony.* (New York, N.Y.: Oxford University Press, 1970), p. 121, Barry John Levy, *The Light in the Valley: The Chester & Welsh Tract Quaker Communities and the Delaware Valley 1681-1750.* (University Microfilms International, Ann-Arbor, Michigan), p. 170.

19. Esther L. Irvine, *Joseph Glick Family Scrapbook.* (1961), p. 343.

20. Personal Communication.

21. Jesse H. Ziegler, *The Broken Cup*, p. 104.

22. Jesse H. Ziegler, *The Broken Cup*, p. 104.

23. Jesse H. Ziegler, *The Broken Cup*, p. 104.

24. Jesse H. Ziegler, *The Broken Cup*, p. 104.

25. J.M. Henry, *In Memory of Father.* (The Gospel Messenger, Volume 84 No. 10, March 9, 1935).

26. Lester S. Flory, Typescript.
27. Ruel B. Pritchett, *On the Ground Floor of Heaven*, p. 54.
28. John S. Flory, *H.C. Early.* (Elgin, Illinois: The Brethren Publishing House, 1943), pp. 125-126.
29. *History of the Church of the Brethren, Eastern Pennsylvania 1915-1965*, Advisory Board District Historical Committee. (Printed by Torrey and Hacker, Lancaster, Pennsylvania, 1965).
30. Maggie M. Moomaw, *Experience of a Minister's Wife.* (The Gospel Messenger, Volume 39 No. 1, March 16, 1901), p. 167.
31. Esther L. Irvine, *Joseph Glick Family Scrapbook.* p. 273.
32. Kermit Eby, *For Brethren Only*, p. 97.
33. Earl W. Fike, Jr., *A Raspberry Seed Under God's Denture.* (Elgin, Illinois: The Brethren Press, 1979). (This source has not been quoted extensively because no collateral evidence was found to indicate that Beahm's conflicts as a young man were typical of the Dunker youth of that day.)

Chapter 7

1. *History of the Church of the Brethren, Eastern Pennsylvania 1915-1965*, Advisory Board, District Historical Committee. (Printed by Torrey and Hacker, Lancaster, Pennsylvania, 1965), p. 249.
2. Kermit Eby, *For Brethren Only*, p. 59.
3. Kermit Eby, *For Brethren Only*, pp. 66-67.
4. Robert E. Mohler, *Out on Broad Kansas Plains.* (1969), p. 47.
5. J.Z. Gilbert, *We Are Our Children's Mirror.* (The Gospel Messenger, Volume 91 No. 29, July 18, 1942), p. 12.
6. Jerome Blough, Typescript.
7. Ruel B. Pritchett, *On the Ground Floor of Heaven*, p. 5.
8. Ernest M. Wampler, *Seeking God's Will For Me.* (Verona, Virginia: The McClure Printing Company, Inc. 1969), p. 10.
9. Jerome E. Blough, *History of the Church of the Brethren of the Western District of Pennsylvania.* (Elgin, Illinois: The Brethren Publishing House, 1916), p. 360.
10. Robert E. Mohler, *Out On Broad Kansas Plains.* p. 29.
11. Samuel Weimer, *Experience of Raising Children.* (The Gospel Messenger, Volume 39 No. 6, February 9, 1901), p. 87.
12. Ralph G. Rarick, *History of the Mississinewa.* (Elgin, Illinois: The Brethren Publishing House, 1917), p. 194.
13. J.E. Miller, The Gospel Messenger, November 19, 1932.
14. E.K. Ziegler, *A Tapestry of Grace*, p. 35.
15. Robert E. Mohler, *Out on Broad Kansas Plains.* p. 3.
16. Glee Yoder, *Passing On The Gift.* (Elgin, Illinois: The Brethren Press, 1978), p. 12.

17. Mary Early Davis, Typescript.
18. J.H. Moore, *The Boy and the Man.* (Elgin, Illinois: The Brethren Publishing House, 1923), p. 40.
19. J.H. Moore, *The Boy and the Man.* (Elgin, Illinois: The Brethren Publishing House, 1923), p. 20.
20. John D. Brooks, *The Dunkard Dozen.* (The Gospel Messenger, Volume 79 No. 8, February 22, 1930.
21. T. Richardson Gray, *The Pull of the Lines.* (The Gospel Messenger, Volume 78 No. 32, August 10, 1944), p. 506.
22. E.K. Ziegler, *A Tapestry of Grace*, pp. 27-28.
23. D.W. Bittinger, *Because I Have Commanded You.* (The Gospel Messenger, Volume 93 No. 18, April 29, 1944), p. 4.
24. Glenn Davis, *Childhood and History in America.* (New York, New York: The Psychohistory Press, 1976), p. 45.
25. Glenn Davis, *Childhood and History in America.* p. 60.
26. Glenn Davis, *Childhood and History in America.* p. 60.
27. Isaac A. Abt (ed.), *Abt-Garrison History of Pediatrics.* (Philadelphia, Pennsylvania: W.B. Saunder Company, 1965), p. 156.
28. Isaac A. Abt (ed.), *Abt-Garrison History of Pediatrics.* (Philadelphia, Pennsylvania: W.B. Saunders Company, 1965), p. 121.
29. Isaac A. Abt (ed.), *Abt-Garrison History of Pediatrics.* (Philadelphia, Pennsylvania: W.B. Saunders Company, 1965), p. 106.
30. Henry R. Kurtz, *The Brethren Encyclopedia*, p. 183.
31. Henry R. Kurtz, *The Brethren Encyclopedia*, pp. 183-184.
32. T.S. Moherman (ed.), *A History of the Church of the Brethren Northeastern Ohio.* (Elgin, Illinois: The Brethren Publishing House, 1914), pp. 125-126.
33. A.C. Wieand, *Interesting the Children in Family Worship.* (The Gospel Messenger, Volume 68 No. 35, August 30, 1919), p. 554.
34. Ruel B. Pritchett, *On the Ground Floor of Heaven*, p. 43.
35. J.Z. Gilbert, *We Are Our Children's Mirror.* (The Gospel Messenger, Volume 91 No. 29, July 18, 1942), p. 12.

Chapter 8

1. Lloyd de Mause (ed.), *The History of Childhood.* (New York, New York: The Psychohistory Press, 1974), p. 6. In de Mause's psychogenic theory of childrearing, projection and reversion were the earlier mechanisms of childrearing. The parents' attitude changed towards their children as the centuries passed; projection decreased, reversion almost disappeared, and by the 1700's the psyche of the people was such that they were able to develop empathy for their children. However, projection, perhaps a little less destructive, has continued to be a component of the parent's interaction with their children up

to the present time, according to the de Mause theory.

2. *The Bonsack Papers*. (Manuscript Division, Perkins Library, Duke University).

3. Edward K. Ziegler, *A Tapestry of Grace*, p. 34.

4. Willis P. Rodabaugh and A.H. Brower, *A History of the Church of the Brethren in Southern Iowa*. (Elgin, Illinois: The Brethren Publishing House, 1924), p. 65.

5. J.H. Moore, *The Boy and the Man*. (Elgin, Illinois: The Brethren Publishing House, 1923), p. 31.

6. Edward K. Ziegler, *A Tapestry of Grace*, p. 17.

7. Kermit Eby, *For Brethren Only*, p. 49.

8. Lawrence W. Shultz, *People and Places*, p. 33.

9. Bess Royer Bates, *Life of D.L. Miller*. (Elgin, Illinois: The Brethren Publishing House, 1924), p. 17.

10. Ernest M. Wampler, *Seeking God's Will For Me*. (Verona, Virginia: The McClure Printing Company, Inc., 1969), pp. 1-2.

11. H. Spenser Minnick, *Brother Bonsack*. (Elgin, Illinois: The Brethren Publishing House, 1954), p. 21.

12. Bess Royer Bates, *Life of D.L. Miller*. (Elgin, Illinois: The Brethren Publishing House, 1924), pp. 49-51.

13. Lawrence W. Schultz, *People and Places*, p. 17.

14. Kermit Eby, *For Brethren Only*, p. 59.

15. Ruel B. Pritchett, *On The Ground Floor of Heaven*, p. 8.

16. Earl W. Fike, Jr., *A Raspberry Seed Under God's Denture*. (Elgin, Illinois: The Brethren Press, 1979), p. 20.

17. Mary Ann Moyer Kulp, *No Longer Strangers*. (Elgin, Illinois: The Brethren Press, 1924), p. 21.

18. Roger E. Sappington, *The Brethren in the New Nation*. (Elgin, Illinois: The Brethren Press, 1976), p. 34.

19. Bess Royer Bates, *Life of D.L. Miller*. (Elgin, Illinois: The Brethren Publishing House, 1924), p. 28.

20. Bess Royer Bates, *Life of D.L. Miller*. (Elgin, Illinois: The Brethren Publishing House, 1924), pp. 59-60.

21. Bess Royer Bates, *Life of D.L. Miller*. (Elgin, Illinois: The Brethren Publishing House, 1924), p. 61.

22. Ruel B. Pritchett, *On The Ground Floor of Heaven*, p. 13.

23. Ernest M. Wampler, *Seeking God's Will For me*. (Verona, Virginia: The McClure Printing Company, Inc., 1969), p. 11.

24. Ruel B. Pritchett, *On The Ground Floor of Heaven*, p. 13.

25. Esther L. Irvine, *Joseph Glick Family Scrapbook*, p. 312.

26. *The Gospel Visitor*, Volume XV No. 12, December 1865, pp. 378-379.

Chapter 9

1. Frederick D. Dove, *Cultural Changes in the Church of the Brethren.* (Elgin, Illinois: Thje Brethren Publishing House, 1932), p. 57.
2. Jesse H. Ziegler, *The Broken Cup,* pp. 60-61.
3. Earl C. Kaylor, Jr., *Out of the Wilderness.* (East Brunswick, New Jersey: Cornwall Books, 1981), p. 150.
4. Joseph F. Kett, *Rites of Passage.* (New York, New York: Basic Books, Inc., 1977), p. 117.
5. Joseph F. Kett, *Rites of Passage,* p. 194.
6. Joseph F. Kett, *Rites of Passage,* p. 229.
7. Joseph F. Kett, *Rites of Passage,* p. 172.
8. Joseph F. Kett, Personal communication.
9. Joseph F. Kett, *Rites of Passage,* pp. 215-244.
10. Earl C. Kaylor, Jr., *Out of the Wilderness.* (East Brunswick, New Jersey: Cornwall Books, 1981), pp. 342-343.

Illustrations

Martin G. Brumbaugh wrote the first history of the Brethren in 1906. There are 77 illustrations among its 559 pages, but there are no pictures of people. This was due to the lingering aversion to "graven images" in the church; it may also have been due to the paucity and quality of the pictures available. (Many of the illustrations in this text are not in the correct time frame,) but they show the substance of Brethren life and activities prior to 1900.

Crystal Driver Wakeman and Anna Blough Williams contributed most of the pictures.

PLATE 1. Abram L. Conner was the son of Jesse Conner (Mennonite?) and Susannah Landis (Mennonite) who became members of the German Baptist Brethren sometime after they were married. This family portrait illustrates the gradual disappearance of distinctive dress. Except for W.K. Conner and Dr. S.S. Conner (not pictured), this family lived within 2 miles of each other and attended the Cannon Branch Church. The second generation all married Brethren. This grouping of the family provided security for the young. It also was a stimulus to conform to family values.

Conner Reunion, 1914

Seated: Abraham Conner, Lovina (Kinsel) Conner
Front Row: Harold Conner, Sarah Conner, Joseph Conner, Agnes Thomasson, Elizabeth Thomasson, Etta May Hottle, Clyde Conner, Katherine Conner, Frances Conner, Alice Conner, Gladys Conner, Anna Blough, Leslie Blough
2nd Row: William K. Conner, Mildred (Bowman) Conner, Sally (Conner) Thomasson, Lizzie (Conner) Hottle, Archie Conner, Elmer H. Conner, Jesse J. Conner, Bessie (Kerlin) Conner, Virginia (Hockman) Conner, holding Norma

Conner, Jacob K. Conner, Alice (Conner) Blough, E.E.
Blough
Back Row: W.T. Thomasson, holding Claudia Thomasson, M.J.
Hottle, holding Margaret Hottle, William A. Conner,
Lola Conner, Mildred Conner, Ruth Conner

PLATE 2. Leslie Blough, son of E.E. and Alice Blough, probably
wore a dress until 4 years of age. This custom was not unique to
the Brethren.

PLATE 3. Children's play is used as a diagnostic tool by
psychologists. These Brethren children at play demonstrate
subculture values: non-conformity to the world through distinctive dress and large families, evidenced by the dolls. Rachel
Thrasher (Driver); Crystal Wakeman (Driver); Virginia Merryman;
and Lydia Diehl (Driver).

PLATE 4. Group activities within the congregation were infre-
quent forms of entertainment for the early Dunkers. The church
building was not used for these. Sunday School picnics occurred
mostly after 1900.

PLATE 5. Group activities confined to the young people of the
church were encouraged. These activities provided a matchmak-
ing forum, shown in part by the dress of the group.

PLATE 6. Swimming was enjoyed by the children and young
adults before 1900. No references were found to suggest that this
was a common family recreation, however. The Casper M. Driver
and John DeBolt families enjoyed a swimming outing in 1922.

PLATE 7. Young adults enjoyed skating on ponds and rivers. They
and younger children also had individual sleds as well as the
larger horse-drawn sled to enjoy. Benjamin O. Wakeman, unknown, Levi B. Miller, Russell M. Miller, and Roland Miller.

PLATE 8. Trine immersion forward in a stream of running water
was considered the gospel form of baptism by the Brethren and
was practiced into the 1900's. However, in 1877 the AM validated
baptisms performed in church pools or baptistries, in recognition

of the circumstances of city churches. Baptisms were religious exercises and did not give rise to social celebrations.

PLATE 9. Unlike other sectarians, the Dunkers did not establish exclusive schools to train and educate their young. However, the clustering of their families in one general area caused the enrollment in the public school serving that area to be heavily Brethren. Over half of these students came from Brethren homes.

Cannon Branch School, 1890
Deb Wheeler, teacher
Front Row: Daisy Hornbaker, Myrtle Hornbaker, John Hornkbaker, Warren Baker, Vernie Baker, Roy Baker, Sallie Conner, Samuel Conner, Lizzie Conner, Tommy Gulick, Rennie Gulick, Mamie Gulick, Joseph Gulick, Lizzie Runaldue.
2nd Row: Jesse Conner, Walter Weir, W.B. Baker, Ellie Baker, Amrie Harley, Clara Lamb, Bertie Lamb, Alice Conner, Angie Hornbaker, Jacob Conner, Will Gulick
Back Row: Dean Holsinger, Allen Harley, Will Conner, Eli Holsinger, Bob Weir, Charlie Holsinger, Bill Runaldue

PLATE 10. The Brethren young used what was available in their play. This included walking fence rails, skipping rocks over water, having rock fights, and climbing trees. Of course, John C. Driver had to climb higher than his sisters Bessie Legg (Driver), Rachel Thrasher (Driver), and Lydia Diehl (Driver).

PLATE 11. Although even the smallest was expected to walk the several miles to school, there were times when the weather made this unsafe. Fathers provided riding horses, buggies, or sleds for those occasions. Young boys learned early how to drive a team of horses.

PLATE 12. William T. Kahle discarded his Methodist suit for the Dunker garb after marrying Cynthia Hutchinson. He has a mustache, unusual for a Brethren man during that period.

PLATE 13. Elder Conner became a minister sometime after 1870. Many ceremonies of this period and much later charged the wife to obey her husband. His charge was the same to both: "Be faithful and affectionate, forsake others and cleve one to the other."

PLATE 14. The minister used a riding horse or a horse-drawn carriage of some type while carrying out his duties. In this picture Casper M. Driver and Mabel Layman Driver are going to visit members in the mountains of Greene County, Virginia in 1923. The Reverend Driver was trusted by those who lived in the hollows and could travel freely without fear of being shot. This method of visitation had changed little over the previous two hundred years.

PLATE 15. Orville Hersch and Mabel Harley Hersch taught, farmed, and served the church. Orville accepted the Brethren garb when he married Mabel, a condition imposed when "unequals were yoked." Orville was not reared in the Brethren church, but became an argumentative defender of its practices and beliefs.

PLATE 17. Mabel Layman Driver and toddler Lowell Bollinger feed the chickens behind the parsonage in Greene County, VA in 1922. This early involvement of the child in the work of the day both trained him to labor and developed work habits and values.

PLATE 18. Elmer H. Conner and Jacob K. Conner took pride in their springboard and team of horses. This photograph obviously was taken to show the horses.

PLATE 19. The proscription against photographs (graven images) had weakened by 1895 when Miriam Canard had this studio picture taken. The rule was eliminated in the AM of 1904. Miriam Canard probably donned the garb when she married.

PLATE 20. The students of Juniata College were drawn primarily from Brethren homes. In this group, a variety of dress suggests that most had not accepted the discipline of the dress code. Note the young E.E. Blough with a bow tie and an older E.E. Blough in a previous picture.

Class of 1895—Juniata College

1st Row: Lucy Leatherman (4); Vinnie Mikesell (6); Lena Mohler Johnson (8); Orra Hartle (9)

2nd Row: William L. Shafer (1); Elijah E. Blough (3); Jesse L. Hunsberger (4); Nelson Cupp (5)

3rd Row: John M. Hooley (2); Joseph W. Yoder (4); Edmond Isenberg
     (8)

PLATE 21. Dr. Sanger had an outstanding career in education. His
father, Elder S.F. Sanger, was a minister, businessman, and
churchman. Though from a conforming Dunker family whose
lineage dated back to 1732, the Sanger chidren were allowed to
select their own place in life as well as vocation.

PLATE 22. Jacob M. Blough and Anna (Detwiler) Blough wear the
approved dress of their time. Mr. B.O. Wakeman remembered that
a couple, returning from a long stay in a foreign mission, found
that manufactured clothes had become much less expensive than
the garb. They discarded the garb. This was about 1915.

PLATE 23. The Bull Run Church was built after 1910. It had two
doors, one on the right for the women and one on the left for the
men. The sexes were separated so that "impure" thoughts would
not interfere with worship. The young children sat with their
parents. When older, they were allowed to group in the back rows
on their respective sides.

PLATE 24. Hebron Seminary was among many secondary
schools established by the Brethren before and after 1900 to
prepare Brethren youth for college. The preponderance of girls
suggests that the Brethren believed in equality of sexes and in
co-education.

Class of 1918

1st Row: Mr. Shidler, Pres.; Mrs. Shidler; Mildred Conner; Denise
     Hollinger; Marjorie Graybill; Mabel Pence; Edgar Cari-
     cofe
2nd Row: Mary Sines; Mabel Harley; Russell West; Viola Miller;
     Wilmer Kline; Nora Harley; Lola Conner

PLATE 25: Though the Blough family was traditionally Dunker for
generations, producing farmers, teachers, and preachers, the
members had begun to adopt the modern dress in 1903.

Reunion of the Emmanuel Blough family, 1903

Back Row: E.E. Blough, Alexander Beam, S.S. Blough, Mary (Wertz)
Blough, J. Frank Dietz, J.E. Blough

2nd Row: Alice (Conner) Blough, Amy (Blough) Beam, Emanuel J. Blough, Sally (Barndt) Blough, Jemima (Blough) Dietz, Mollie (Dietz) Blough
Seated in front: J.M. Blough, Anna (Detwiler) Blough

Personal Index

Bibliography

1. Abt, Isaac A., MD (ed) and Abt, Arthur F., MD, *Abt—Garison History of Pediatrics*. Philadelphia, Pennsylvania: W.B, Saunders Co., 1965.
2. Aries, Philippe, *Centuries of Childhood*. New York: Alfred A. Knof, 1962.
3. Arnold, Eberhard, *Children's Education in Community*. Rifton, New York: Plough Publishing House, 1976.
4. Beckman, Daniel, *Mechanical Baby*. West Port, Connecticut: Lawrence Hill and Co., 1977.
5. Billings, W.E., *Tales of the Old Days*. North Manchester, Indiana: The News-Journal, 1926.
6. Bittinger, Emmert F., *Heritage and Promise*. Elgin, Illinois: The Brethren Press, 1970.
7. Brammell, Roy P., *Brother Harvey*. Elgin, Illinois: The Brethren Press, 1976.
8. Brenner, Scott F., *Pennsylvania Dutch—The Plain and The Fancy*. Harrisburg, Pennsylvania: The Stackpole Company, 1957.
9. Brumbaugh, Martin G., *A History of the Brethren*. Mount Morris, Illinois: The Brethren Publishing House, 1899.
10. Clark, Elmer T., The Small Sects in America. Abingdon-Cokesbury Press, 1937.
11. Davis, Glenn, *Childhood and History in America*. New York: The Psychohistory Press, 1976.
12. deMause, Lloyd, *The History of Childhood*. New York: The Psychohistory Press, 1974.
13. Durnbaugh, Donald F., *European Origins of the Brethren*. Elgin, Illinois: The Brethren Press, 1958.
14. Durnbaugh, Donald F., (ed). *The Brethren in Colonial America*. Elgin, Illinois: The Brethren Press, 1967.
15. Fisher, Nevin W., *The History of Brethren Hymnbooks*.

Bridgewater, Virginia: The Beacon Publishers, 1950.

16. Fisher, Virginia S., *The Story of the Brethren*. Elgin, Illinois: The Brethren Publishing House, 1957.

17. Fletcher, Stevenson W., *Pennsylvania Agriculture and Country Life 1640-1840*. Harrisburg, Pennsylvania: Pennsylvania Historical and Museum Commission, 1950.

18. Frantz, Evelyn, *A Bonnet for Virginia*. Elgin, Illinois: The Brethren Press, 1978.

19. Hostetler, John A., *Amish Life*. Scottdale, Pennsylvania: Herald Press, 1981.

20. Hostetler, John A., *Hutterite Society*. Baltimore, Maryland: The Johns Hopkins University Press, 1974.

21. Kissinger, Warren S., *The Buggies Still Run*. Elgin, Illinois: The Brethren Press, 1983.

22. Lefever, Ernest, *Ethical Characteristics of the Church Sect Motif*. Oak Brook, Illinois: Manuscript in Library of Bethany Seminary, 1944.

23. Lehman, James, A., *The Old Brethren*. Elgin, Illinois: The Brethren Press, 1976.

24. Levy, Barry J., *The Light in the Valley: The Chester and Welsh Tract Quaker Communities and the Delaware Valley, 1681-1750*. Ann Arbor, Michigan: University Microfilms International, 1983.

25. Long, Lucille, *Anna Elizabeth, Seventeen*. Elgin, Illinois: The Brethren Press, 1946.

26. Neff, Joel B., *The Biography of Cain Lackey*. Roanoke, Virginia: Toler and Company, Printers, 1976.

27. Payne, George H., *The Child in Human Progress*. New York: The Knickerbocker Press, 1916.

28. Rupel,Esther Zern, *An Investigation of the Origin, Significance, and Demise of the Prescribed Dress Worn by Members of the Church of the Brethren*. Ann Arbor, Michigan: University Microfilms International, 1980.

29. Sappington, Roger E., The Brethren in the New Nation. Elgin, Illinois: The Brethren Press, 1976.

30. Smith, Elmer L., *Meet the Mennonites*. Witmer, Pennsylvania: Applied Arts, 1965.

31. Winger, Otho, *History and Doctrines of the Church of the Brethren*. Elgin, Illinois: The Brethren Publishing House, 1919.

32. Ziegler, Edward K., *Simple Living*. Elgin, Illinois: The Brethren Press, 1974.